# What Works in Computing for School Administrators

Edited by
Gary Ivory

The Scarecrow Press, Inc.
A Scarecrow Education Book
Lanham, Maryland, and London
2001

SCARECROW PRESS, INC.
A Scarecrow Education Book

Published in the United States of America
by Scarecrow Press, Inc.
4720 Boston Way, Lanham, Maryland 20706
www.scarecroweducation.com

4 Pleydell Gardens, Folkestone
Kent CT20 2DN, England

British Library Cataloguing in Publication Information Available

**Library of Congress Cataloging-in-Publication Data**

What works in computing for school administrators / edited by Gary Ivory.
    p. cm. — (A Scarecrow education book)
  Includes bibliographical references and index.
  ISBN 0-8108-4174-6 (pbk. : alk. paper)
  1. School management and organization—United States—Data processing. I. Ivory,
Gary, 1947–.
LB2806.17 .W43 2001
371.2'00285—dc21                        2001042018

To: Marjory and Alvin Ivory

Mom and Dad, thanks for letting me join the Weekly Reader Book Club.
Thanks for all the other opportunities you have given me as well.

# Contents

# Preface

I have put this book together because I think about computers differently from a lot of experts in the field. A lot of experts preach that administrators *ought* to learn about technology, or somehow they are inferior human beings. I do not think you have an *obligation* to learn about computers. In fact, I just stopped being a school administrator after fifteen years, and I think you already have enough obligations. The argument that you *should* learn about computers strikes me as coming most strongly from (and appealing most strongly to) those who are not happy unless someone is tweaking their guilty consciences. Many of us aspire to do more: spending quality time with our kids, staying physically fit, keeping up with current events, mastering a foreign language, seizing opportunities for professional advancement, (and, oh yes, finding time to be meditative, reflective, and calm). The problem is that our aspirations so often bump up against real life.

The you-ought-to-be-doing-more argument seems particularly repellant when applied to school administrators. You *ought* to be skillful stewards of time and resources, instructional leaders, proactive strategic planners, inspirers of students, and empowerers of teachers—all in addition to the list of daunting personal "oughts" in the first paragraph. I read an article recently commenting on the old "in-basket" tests of aptitude for school administration. It said that these tests are inadequate because they measure administrators' abilities to deal only with problems that come to them. Truly skilled administrators will identify problems before they come to them. Is that depressing or what?

It grates on me, therefore, like fingernails on a blackboard, to hear that the prevalence of computers creates some additional obligation on administrators to stay up-to-date. First of all, as a wise friend of mine said once, "There's no such thing as being good at technology. It's too big. It's like saying someone is good at literature." Second, we do not need more things that we ought to be good at. The perception that we all ought to be getting better and better at things is a kind of insanity, one that is counterproductive to real intelligent reflection and construction of meaning in our lives. And I use the word "insanity" advisedly. Perhaps the ultimate absurd example I have seen was in an article on stress reduction. It urged people to find more time to relax. "If you have trouble finding such time," the writer urged, "try getting up earlier."

This book is for you if you want to know what computers can do to help you get through your day. Administrators have to schedule appointments, use time and money efficiently, stay in touch with others, clarify and persuade, keep track of people and products, process information, monitor effectiveness, motivate staff, mollify the angry, and yes, learn new things. Computers will not do those things for you, but they can help you do many of them better. If you are already doing them as well and as much as you like, and if you are going to be able to keep doing them as well and as much as you like, then this book is not for you  But if you want to know how to be more proficient with those things, then this book contains ideas that will help. And that can enable you to find more time to deal with loftier goals: making schools be good places for children, supporting teachers' efforts, and having a meaningful career for yourself. Are not those the reasons we got into this profession in the first place?

So here is what we have: In chapters 1, 2, and 3, Irma Trujillo, Steve Leask, Mario Martinez, and I introduce you to three relatively easy-to-learn pieces of software that can give you great leverage in important administrative tasks: communicating with groups, crunching numbers, and managing your time. Chapter 4 is about database management systems. These are considerably more difficult to learn, but Tom Ryan tells how they helped him streamline a cumbersome process, handling high school discipline referrals. Next, in chapters 5 through 8, Anne Moore and Tom Watts demystify two intimidating components of technology, library/Internet searching, and computer networking. Chapters 9 and 10 are two of my favorites, because in them Bruce Baker introduces an application that was new to me, using computer simulations to help us think about problems in new ways. He even tells you how to find a free demo of the software on the Web. Then in chapter 11, Mario Martinez returns to answer a question the publisher asked me to address: How do you decide when you are in such deep water with a technology issue that you are just going to have to pay a consultant to help you make the best decision? And how do you hire a consultant without getting taken? Finally, in chapters 12 and 13, Carmen Gonzales and Karin Wiburg help us look to the future. Once we find that technology helps us do our jobs, how do we help others discover how it might help them?

One final note: This book introduces you to some websites that you may find helpful. There is some irony in using a book, a stable medium, to introduce websites that may move or change from time to time. To compensate, I am creating a web page that will update ad-

dresses of an sites that change after the book is published. My site is at
<http://education.nmsu.edu/emd/ivory/>.

I am grateful to several people besides the authors for the completion of this book. María Luisa González suggested that I take it on at a
time when it would not even have occurred to me to do so. She has
supported me throughout its development. Joe Eckenrode gave my proposal a thoughtful hearing and suggested ways to improve it. Four
graduate assistants made substantial contributions: April Padilla and
Rachel Ortiz made helpful comments on early versions of the manuscript; Lizbeth Ascencio waded fearlessly into the *Chicago Manual of
Style* and did a great job of editing and formatting chapters; and Kara
Schlosser has been a great wordsmith and organizer, striving tirelessly
to work author's good ideas into the most consistent and readable
forms. Finally, Teresa Lao's and Robert Kramer's facility with the in-
tricacies of Microsoft Word got the manuscript ready for the camera. I
appreciate all of them.

Gary Ivory
March 2001

# 1

# Selling Your Ideas
# with Presentation Software

## Irma H. Trujillo and Steve Leask

## Introduction

### Why Use Presentation Software?

As administrators we are often called on to speak to teachers, parents, students, fellow administrators, and community audiences. We must inform or explain; we must persuade and motivate. Speakers long ago realized the power of visuals when conveying ideas or information and have armed themselves with chalk, charts, overhead transparencies, carousel slides, and other visual aids. Presentation software now joins the list of tools to assist administrators in getting messages across. Presentation software gives you the power to create attractive eye-catching slides quickly. You can then convert these slides to overhead transparencies or project them directly from the computer.

If you are as busy as most school administrators, the thought of learning new software may be daunting. In fact, even the language of presentation software—*templates, layouts, fonts, backgrounds,* and *clipart* may discourage you. Furthermore, people who are very proficient with technology often create a "technology mystique" that makes the rest of us feel inept and unable to create the very polished products that the technocrats produce. Put your fears aside. Do not be concerned with what you do not know. As you learn to use presentation software, stick with the basics (even the basics can give you fantastic results) and then add to your repertoire. Take one step at a time. You are not in competition with the "techies." You only want a few slides to help you make your point.

## Software and Hardware

There is a variety of presentation software to choose from. The two of us have extensive experience with *Adobe Persuasion* on the *Macintosh* platform and *Microsoft PowerPoint* for both Mac and PC platforms. We have recently learned some things about *Corel Presentations 8* for PCs, but do not have much experience with it. Mac lovers tell us that *Persuasion* is more powerful than *PowerPoint*, but our experience is that it is also more complex and difficult to use. This chapter will use examples from *Microsoft PowerPoint 97*. If you become familiar with the terminology and methodologies of *PowerPoint 97*, you will be able to transfer your knowledge to other packages.

# Creating Your Slides

## Starting Out

There is more than one way to create a presentation in *PowerPoint*. In this chapter we will be creating a new presentation using the *Auto-Content Wizard*. Open your presentation software. If the *Tip of the Day* window is open, close it. You should see the *PowerPoint* window (figure 1.1) that allows you to select one of four options.

- AutoContent Wizard: This application contains sample presentations for a variety of topics. These samples are easy to modify for your particular needs.
- Template: Here you will find color schemes and font styles. By applying a new template you can alter the look and feel of your presentation. The *PowerPoint* application contains many preformatted templates. Select the template radio button and explore the *New Presentation* dialog box.
- Blank Presentation: As its name implies, this one starts you with a blank first slide and the default colors and fonts. You add content, format text, and select colors, to create presentations that are uniquely your own.
- Open an Existing Presentation: This selection allows you to open a saved presentation. The presentation file may be on a floppy or hard disk or located on a network.

**Figure 1.1: Beginning with the AutoContent Wizard**

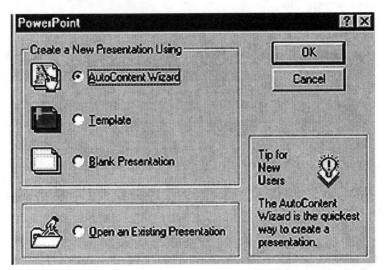

As we said above, we are going to use the AutoContent Wizard. So select that radio button and click on OK. The AutoContent Wizard dialog box takes you through a six-step process to help you create your presentation.

Click *Next*. A window appears that allows you to select the type of presentation you are going to give.
Click the *All* button and then select *Generic*.
Click Next and select Presentations, informal meetings, handouts. For output select On-screen presentation and for handouts select Yes.
Click *Next* and enter the requested information. For this exercise any title will do.
Click *Finish*. *PowerPoint* will then create a generic presentation with titled slides, a color scheme, and a background image. To view your presentation, move the cursor to the *menu bar*.

Click    View
                   Slide Show.

Click the left mouse button to move from slide to slide. Get out of Slide Show by hitting the *[Esc]ape* key. Take some time to explore some of the other presentation formats. You may find them useful for future presentations.

Now it is time to emphasize absolutely the most boring—and simultaneously the most important—advice about working with computer software: *REMEMBER TO SAVE YOUR PRESENTATION OFTEN WHILE YOU ARE WORKING ON IT!* If you do not save often, and the computer fails, you will lose the results of a lot of hard work.

## Modifying Slides

One way that presenters like to work on the slides is in *Outline View*. To get to Outline View:

Click      View
                    Outline.

You should see an outline of your presentation (see figure 1.2) with slide titles and contents on the left side of the screen and a representation of the slide on the right.

**Figure 1.2: Outline view of a presentation (with components labeled)**

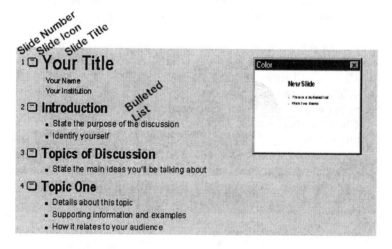

From the outline view you can enter and edit your presentation material very quickly. For example, to change the title of your presentation, simply move the cursor to the title slide, type in the new material, and delete the old.

All of the existing slides can be edited in the same fashion. Edit the slide titles and the bulleted lists, spell check your work, and save your presentation as a new file. Your presentation is now complete. But you are not stuck with just these slides. For example, if you want to add a new slide between slide two and three, position the cursor just after the little slide icon and before the text and press *Enter*. A new blank slide will appear. Type a title for this new slide and press Enter again.

Press the *Tab* key to create a new bulleted item for this new slide.

To add additional bulleted items to the slide, move the cursor to the end of the line and press Enter. Then type your new text.

To delete a slide, click on the slide icon and press the [*DelJete*] key.

# Another Approach to
# Creating and Editing Slides

Some presenters prefer to work on slides from within *Slide View*.

Click     View
               Slide View.

Try editing individual slides while in this view. You can move from slide to slide by using the scroll bar on the right side of the window. If you feel more comfortable editing your presentation from this view then use it instead of the Outline View. Again, to see what a finished slide looks like on the screen:

Click     View
               Slide Show.

Exit Slide Show by hitting [Esc]ape.

# Showing Your Slides

Now you are ready to display your slides to the world. The computer that you use for your presentations (and it is usually a laptop) must have a *video port*, that is, a place to connect the projector. PC laptops usually come with a video port. The newest Macs do as well, but if you have an older Mac, you must purchase a video port for it. You will run a cable from the video port to either a projector or to a *liquid crystal display* (*LCD*) panel that works with a regular overhead projector.

## Projector Problems to Beware

Let us begin with a warning: A projected slide show will not look as nice as one on a computer monitor. Backgrounds will fade, colors will blend, and contrasts will disappear. Illustration details that stand out clearly on the computer monitor may become invisible when projected. Finally, the margins may differ on the projector, so that slide content that fits perfectly on your computer screen will not fit on the screen. Make sure that you preview your presentation on the actual screen before "showtime" and make any needed adjustments.

Furthermore, if your computer is top-of-the-line, and the projector is not, your slides' requirements may be incompatible with the projector's capabilities. Older projectors are often limited to a maximum resolution of 640 x 480, while newer laptops are capable of producing slide shows having a resolution of 800 x 600 or higher. Your computer monitor settings may need to be adjusted for your presentation to appear as designed. If you are unsure how to perform this task, you should consult one of your institution's technology personnel.

Finally, projectors sometimes fail. You can prepare for that possibility by using *PowerPoint* to print a set of overhead transparencies from your slides. Then, if your projector (or computer) fails, you can go back to the old familiar overhead projector, but with your dynamite new slides. You can print these in color on either a color inkjet or laser printer. If you do not have a color printer, you can print them in grayscale on a regular black ink printer.

## Finishing Touches

Once you have created your basic presentation there are a number of changes and additions that you can make. In this section we will explain how to view the slides from different perspectives, reorder the slides, change font style, size, or color, add clip art, and insert slide *transitions*. Once we have completed those actions we will use the *Pack and Go* feature.

## The View Buttons

As you develop your presentation you may want to shift between the different views to examine your work. In addition to using the View menu at the top of the screen, you can also use the group of buttons located at the bottom left side of the window (See figure 1.3).

**Figure 1.3: The view buttons (with choices labeled)**

*Slide View*: allows you to type in text, draw, add clip art and graphics, and change the appearance of your presentation.

*Outline View*: allows you to edit the individual slide titles and the main text. You can also change slide order easily and even the order of bulleted points within a slide.

*Slide Sorter View*: shows a number of slides at once in thumbnail (small picture) views with graphics and text. Allows you to delete, insert, and reorder slides easily.

*Notes Page View*: shows an area below each slide in which you can type speaker notes. You can then print the speaker notes to serve as a support while you speak.

*Slide Show*: shows what the finished slide looks like filling the screen. You can use the left mouse button to run through several slides and see the transition effects.

## Reordering Slides with the Slide Sorter

The Slide Sorter View, accessible through the View menu or the buttons on the lower left side of the screen, allows you to change the order, hide, or delete some of your slides. When in the Slide Sorter, select a slide by clicking on it and then drag it to another position. Once you release the mouse button, the slide will be located in the new position. A slide can be deleted by selecting the slide and then pressing [Del]ete or by going to the Edit menu and selecting *Delete Slide*. You can also make a copy of a slide by clicking on the slide, and then selecting *Copy* in the Edit menu. Once copied, an exact copy of the slide can be pasted anywhere in the presentation. This is a handy way to copy slide formatting and layout to a new slide and to create additional slides with only minor editing.

Slide Sorter view also offers you the option of hiding slides you may not want to use for one presentation, but that you want to keep for future use.

Click     Slide Show
          Hide Slide.

## Changing Text Attributes

*PowerPoint* allows you to change *font style*, *font size*, and *font color* on your slide. Font style refers to its being **bold**, *italic*, <u>underlined</u>, or shadowed. There are numerous possible combinations of style, size, and color; we will explore only a few. If the file you created earlier is not open, open it now.

Move to the second slide of your presentation, "Introduction," and click on the title. A *text box* with *handles* (small squares) will appear around the text. To move the title, click on the text box and then drag, and drop in a new location. If you want to resize the text box, click on one of the handles and drag to the desired size. By clicking on the text box and clicking

Format
    Alignment,

you can change text justification (left, center, or right) within the text box.

If you want to change the appearance of the text, click on the text frame and use the tools available on the Formatting menu (shown in figure 1.4) to make your changes.

Explore the formatting tools to see what your title might look like if you used a different font, size, or style. You can change the color of the text by using the Font dialogue box on the Format menu or by using the Font Color Button on the *Drawing* menu. Remember, make changes that will help emphasize your key ideas; do not let glitz bury your ideas.

## Adding Clip Art and Other Images

Pictures are a great way to keep your audience's interest and provide them with valuable information about your topic. You can place a picture on a slide from the *Clip Gallery* or from a file:

Click    Insert
                Picture
                        Clip Art . . . or
                        From File . . .

When you select Clip Art, *PowerPoint* will open the Clip Gallery with an array of choices that are categorized by topic. Once you have chosen an image click *Insert* and it will appear in your slide. You can move the image by dragging it to the desired position. You can resize it by using the handles in the image. Other images, such as those from a digital camera or from the Web, can also be inserted by clicking on the From File option.

## Slide Transitions

A *transition* is the movement from one slide to another during a slide show.

Click    View
                Slide Show

to view your presentation. Click the left mouse button to move to the next slide. You should not see any type of transition, only a quick movement to the next slide. That is how a slide show appears without any transitions. You can add transitions either in Slide View or in the Slide Sorter View. The main difference is that in Slide Sorter View, you can select particular slides to add a transition to all at once. For now, let us work in Slide Sorter View.

Select the slide or slides to which you want to add a transition. You can select multiple slides by holding down the *Shift* key and clicking on each slide. To select all of the slides press CTRL + A. For our exercise, select all of the slides.

Click      Slide Show
                   Slide Transition

The Slide Transition *dialog box* should appear as shown in figure 1.5. Under *Effect,* click the down arrow beneath the graphic and scroll down to and select *Fade Through Black*. Set the transition speed to *Medium* and click OK. You can click *Apply to All* to apply a slide transition to all of the slides.

Take a look at your new transitions by clicking on your title slide and then on the Slide Show button. Now when you move from one slide to another you should see the Fade Through Black transition. You can also add a transition from the Slide View by using the Slide Show, Slide Transition option.

## Pack and Go

There are many times when administrators need to run slide shows on computers other than their own. If you find yourself in such a situation, you can use the *Pack and Go Wizard*. The wizard will pack all of the files, including linked files and fonts used in your presentation, together on a disk or disks. If the computer on which you are going to run your presentation does not have *PowerPoint*, you can also include the *PowerPoint Viewer* on the disk(s). The Viewer is a small application that will show slide presentations. To pack up a presentation for use on another computer, first open the presentation.

Click      File
                   Pack and Go

**Figure 1.4: Formatting menu (with functions labeled)**

and then follow the instructions in the Pack and Go Wizard. Insert another disk when prompted. Even if the other computer has *PowerPoint*, it may be a different version than yours, so it is a good idea to include the Viewer whenever possible. It is important to remember that if you make any changes to your presentation you will need to update your files by running the Pack and Go Wizard again.

When you need to unpack the presentation on the other computer, all you have to do is insert the disk with your packed presentation into the computer, go to the disk location (usually the 3 1/2 floppy in *My Computer*), and then double-click the file *Pngsetup.exe*. When prompted, enter the destination for the file, i.e., to what directory of the hard drive you want it to be copied (e.g., c:\My Documents). To run the slide show, double-click *Ppview32* and then click your presentation. The best advice we can give you is to practice this operation a couple of times before you have to use it in a real presentation.

**Figure 1.5: Slide transition dialogue**

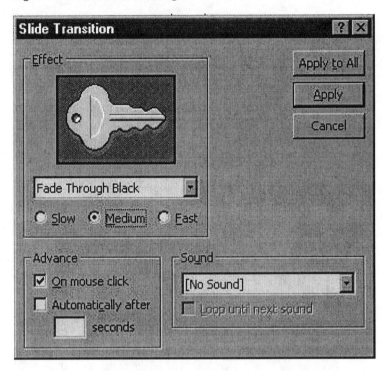

# But What About the Audience?

Slides are great! You can present information in many creative ways
including graphics, tables, organization charts, and pictures. Presentation
software allows you to make a slide or even portions of a slide appear
and disappear in interesting ways. They can fly up, fly down, emerge
from the center, or dissolve. You can make text multicolored or three-
dimensional, you can have it read sideways, and you can even get it to
twirl. When we started using presentation software we used every new
technique available because it was fun! As we saw our audience's
reactions, however, we began to suspect that all the glitz was
distracting them from our messages. Now we tend to keep our slides
very basic. If we use any fancy transitions from slide to slide or from
one point to another, we make sure the movement contributes to our
message. You can learn from our mistakes. During your presentations,

check your audiences to see if they seem to be following your ideas rather than just being entertained. Our advice, like the advice of so many other contributors to this book, is to keep your purpose in mind, and make sure the technology serves your purpose. Know your audience as well as you can; monitor their reactions; and work to involve them in your message. When you first start, we recommend that you practice and get feedback about your slides from others.

# Some Tips for Effective Presentations

The following advice should help you design effective presentations to portray your message in a motivating way:

### Keep it simple and straightforward (KISS).

Be consistent. Use a consistent format for all your slides. Find a good relationship between the format and the content. Changing slide formats can make it difficult for your audience to follow your presentation. You are the one who must deliver the message—slides only help. Limit the information on your slide and do not read your slides to your audience. Use only one major thought or idea per slide. Relate any additional content to the central theme of the slide.

### Know your delivery medium.

Remember that your slides will lose clarity and subtlety when they are projected on a screen or displayed on a TV. They just will not look as good! Use large plain fonts and make them bold. Use simple illustrations.

### Check your equipment.

If possible, practice your presentation on the equipment you will be using. Since you can never be sure that everything will be working properly, prepare for the unexpected.

## Know Your Audience.

Understand and respect those who are attending your presentation. Do not become so infatuated by your elaborate slide show that you lose the focus of your message or forget to monitor audience reaction.

## Do Not Present Too Much Text.

A good rule of thumb, the 7 x 7 rule, states that you should have no more than seven lines of text per slide and no more than seven words per line. You want your slides to punctuate your words by having your audience see a few key words—even just one word! Use the slides just to emphasize key points.

## Do Not Fall in Love with the Sound of Your Own Voice.

Speak no more than thirty to forty-five minutes without audience interaction, a break, or a hands-on activity. A slide presentation of thirty to forty-five minutes will generally consist of ten to twenty slides. A fifteen-minute presentation that leaves the audience with a few specific points is much better than a detailed two-hour presentation. Your audience will spend the second hour wishing for the last slide!

## Keep on Learning.

As in all learning, persistence is important. Using presentation software will make your presentations more effective and efficient. In the short run, however, you will need to devote blocks of time to learning how to use the software. We can now generate a finished fifteen-slide presentation in thirty minutes, even right before the presentation. But we had to invest time to get to this point.

You might consider investing in training as well. You can learn presentation software on your own, as we did, but a half-day training session taught by an expert could save you time. Such training may be available from your school district or local university for a small fee.

Do not be afraid to play with the software. Even after you read the manual, some things are not clear until you use them several times. It is also beneficial to talk to other users of the software or call for technical assistance when something baffles you.

## Practice Makes Perfect.

The only sure way to learn how to use a presentation software application is practice. Develop some rudimentary presentation formats with fonts, graphics, and colors that will suit your needs. This will provide some needed practice as well as a head start on that presentation they ask you to do on short notice. That is because modifying an existing presentation usually requires less time than creating a new one.

Like most computer applications, presentation programs require an investment of time and energy, items that are usually in short supply. Remember, though, the purpose of these programs is better communication. Your investment in learning how to create a presentation in *PowerPoint* or any other presentation software program will be worth the effort if it enhances your ability to communicate.

# 2

# Prison Cells and Spreadsheets

## Mario Martinez

Travel back in time to your first teaching job and imagine that it was with a public school teaching math. Since it is in the public schools, you will be dealing with the state, and you know there are always extra rules and procedures that you must consider. You cannot call students by regular names for fear of a lawsuit if you mistakenly refer to somebody by the incorrect name. Since this is a math class, students can be referred to (or referenced) only by a combination of numbers and letters (the state feels there is less risk for lawsuits if you mistakenly call somebody a wrong letter). It is up to you to figure out a scheme for giving each student a new name.

Although one of your college professors said that the traditional arrangement of neatly aligned rows and columns of our schools is reminiscent of factories and prisons, you decide the most logical thing to do, especially in light of new state regulations, would be to stay with tradition. Fig. 2.1 shows the arrangement of your class.

Come to think of it, the arrangement of your class does resemble a prison. Each student's area looks a little bit like a prison cell. Just as the prison analogy will be helpful in giving you a conceptual layout of a spreadsheet, perhaps it is equally beneficial to think of each student's area as a cell. Now, how should you name each student, or cell? To remember each student, you can use letters, numbers, or a combination of the two. Since the layout of your class is two-dimensional (there are rows and columns), it might be better to name each cell with a combination of letters and numbers. Let us label each column with a letter, starting with the leftmost column being column A, the next column labeled B, and so on. We can define the rows similarly, except using numbers.

As fig. 2.2 illustrates, the rightmost student (the teacher's right) is now named A1. If you move down one cell, you will find student A2. The other students' names depend on which letter and number labels their cell intersects, as shown in figure 2.2. This labeling and cell-naming scheme is the premise for how a spreadsheet application is designed. For our purposes, I will demonstrate some essential features and functions of a spreadsheet application using *Microsoft Excel*. There are many good spreadsheet application products on the market, but I will demonstrate using *Excel* simply because it is ubiquitous and conceptually demonstrates the power of any spreadsheet software.

**Figure 2.1: Classroom arrangement**

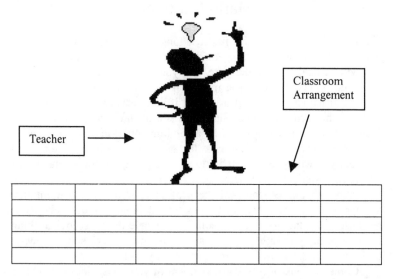

The goal of the chapter is to introduce you to spreadsheets, highlighting what they can do and how they can help you. I assume that many of you do not find particular joy in sitting in front of a crackling fireplace, curling under a cozy blanket, and pulling out a user's manual on how to use a spreadsheet. Thus, my aim is to give you an introduction to spreadsheets by examples and words that you can relate to. I will not go into every detail or technical aspect of your spreadsheet application, because a user's manual for your software can give you additional information about the topics we will be discussing. The chapter is meant to be one of practical application, however, so you will probably get more out of it by starting your computer and launching your spreadsheet application software.

**Figure 2.2: Classroom layout or spreadsheet layout**

| | A | B | C | D | E | F |
|---|---|---|---|---|---|---|
| 1 | A1 | B1 | | | | F1 |
| 2 | A2 | | | | | |
| 3 | | | | | | |
| 4 | | | | | | |
| 5 | | | | | | |
| 6 | | | | | | |
| 7 | | | | | | |
| 8 | | | | | | |
| 9 | A9 | | | | | F9 |

# Sink or Swim: Learning Financials

In figure 2.2, we saw the basic layout of a spreadsheet using the analogy of your classroom. Let's leave that analogy and get on to a practical problem that confronts many administrators: suddenly finding out that they need to know how to budget. One reason administrators may find themselves in this position is because their district may have implemented site-based management. Another reason may be that administrators increasingly are being asked to defend their requests for resources, such as supplies or teacher's aides. These are areas that principals of the past may not have known that much about because they were basically taken care of at central office. So, many administrators may not have the training to budget properly, or, if they had the training, it may have been a long time ago. Another issue is that administrators may not know what tools are available to help them become more financially savvy.

If you are an administrator or aspire to be one, budgeting will certainly be a task you will have to confront. The spreadsheet is one tool that you may not have known can help you in the area of finance and budgeting, and it is probably already on your computer or can be readily purchased for under $100.

We will be using the example of site-based management as a vehicle to learn about spreadsheets. Even if site-based management is not part of your environment, think of this example as one way to see the power of spreadsheets.

When your spreadsheet application comes up on your computer, your screen should look very similar to figure 2.2. There will be several *icons* (miniature pictures) on the top and bottom of the screen. Icons are "shortcuts" that allow the user to quickly perform a spreadsheet function. However, we will first do things the long way, using the keyboard, mouse, or a combination of the two to perform functions. This will allow you to visualize the steps that a given icon automatically performs.

At the very top of your spreadsheet, near the top of the screen, you should see several words with the first letter underlined (File, Edit, etc.). These words appear on what is called the command menu, and each performs a specific function ranging from saving a file to alphabetically sorting your spreadsheet information. To see an example of how to access a command on the command menu, position the mouse cursor on the word *Data* and press the left mouse button. You should see an entire menu below the Data command. Press the *Esc* key or click your mouse on any cell in the spreadsheet to get rid of the menu. Another way to access a menu command is by using the keyboard. Press the *Alt* key on your keyboard and hit the letter "D" at the same time (hereinafter referred to as "ALT+[the other key]," e.g., ALT+D). You will automatically see the menu you saw a moment ago. Under the Data command menu, there is a menu of words, and each word has one letter that is underlined. If you are using the keyboard, you can access commands or functions within the Data command by simply pressing the underlined letter of the word that describes the command you wish to execute. If you are using the mouse, you would click on the word Data to see the menu, let go of the left mouse button and position the cursor to the desired command. Clicking the left mouse button will then invoke that command. Press Esc to get back to the spreadsheet.

I have given you these examples to demonstrate two ways of doing the same thing. Some people prefer to use the keyboard because they are fast typists, while others like to use the mouse. Not all the functions appearing on the command menu have a corresponding icon, so we will use an icon when an appropriate opportunity arises. For now, we will be using a combination of the mouse and keyboard, but you can use only one method if you prefer.

Now, in spreadsheet applications, each cell is given a name, or a reference, as we saw in figure 2.2. Each cell, however, is empty until you type in some contents to occupy its cell space. The contents can be letters, numbers, formulas, or labels. Once you have typed the desired contents into a particular cell, it is full. The contents of a cell can be changed, however, by simply clicking your mouse cursor on that cell and typing in the new information.

Now that you have seen the basic layout of the spreadsheet, let's proceed with a scenario to help you gain some expertise. Assume that the central office in your district has delivered a document to you that looks like figure 2.3.

**Figure 2.3: Budget spreadsheet from central office**

| | Microsoft Excel - Book1 | | | | |
|---|---|---|---|---|---|
| File | Edit | View | Insert | Format | Tools  Data  Window  Help |

| | A | B | C | D | E |
|---|---|---|---|---|---|
| 1 | | | **2001** | | |
| 2 | Line # | Budget Item | | | |
| 3 | 6100 | Salary | $900,000 | | |
| 4 | 6200 | Consulting | $5,000 | | |
| 5 | 6300 | Supplies | $7,500 | | |
| 6 | 6400 | Travel | $3,500 | | |
| 7 | 6500 | Capital Equipment | $15,000 | | |
| 8 | | **Total** | $931,000 | | |

You received a memo attached to the document that informs you that this is how your money was spent in 2001. The memo also informs you that you are to turn in a proposed budget (often referred to as "forecasted budget" in financial circles) for 2002. This means that you must try to predict how much you think you are going to spend in 2002. Although you are now in charge of your own budget, central administration wants to ease you into it, so they have attached some guidelines that might help ensure that your budgeted forecast will be approved. Here are the additional points in the memo that you should probably consider as you try to forecast:

- There are twenty teachers in your school who make up $600,000 of the salary line.
- Teachers are due for a 5 percent pay raise next year.
- Capital equipment in 2002 will be cut to only 1.5 percent of your total 2001 spending.
- There has been an emphasis on professional development, so you can increase your travel budget by ten percent (above travel for 2001) to send your employees to training, conferences, etc.
- Central office is open to growth in consulting and supplies, though you will need to justify any increases.

- If you choose to include 2003 forecasts, assume all categories can only grow 1 percent above the 2002 forecast.

To complete your task, you must first understand the memo and spreadsheet document that has been sent to you. A good strategy might be to dissect the information one piece at a time.

Let us start by examining the contents of the budget that was sent to you by looking at figure 2.3. First, Column A contains numbers that correspond to each budget item description. There is no magic to the numbers, only that the line item numbers are used to label each budget item description in Column B. Column C contains the actual spending for each line item number and budget item. The complete information for any given budget item appears in a given spreadsheet row (for example, Row 6 contains three pieces of information about Travel). Second, the budget item descriptions are useful because they tell you in words where certain monies were spent. The memo has included some information (the bullet points given above) to help guide you through the forecasting process.

The central office has sent you a spreadsheet printout, so you will have to type the information in figure 2.3 into your spreadsheet. Our first task will be to make your spreadsheet look exactly like figure 2.3. Start by typing in the line numbers shown in Column A. Point your cursor to Cell A2 and click the left mouse button. This puts you in Cell A2, which is currently empty. Type "Line #" as shown in figure 2.3 and then press *Enter*. Pressing Enter automatically enters your information and moves you to Cell A3. Type in the line item numbers in the remaining rows of Column A as shown in figure 2.3 (we will worry about formatting in just a moment). Now do the same for Column B.

Position your mouse cursor to Cell C2 and begin entering the numbers in this column. Do not worry about commas and dollar signs yet; we will get to formatting in a moment. Enter the information for Column C, starting with Cell C1. Do not enter a number in Cell C8, which contains the total for your 2001 budget. Finally, go to Cell D1 and enter the final label "2002."

Your spreadsheet probably looks something like figure 2.4, so a bit of formatting is needed to make it look like figure 2.3. It is always a good idea to spend a little time formatting at the beginning stages of designing your spreadsheet; this way, things look nice and neat from the beginning. As we format the spreadsheet, you will begin to notice that formatting a spreadsheet is very similar to formatting text in a word processor or a database management program such as *Access*.

**Figure 2.4: Budget spreadsheet just after you type it in, without formating**

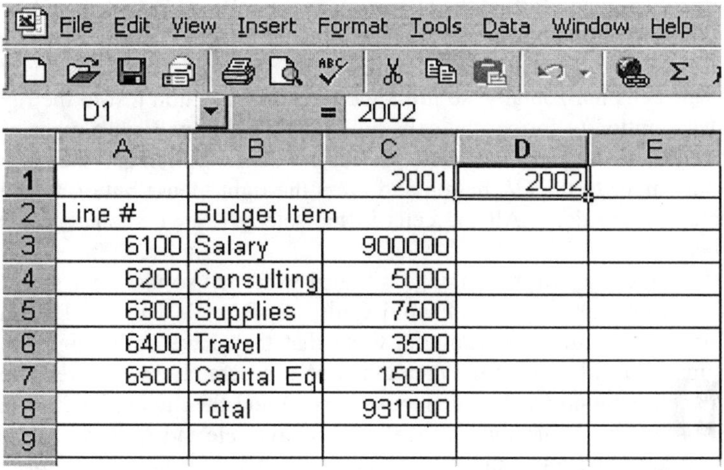
File Edit View Insert Format Tools Data Window Help
D1
= 2002
A
B
C
D
E
1
2001
2002
2 Line # Budget Item
3 6100 Salary 900000
4 6200 Consulting 5000
5 6300 Supplies 7500
6 6400 Travel 3500
7 6500 Capital Eq 15000
8 Total 931000
9

## Formatting

Probably the first difference you notice between figures 2.3 and 2.4 is that the budget item descriptions in Column B, figure 2.4, do not fit in the cells. To widen Column B so that each of the descriptions fit into the cell spaces, point your cursor to the column labeled "B" (see figure 2.2). Move the cursor to the line that separates label "B" from label "C." You should see a little cross; hold down your left mouse button and move the mouse to the right just enough so that the longest description (Capital Equipment) fits into the space.

Another obvious difference between the figures is that the information in figure 2.4 is not centered. To center all of the items, highlight the cell range A1 through E8 (hereafter such a range will be denoted A1:E8) so that *Excel* knows what you want to format. To do this, click on Cell A2, press the left mouse button down, and, keeping the button pressed, drag your mouse cursor to Cell E8. The entire range should now be highlighted. Press ALT+O. This will take you to the format command on the menu bar. Now let go of both keys and hit the letter "e" to tell the application that you wish to format the cells you have highlighted. A window, commonly known as a *dialog box*, now appears. This dialog box contains folders, and each folder contains a tab at the top of it, much like the manila folders you would find in your metal file cabinet. The tabs describe what it is that we might want to format in the cell range: fonts, numbers, borders, etc. In this case, we are only going to format the alignment of the cells we have selected.

Use your mouse to select the *Alignment* folder. There is a box that allows you to format the cells horizontally. We will center the contents of the cells horizontally, so press the little arrow button just to the right of the option to format the cells horizontally. You will see a menu appear when you press the arrow. Select the *Center* option and then point your cursor to the *OK* button and press the right mouse button to indicate you are done. All the cells in the selected range should now be centered.

There are two more things we need to format so that your spreadsheet looks like figure 2.3: bold Cells A2, B2, C1, E1, and B8; and format the numbers in Column C so that they have dollar signs and commas. Bold each of the mentioned cells separately by first selecting the cell location (with your mouse cursor) and then going back to the *Format* menu command. Also, after you have selected ALT+O, release those keys and select the letter "e" again to indicate you wish to format a cell. The folders will appear once again. This time choose the folder with the *Font* tab. After you have chosen the Font folder, look for the box that allows you to choose a font style (about the middle of the dialog box). Use your mouse to select the option *Bold* and then click the left mouse button and click on OK. You have now bolded your first cell. Bold the remaining cells according to figure 2.3.

To format the numbers in Column C, select the range C3:C8. Cell C8 does not have a number in it yet, but you can still format it. For this exercise we will use the mouse instead of the keyboard.

Click     Format
                Cells.

Release the left mouse button and the formatting folders will reappear. The very first tab is titled *Number*. Select it if it is not already chosen. There are several options that allow you to format your numbers. Use your mouse to choose the *Currency* option. Next, you will see a place in the folder where you can also designate the number of decimal places. Point your mouse to the default (which is 2) and change this number to "0." Click OK and all of your numbers should now be reformatted. Your spreadsheet should now look like figure 2.3, without a total calculated 2001 amount in Cell C8. If it does, we are ready to begin filling in additional information. If it does not, return to the beginning of this section and see if there are any steps you may have missed.

## An Example of an *Excel* Function

Spreadsheet programs are designed for mathematical calculations. *Excel* can perform basic mathematics as well as statistical calculations. Let us automatically add a series of numbers to get an idea of *Excel's* mathematical capabilities. Select Cell C8 so that we can enter a formula to calculate all of your budget items in 2001. You could just enter the number you received from central office, but for this discussion, suppose you want to enter a formula to automatically calculate it. For one thing, this will help you verify the central office calculation. We are now going to insert a formula using a built-in *Excel function*. The function is the *SUM* function, and it adds the numbers you tell it to (by specifying their cell locations). Click your mouse button on Cell C8. Using the keyboard, press ALT+I. Let go of both keys and press "F" to select Function. A dialog box now appears. One of the choices on the right-hand side of the box is the SUM function. Use your mouse to select the SUM function. Now go to the bottom of the dialog box and use your mouse to select OK. Another dialog box will come up. This box is where you can specify which cells you want the function to SUM. In our case, we want the range C3:C7. You will notice that *Excel* has already made an educated guess as to which cells should be summed, so the proper parameters may already be specified (C3:C7). In the event that your range has not been properly specified, point your mouse to the dialog box where the data range can be specified and enter "C3:C7" and press the *Enter* key. Cell C8 should now have a number in it, as the function SUM has added all of the budget items above it. Your spreadsheet should now look exactly like figure 2.3.

## Copying and Cutting

Before we get on with the business of forecasting your 2002 budget, let us go over some frequently used commands in *Excel*. The first two commands we will review are *Copy* and *Cut*. First, let us go over the Copy command. Assume that you decide to ignore the memo that came from central office. To make life easy, you will simply predict that next year's spending will be exactly equal to last year's. To do this, you have only to copy cell range C3:C8 (budget for 2001) to cell range D3:D8 (2002). Select cell range C3:C8 using your mouse. Press ALT+E. This tells the spreadsheet that you are going to perform some type of *Edit* function. Let go of both keys and press "C" indicating that you are going to copy the contents of the selected range. Move your mouse to Cell E3 and simply press Enter. The information in Column E should look exactly like the information in Column C. *Excel* copied the contents of one cell range and pasted them into another cell range.

Remember that Cell C8 contains a formula (using the SUM function); so what do you think happened when you copied the contents of Cell C8 to Cell E8? Select Cell E8. You will notice that Cell E8 also has a formula, but the range of cells that it added together is E3:E7. When *Excel* copied the formula from C8 to E8, it automatically changed the variables in the original function (C3:C8) to correspond with the column containing the newly copied function (Column E), thereby automatically changing the formula to SUM the Cell range E3:E7. We will talk more about this when we figure out a 2002 budget that is different from 2001's.

Let us *Undo* the copy command that we just performed. Use your mouse this time.

Click     Edit
                Undo.

The numbers that were copied in Column E should now be erased. The cell range you copied may still have a blinking box around it (called a *marquee*). Hit Esc to get rid of the marquee.

Now, when we copied the range from Column C and pasted it to Column E, we simply pressed Enter. We did not have to explicitly tell *Excel* to paste the copied contents to the new range. We can specify the *Paste* function as well, but this is not necessary unless we are doing something a little fancier. Say, for example, that you wanted to copy only the total budget value for 2001 into the total for 2002, but not the formula. Select Cell C8 and then choose the Copy command using your mouse. Select Cell E8 and choose the Edit menu again. You will see several options. Choose the *Paste Special* option. A dialog box will come up, and you will see an option to paste the *Formula, Values*, etc. Choose the button beside Values, and click OK. Press Esc and go to Cell E8. You should see that *Excel* now copied only the value of Cell C8 into Cell E8, not the formula. Undo this paste command by choosing the Edit command from the menu and choosing Undo.

Let us compare all that we just did to the Cut command. The Cut command allows you to select a cell, or ranges of cells, just like the Copy command. IMPORTANT: The difference is that the original cell range will be cleared after you initiate the Cut command. Use your mouse to select cell range C3:C8. Press ALT+E. Release both keys and press "T" to cut the contents of this range. Point your mouse to Cell E3, then press ALT+E. Let go of both keys and press "P" to paste the information. You have now moved the information from cell range C3:C8 to E3:E8 by cutting it and pasting it to a different location. Press ALT+E and then "U" to undo the cut and paste commands that you just completed.

The Cut command is much different from the Copy command. The Copy command leaves the original contents of the cells from which you are copying exactly as they were, whereas Cut clears the original contents so that the cells are "empty" or contain no information.

Both the Cut and Copy commands use what is called a *clipboard*. You cannot see the clipboard, but conceptually it is like an actual clipboard that holds information that you copy or cut. The clipboard only has the ability to hold the contents of the cell(s) that were last copied or cut. Thus, if you Copy or Cut some information from a cell range, forget about it, then Copy or Cut information from another cell range, you will loose the information that you first Copied or Cut. The information that you copied most recently will now occupy the clipboard. When you use the Cut command, you can either place the contents of that which you Cut somewhere else in the spreadsheet, or you can simply do nothing, and the information will be placed on the clipboard. The contents will be lost once you close your application or replace the clipboard with information from another Copy or Cut command.

## Deleting and Inserting

Let us go over two more fundamentals before we forecast your 2002 budget. Your spreadsheet should once again look like figure 2.3. Suppose you want to impress central office by eliminating some expenses, so you decide that nobody will get any supplies in 2002. You might as well just eliminate the Supplies line item for the purposes of your 2002 budget. This can easily be done with a few commands.

Click your mouse on the row label number 5, to the left of Line # 6300. The entire row should automatically be highlighted. Press ALT+E, then "D" for Delete. You have now deleted the entire row. Select Cell C7, where your formula now resides. You will notice that the formula automatically adjusted the cell range it is using in its calculation. Before you deleted the row, the range was C3:C7, now it is C3:C6. Another feature of *Excel* is that it does its best to adjust formulas when you make changes, but you must always check your formulas to make sure something unexpected hasn't occurred.

Now, let's say you quickly change your mind about deleting this line item because you just remembered a summer workshop you attended, and the trainer said cutting corners on the small stuff will really decrease teacher morale. Better reinsert the Supplies line item. Press ALT+E, then "U" to undo the last command. This should restore the row that you have just deleted. To delete an entire column, you would follow the same logic.

Assume the thought came into your mind of really pushing the envelope with central administration, and you want to ask for money to have several recreational activities with your staff. Sounds like you need to insert a new budget item called "Personal Enrichment." You decide to put this line item between Supplies and Travel (maybe they won't notice it), so you should click your mouse on row 6.

Click     Insert
                 Rows.

*Excel* has automatically inserted a new row for you, and you can type in the appropriate information. Again, you will notice that the formula has been recalculated (Cell C9) and the variables now incorporate an additional row of data.

Once again you decide this change is not a good idea. Undo the row that you just inserted, using the mouse or the Alt key functions. Now you decide to get serious. It is time to fill in the forecasted budget for 2002, using the memo and the initial spreadsheet in figure 2.3. Formatting data, entering data and formulas, and gaining familiarity with various *Excel* functions was just my way to get you comfortable navigating around the spreadsheet.

We have covered some basic *Excel* commands, written a formula, and experimented with several formatting features. Now you will learn some of the finer points of your spreadsheet's capabilities.

Read all of the bullet points from the central office budget instructions and then look at the spreadsheet again. Figure 2.5 is different from the original document in figure 2.3, because the first row now contains headings for three years. The last bullet point of the memo informs you that you may forecast 2003, so let's go ahead and do that. Type "2002" in cell D1 and bold it. We are now ready to forecast for 2002, and the projections will reside in Column D.

The first two bullet points have to do with the Salary line. In 2001, salary expenses amounted to $900,000. Your school is fairly small, and twenty teachers' salaries made up $600,000 of the $900,000, or two-thirds of the salary. This means $300,000 (or one-third) went for administrative and other staff salaries. From the second bullet point, you assume that no administrative personnel will be getting a raise in 2002, but the teachers ($600,000) will be receiving a 5 percent raise. Based on this information, you can write a formula in Cell D3 to calculate the 2002 forecast for salaries. Go to Cell D3 and type the following formula:

=(C3/1.5*1.05)+(C3/3)

Hit Enter after you type any formula.

**Figure 2.5: Budget spreadsheet after formatting**

|  | A | B | C | D | E |
|---|---|---|---|---|---|
| 1 |  |  | 2001 | 2002 | 2003 |
| 2 | Line # | Budget Item |  |  |  |
| 3 | 6100 | Salary | $900,000 |  |  |
| 4 | 6200 | Consulting | $5,000 |  |  |
| 5 | 6300 | Supplies | $7,500 |  |  |
| 6 | 6400 | Travel | $3,500 |  |  |
| 7 | 6500 | Capital Equipment | $15,000 |  |  |
| 8 |  | Total | $931,000 |  |  |

The first part of the formula takes the total amount for the 2001 salaries and divides it by 1.5 (which is the same as multiplying by two-thirds) to give you the $600,000 in teacher salaries. This amount is then multiplied by 1.05 to produce the 5 percent raise. The second part of the formula figures out the administrative and staff salaries, which is the total 2001 amount divided by three. This amount is simply added on to the teacher salaries for 2002, since administrators and staff will not get a raise.

Notice in the formula, cell locations, rather than numbers, are used wherever possible. To understand why, imagine you got a call from central office. The finance person tells you that there was a mistake in your 2001 Salary line. Instead of $900,000, it was supposed to read $950,000. If you go to Cell C3 and change the $900,000 to $950,000, Cell D3 will automatically recalculate. This is an extremely useful and powerful feature of spreadsheet applications. If you had not used cell references and instead had used numbers in the formula in Cell D3, you would have to change the formula in Cell D3 and Cell C3.

Before you continue with the memo, it would be helpful to keep a running total of your 2002 expenses as you calculate them. Using the Copy command, copy the formula in Cell C8 to Cell D8. Your total for 2002 only includes the salary line so far, but it will be updated as we add more information.

The third bullet point concerns your Capital Equipment and Travel lines. Current spending on Capital Equipment is about 1.6 percent of total 2001 expenses ($15,000/$931,000), but you need to pare it down to 1.5 percent of the total for 2001. Your total for 2001 appears in Cell C8, so your formula for 2002 Capital Equipment will be 1.5 percent of the contents of Cell C8. Go to Cell D7 and type the following equation (only what is inside the brackets, <>): <=C8*.015>. Next, in Cell D6, increase your 2002 Travel line by 10 percent above 2001 by typing: <=C6*1.1>.

The only thing left to do is predict the Consulting and Supplies line items. The fourth bullet point indicates that you have some latitude in forecasting these two line items. You know that supply costs will be increasing and some additional consultants will be needed to help train the teachers on some new computer equipment that was acquired this year. In essence, your spending on these two line items should increase over the 2001 levels. You have also talked to other administrators who have told you that supplies account for about 1.5 percent of their total budget (currently 0.8 percent of your total budget) and consulting about 1 percent (currently .5 percent of your budget). If you apply these percentages to the 2001 totals to determine 2002 Supplies and Consulting, the actual dollar amounts will almost double, but you feel you can justify it. You decide to give it a try. Let us figure that your 2002 consulting will be 1 percent of your total 2001 budget (Cell C8). Go to Cell D4 and type the following formula: <=C8*.01>. Next, copy the formula from Cell D4 to Cell D5.

Now, go to Cell D5 and change the .01 to .015 and press Enter. You will notice that the value in Cell D5 is zero. Go to Cell D5 and look at the formula again. Notice that you wanted to multiply the total 2001 budget by 1.5 percent, but the variable in the formula is referring to Cell C9, not the total budget amount in C8. Remember that you copied the formula from Cell D4 to D5, and the formula in Cell D4 correctly refers to Cell C8 (the 2001 total budget amount). Since you copied the formula from D4 to D5 (which is one row below D4), *Excel* automatically changed the reference in Cell D5's formula to be one row below C8. When *Excel* copies a formula from one cell to another, it assumes that the formula will still perform the same operation, but that the variables (or cell references) will change depending on where you copy the formula. This is called relative referencing. Go back to Cell D4 and retype the formula: <=$C$8*.01>.

Now, copy the formula to Cell D5 and change the .01 to .015. Notice that the C8 did not change to C9 this time. As you typed the formula in Cell D4 this time, you put dollar signs ($) in front of the column and row designation for your 2001 total budget cell designation ($C$8). In most spreadsheet applications, a dollar sign can be placed in front of the row (8, in this case) and/or column (C, in this case) variable designations to make it absolute. That is, there will be instances when you want to copy a formula, but you want one or more cell references to stay the same or to stay absolute.

Finally, we have again used a variable in the formulas for Cells D4 and D5, even though we want both formulas to refer to the 2001 total budget amount. Again, if for some reason, you have to make adjustments to the 2001 budget, all of the 2002 items, individual line items, and totals will be automatically recalculated. You won't have to adjust any formulas.

The use of formulas, with relative and absolute references, where appropriate, offers the user great flexibility in using one formula for multiple calculations. This is more efficient because it saves you time. Your comfort with formulas and references will increase with practice.

Now, the last step to complete our calculations is to forecast for 2003. At this point, your spreadsheet should look like figure 2.6. The 2003 forecasts will be fairly simple. You will simply take each line item, and increase it by 1 percent for 2003. The challenge is to figure out how to type one formula for the first line item (Salary) that will automatically make the appropriate changes when you copy it to the remaining line items. The answer, of course, is to make use of relative and absolute references. You know that you always want to refer to the 2002 amount, and 2002 amounts reside in Column D. This means that any reference to Column D should be absolute. The rows will change depending on the budget item for which you are forecasting. So, the row reference should be relative, and it should not include a dollar sign. Type in the following formula in Cell E3 to see how this works: <=$D3*1.01>. Then, copy this formula to Cells E4, E5, E6, and E7. You can select Cell E3, copy the contents, and then select the range

E4:E7 and hit Enter. Your spreadsheet should now look like figure 2.7. If you look at the formulas in Cells E4:E7, you will notice that the row numbers in the formula changed (relative), but the Column designation did not (absolute). The final task is to copy the formula that calculates the total budget amount from 2002 to 2003. Copy Cell D8 and paste the contents to Cell E8. You now have your 2003 total. We will conclude this chapter with some spreadsheet functions that allow you to manipulate and graph your information, should the need ever arise.

**Figure 2.6: Budget spreadsheet with forecast for 2002**

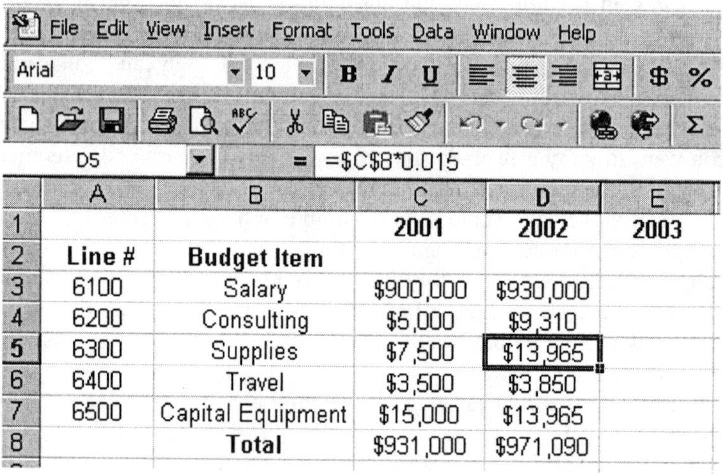
File Edit View Insert Format Tools Data Window Help
Arial
10
D5
=$C$8*0.015

| | A | B | C | D | E |
|---|---|---|---|---|---|
| 1 | | | 2001 | 2002 | 2003 |
| 2 | Line # | Budget Item | | | |
| 3 | 6100 | Salary | $900,000 | $930,000 | |
| 4 | 6200 | Consulting | $5,000 | $9,310 | |
| 5 | 6300 | Supplies | $7,500 | $13,965 | |
| 6 | 6400 | Travel | $3,500 | $3,850 | |
| 7 | 6500 | Capital Equipment | $15,000 | $13,965 | |
| 8 | | Total | $931,000 | $971,090 | |

## Sorting and Graphing

In figure 2.7, your budget items are in numerical order, according to their line number, but they are not in alphabetical order. Suppose, for internal purposes, you wanted to look at the information alphabetically. Most spreadsheet applications have basic data manipulation capabilities, though database management software (as described in chapter 4) is the more appropriate vehicle for handling large amounts of data.

Go to Cell A3 and select the range A3:E7. Notice that you are not selecting the labels or the totals. The totals will automatically recalculate when you sort. In addition, several of the line items have formulas in them, but we should get the exact same totals as in figure 2.7, even if we sort our spreadsheet alphabetically. That is, if we have used the correct combination of relative and absolute references for those cells that contain formulas.

Now, using your mouse, go to the menu bar.

Click    Data
                Sort.

**Figure 2.7: Budget spreadsheet with forecasts for 2002 and 2003**

| | File Edit View Insert Format Tools Data Window Help |
| --- | --- |

| Arial | ▼ 10 ▼ | **B** *I* <u>U</u> | ≡ ≡ ≡ ☰ | $ % |

E8 ▼ =

| | A | B | C | D | E |
| --- | --- | --- | --- | --- | --- |
| 1 | | | **2001** | **2002** | **2003** |
| 2 | **Line #** | **Budget Item** | | | |
| 3 | 6100 | Salary | $900,000 | $930,000 | $939,300 |
| 4 | 6200 | Consulting | $5,000 | $9,310 | $9,403 |
| 5 | 6300 | Supplies | $7,500 | $13,965 | $14,105 |
| 6 | 6400 | Travel | $3,500 | $3,850 | $3,889 |
| 7 | 6500 | Capital Equipment | $15,000 | $13,965 | $14,105 |
| 8 | | **Total** | $931,000 | $971,090 | |

From the dialog box, we will use the mouse to choose some options to sort the data alphabetically. The data that we highlighted are exactly the data we want to sort. *Excel* automatically makes an assumption about whether the highlighted data contains labels. If *Excel* did not assume the *No Header Row* option, select the No Header Row option to indicate that there are no extra labels or headings in the data you highlighted. All we have selected are the data we want to sort. Selecting the No Header Row option should automatically change the *Sort By* option at the top of the dialog box. Ensure that the *Ascending* button is chosen and that you are going to sort by Column B. If Column B is not selected (Column A is probably the default) in the Sort By option, select the arrow in the Sort By rectangular box and choose Column B. *Excel* now knows that you wish to sort the data by budget item, and that the descriptions are *alphanumeric*. By selecting a sort in ascending order, the command will arrange the data from A-Z. This is all the information you need to give *Excel* for now, so click OK in the dialog box. The entries of your spreadsheet should now be alphabetically arranged as shown in figure 2.8—or are they? It looks like the data were correctly sorted, but there seems to be an error in the Capital Equipment line. The amounts seem very low. Quickly go to the menu bar, select the Edit command and Undo the sort that you just performed. Now, your spreadsheet returns to its original form. Go to Cell D7 and look at the formula. Notice that we forecasted Capital Equipment based on the 2001 total (C8*1.015). Why did the amount change when we performed the sort? The answer is that we used a relative reference instead of an absolute reference. The formula should always refer to the 2001 total, so we need to use the "$" in front of both designations. Go to Cell D7 and change your formula to look like: $C$8*1.015. Enter the new formula. Even though we made a mistake with the formula, *Excel* was very forgiving in letting us Undo a command and search for the error. Now, select the range A3:E7 once again. Perform the sort function again, and your spreadsheet should now look like figure 2.8. All the totals should match figure 2.7.

**Figure 2.8: Budget spreadsheet sorted in alphabetical order**

| | File Edit View Insert Format Tools Data Window Help | | | | |
|---|---|---|---|---|---|
| Arial | ▾ 10 ▾ **B** *I* U ≡ ≡ ≡ 📰 $ % | | | | |
| | B11 ▾ = | | | | |
| | A | B | C | D | E |
| 1 | | | **2001** | **2002** | **2003** |
| 2 | **Line #** | **Budget Item** | | | |
| 3 | 6500 | Capital Equipment | $15,000 | $13,965 | $14,105 |
| 4 | 6200 | Consulting | $5,000 | $9,310 | $9,403 |
| 5 | 6100 | Salary | $900,000 | $930,000 | $939,300 |
| 6 | 6300 | Supplies | $7,500 | $13,965 | $14,105 |
| 7 | 6400 | Travel | $3,500 | $3,850 | $3,889 |
| 8 | | **Total** | $931,000 | $971,090 | $980,801 |

The final thing we will do is to create a graph from the spreadsheet data. This is a useful feature of *Excel*, particularly because graphs are more useful for presentations than are spreadsheets full of numbers that an audience cannot understand, or even see.

We are going to make a pie graph of our 2001 spending. Select the range B3:C7 and then

Click    Insert
                Chart.

A dialog box will appear in the middle of your screen. The dialog box has several areas that allow you to make choices regarding the graph you are about to create. On the far left of the dialog box, Chart Type allows you to specify whether you would like a bar graph, a pie graph, etc. Select the *Pie* option. Once you select Pie, the *Chart sub-type* option gives you several types of pie charts from which to choose. We will keep it simple and select the upper left-hand corner and just create an easy-to-understand pie graph. Go to the bottom of the dialog box and Click on the *Next* button to further tailor your graph.

The next dialog box gives you a picture of what your graph looks like so far. Click Next to get to more options. The next dialog box gives you the option of inserting a title. Click on the *Chart Title* box and type: "2001 Spending." Click Next for your final dialog box.

The final dialog box asks if you would like to insert the chart as an object in the same spreadsheet that contains the numerical data from which the chart was constructed. Select the option to create a new sheet and press *Finish*. You should now see a full screen picture of your pie graph. In the last option you choose to create a new sheet for the graph. If you look at the lower left-hand corner of the spreadsheet, you will see several tabs. The first tab has the label *Chart 1* and the second tab *Sheet 1*. If you click your mouse on "Sheet 1" you will see your original spreadsheet. What you just did was create a separate sheet for your chart so that it would not appear in the same sheet as your numerical data. Both sheets, however, are part of the same file, and both will be saved when you save the file.

A final feature of the Chart command is *Excel's* ability to automatically update the chart if any numerical data are changed. Go to Sheet 1 and select Cell C3, which is now the 2001 Capital Equipment line. Change the $15,000 entry to $75,000 and hit Enter. Select the Chart 1 tab and notice that your pie graph has automatically updated. That is, the Capital Equipment segment of the pie is a greater portion than it was originally.

## Conclusions

We have seen that spreadsheets have the ability to manipulate and display data in different ways. The spreadsheet has some capabilities, such as the sort function, that allow the user to perform functions that other software applications are specifically programmed to handle. So, if you needed to sort a massive amount of data, and this was your primary purpose, *Excel* may not be the optimal application. Still, this availability gives the average user the flexibility to manipulate data in basic ways without ever leaving the spreadsheet application.

The power of the spreadsheet is to perform numerical calculations and help you with any task related to numbers. It is likely that you, as an administrator, will not have to delve into the painful details of spreadsheet analysis, but now you have a basic understanding of a powerful tool that can be a tremendous aid in decision making, tracking data, and forecasting the future. Now, you also have an application that you can recommend to the fortunate individual to whom you delegate the task of budgeting.

# 3

# Keeping Track of Tasks and Appointments: Software for Time Management

## Gary Ivory

## The Most Important Book

In 1977, I was a junior high school reading teacher taking a course in school administration at Texas Tech. A fellow student showed me a thin paperback about time management and announced that it was the most valuable book he had ever read for school administrators. Indeed, time is a critical issue in our profession. The very nature of school administration is that it places infinite demands on our time. The frustration of school administration is that we come to it wanting to do good things for children, and then find ourselves consumed by tasks that seem only tangentially related to that goal. Good time management increases the odds that we will get to do the things we value.

The book my colleague showed me was Alan Lakein's *How to Get Control of Your Time and Your Life* (1973). That was more than twenty years ago. Since then, I have been a teacher for four years, and an administrator for fifteen, and I am now venturing on to college professoring. I have to say that when it comes to being productive, there is a sense in which the ideas in that thin paperback have helped me in a way that nothing else has. Lakein took my own problems (I am too busy to get around to what I want to do; I lack self-discipline; I am a procrastinator) and discussed them in such a way that I could see a way out of my difficulties.

You have to read Lakein's book for yourself. I cannot do it justice here. But I will show you how one component of his program can now be computerized. Furthermore, it is the component that requires the most self-discipline. Since self-discipline is not my strong suit, it is nice to have computer assistance with it.

# The List with a Twist

At the center of Lakein's method is your identifying of goals and then making a To-Do list of activities to reach those goals. Making To-Do lists is not new, and it is often not helpful. Anyone can make a list: turn this school around, become the last of the red-hot lovers, win a Nobel Prize, etc. Lakein's genius as a time management expert is to take the To-Do list, which many people use as a pie-in-the-sky time waster, and show you how to use it as a tool of daily decision making.

Lakein's twist is that you do not just make a list—you remake a list each day. Then you rank the items on the list in importance. The ones that are most important to you are coded A; the ones you would very much like to get to are coded B; and the ones that are left are coded C. Then you rank the A items in importance. The most important item for you to work on right now is A-1; the second most important is A-2; the next is A-3, etc. Then you start to work on doing the A-1 item. I found maintaining such a list to be helpful in three ways.

First, it kept me reminding myself of what was truly important to me. For example, I might feel uneasy both about not having finished a report for my boss and for not having visited classrooms. If in making my To-Do list for today I had already decided that it was more important to me to visit classrooms than to respond to reporting requirements, then I would be more likely to work on that and thus get more control of my life.

Second, it was a great stress-reliever. This issue is very important to worriers like me. Without the ranked list, I could worry myself to death over "what I was not doing that I should have been." But since I had thoughtfully ranked the items, I had already decided what was the most important item for me to do and, if I was doing it, I could absolve myself from worrying about the things that I was not doing.

Third, it helped me account for my actions to people who wanted me to complete some task. I could say sincerely, "Well, I'm working on my A-1 item right now, but you're A-4 so I'm going to get to your project real soon." It helped them see that they were not forgotten, and it helped me maintain my priorities. Of course if the questioner was someone with power over me who objected energetically to being an

A-4, then I could always reprioritize the items. This fact brings me to the next part of Lakein's program.

The hard part, the part that requires the most self-discipline, comes next: you have to make a new list, first thing, each and every day. Remember: this system is not just about list making—anyone can do that. This is about decision making each day about what is most important to you. It was hard to make myself haul out my old completed list each day and rewrite all the unfinished items, add new ones, and reevaluate the importance of each. Instead of starting a new day by jumping right in, attending to those nagging pressures (such as the person with power who did not like being an A-4), I was supposed to redo my To-Do list. Remember: the book is about getting control of your life, not about surviving while life is controlling you. But it surely was difficult to make myself revise my list each day. Often I did not follow the program.

## How Can Computers Help?

Fortunately, I happened upon a piece of computer software called *Lotus Agenda*. This was a very sophisticated program that could do many things. But as with most computer software, you needed to learn only a small fraction of its capabilities to make it serve you well. I learned only a handful of *Agenda*'s functions—the ones related to Lakein's system. I learned to type my items into a computerized list and save them so that I did not need to rewrite them each day. Then, instead of rushing to redo my list each day, I could just peruse it in a leisurely way, reevaluating the importance of each item and determining whether its rank ought to be changed. If people started complaining that an A-4 item was not finished, I would change it to an A-1. On the other hand, if I started thinking that my boss had forgotten about an A she gave me to do, I would downgrade the item to a C. Then I found out how to make *Agenda* do an automatic sort, to rearrange the items according to my new rankings with the most important items near the top of the list. Since the task of remaking the list was now so much less laborious, I became more likely to do it regularly.

Today, *Lotus Agenda* is considered obsolete, and is no longer available, but I used it for years with good results. Now *Lotus* has replaced it with something called *Organizer*. This chapter discusses *Organizer 5.0*. No doubt newer versions will be available by the time you read this. Other publishers produce software that performs similar functions, e.g., *Microsoft Outlook*. Here I am going to concentrate just on *Lotus Organizer* to give you a flavor of how such systems work. My version of *Organizer* is *Windows*-based. That means that it has a menu bar across the top of the screen that gives you options to choose. Figure 3.1 shows how to get started.

**Figure 3.1: Opening the To-Do list in *Organizer***

Click      Section

        Turn to

                To Do.

When you click on *To Do*, you'll get a really snazzy picture of a three-ring notebook.

You double click with the mouse anywhere on the notebook page entitled "To Do." As figure 3.2 shows, a smaller window entitled *Create Task* appears. In the space called *Description*, you type the task. If you want, you can now click *OK*, and the task will appear on the notebook page.

But it is important to adhere to Lakein's method and assign priorities to tasks. In the same Create Task window where it says, *Priority*, select either *1, 2, 3*, or *No priority*. Then click OK.

**Figure 3.2: The "Create Task" Window**

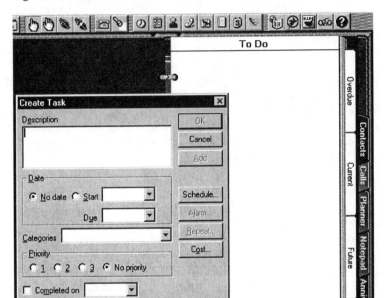

If you have several things to add to your To Do list at one sitting (and if you are a school administrator, that is probably the case), then instead of clicking OK, click the button that says *Add*. The item you just added will go into your list; the Description area will go blank; and you will have a new space place to add a second item. When you finish entering all the tasks, click OK and you will see them nicely entered on the notebook page.

Now you can list the items by priority if you like. Point the mouse at the menu bar running across the top of the screen.

Click     View
                By Priority.

Your notebook will now have three dividers with a tab on each divider, one marked 1, one marked 2, and one marked 3. When you click on each tab, the page under it will appear and you will see the items you coded with that priority.

If you prefer Lakein's classification of A's, B's, or C's, you can have that. Just move the mouse to the menu bar.

Click      View
                  To Do Preferences.

A window will appear with a section called Options, and within that section an item called *Priority As*. Click the Priority As down arrow and it will give you a choice of either 1, 2, 3; A, B, C; or H, M, L (for High, Middle, and Low priority). Select your choice and click OK. The tabs on the notebook dividers (and the priority of each item on the pages) will change to reflect your new choice.

# How Else Will *Organizer* Help?

Just as *Lotus Agenda* did, *Lotus Organizer* performs many applications in addition to keeping your To Do list. And just as with *Agenda*, you can get great benefit out of learning just a few of those. Besides the To Do list, among other functions, *Organizer* provides a Calendar, a place to list Contacts, and a Planner. The great advantage of *Organizer* is that one program keeps such a variety of information. But if you do not have time to learn how to use all of these applications, you can still get benefit from the To Do List and the Calendar.

## The Alarm

I never found a way to make either Lakein's hand-written To-Do list nor *Lotus Agenda* do this next thing: You can make *Organizer* sound an alarm when a deadline is approaching. Hectic and full of interruptions as our lives are, the alarm can be really useful.

When you are entering an item in the Create Task window, look down toward the middle where it says, Date. If you select *No Date*, you obviously do not need an alarm. If, however, you select either *Start* or *Due*, and click on the down-arrow, a small calendar will drop down and allow you to select the due date (figure 3.3).

To the right of the calendar is a button that says *Alarm*. If you click on that button, a new window will appear on which you can select date, time, and the type of alarm sound you want to hear. Just look in the *Tune* menu for an alarm to your liking. Bach or Beethoven, anyone? You anglophiles can even get it to play "Rule Britannia," and (lest they be accused of bias) the *Lotus* staff has also included the "Marseillaise." Click on the *Play* button on the right to hear a preview (See figure 3.4).

**Figure 3.3: Selecting a Start or Due date in the Create Task Window**

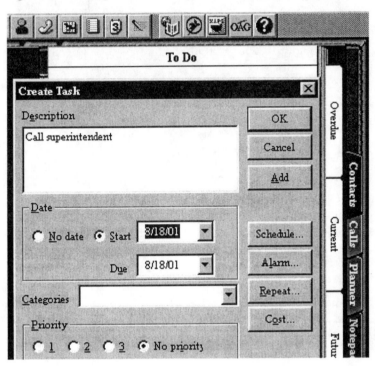

Below the Tune menu, the window says Message. Here you can enter a reminder, such as: "Take a notepad to the meeting so others will think I am interested." When the alarm sounds, the message will appear on the screen. In fact, as long as you have *Organizer* running, you will get the alarm, even if you are working in some other software. You could be composing a letter in your word processing software and when the alarm sounds, you will be taken over to the *Organizer* window where the message will appear.

**Figure 3.4: Selecting a tune for the alarm**

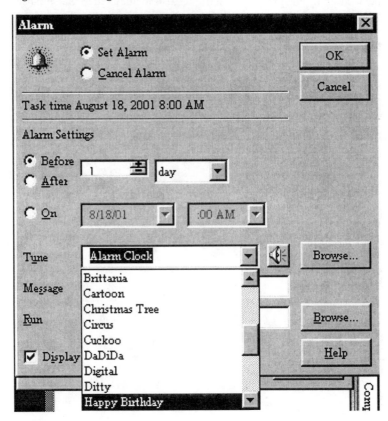

## The *Lotus Organizer* Calendar

The lives of many school leaders are tied closely to the calendar. Maybe that is why when you start *Organizer* running the calendar will appear automatically. If it doesn't, just use the mouse to go to the menu bar.

Click    Section
              Turn To Calendar.

A calendar will appear showing twelve months on one screen. But you have choices as to how much of your calendar to see on the screen at once. Point the mouse at today's date and double click. Then click View on the menu bar. A menu drops down and gives you a choice of several views, for example:

- *Day per Page*—This will give you a typical appointment calendar with today shown on the left-hand page and tomorrow shown on the right-hand page.

- *Work Week*—Monday, Tuesday, and Wednesday on the left-hand page and Thursday, Friday, Saturday, and Sunday on the right-hand page.

- *Week per Page*—All the days of this week on the left-hand page and all the days of next week on the right-hand page.

- *Month*—A typical wall calendar page except that the month starts with today and the week starts with Monday. Saturday and Sunday are scrunched up over on the right.

The great thing about this View menu is that however you enter events, you can always go to this menu and select a different view. That is, even if you started with Day per Page to enter appointments, you can always get a different view without losing or changing the information you have entered. In addition, in many views, the To Do list will also appear in the calendar.

And what about appointments: The school board member's visit? The union leader's request for a meeting? The parent coming to complain because his child's ID number contains the digits "666?" You do not want to miss those. *Organizer's* Calendar can help you remember them all.

Click    View
                Day per Page.

Move the mouse to any point in the day and double click. A *Create Appointment* window appears (figure 3.5) in which you can type in a description of the appointment. Look closely and you will see that you can also specify the need for an alarm, just as in tasks. Once you specify your alarm preferences and click OK in the Create Appointment window, the appointment will appear in your calendar, just as if you had written it onto a paper version.

**Figure 3.5: The Create Appointment window**

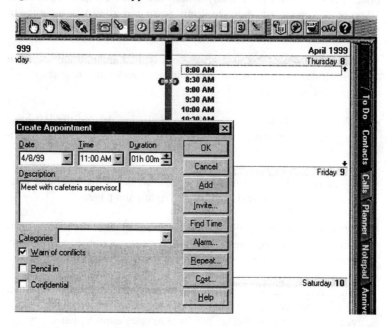

## Repeating Appointments

Then there are the appointments that never go away: the weekly staff meeting, taking Junior for his allergy shots, and giving the dog her heartworm pills each month. *Organizer* really handles this well. The Create Appointment window has a *Repeat* button. Click on it and you can select how you want *Organizer* to automatically schedule the appointment: daily, weekly, monthly, or yearly. Do you have a weird recurrence, such as the school dance every six weeks? Changing the oil in the car every six months?

Select *Custom*; click on the *Custom Dates* menu (figure 3.6); and a small calendar will appear. Click on any dates you like; click on the right arrow at the top of the calendar to select dates in the future. After each date that you select, click the *Add* button, and the date will appear in the box just above Custom Dates. You may never have to worry about missing an appointment again. Furthermore, your dog *and your crankcase* will thank you.

**Figure 3.6: Customizing the calendar for unusual recurrences**

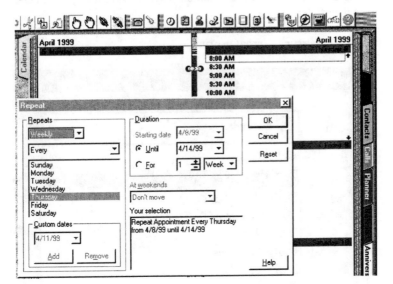

## Carrying Your Calendar in Your Pocket

This one took me a while to figure out. I would sit in a meeting at which we had to (you guessed it) plan our next meeting. Everyone would pull out their calendars and start looking for available dates. I always hoped no one would notice that I did not have a calendar with me. It was on my computer—which I did not want to lug from meeting to meeting. So that was my dilemma: I could have my calendar on my computer, which did lots of things automatically but was not portable, or I could have my calendar on a piece of paper, which was totally portable but did not do anything automatically.

Fortunately, *Organizer* allows you to print your calendar. Then you can have the best of both worlds in your shirt pocket or purse. Use the mouse to point at the menu bar.

Click     File
                    Print.

A *Print* window will appear. Under the Section menu, select Calendar. Under the *Layout* menu (figure 3.7), select the format you prefer. There are many choices; you will have to try them out until you find your preferences. Under the *Range* menu, select the beginning and ending dates that you desire. Then click OK and retrieve your calendar from the printer.

**Figure 3.7: Selecting a layout to print**

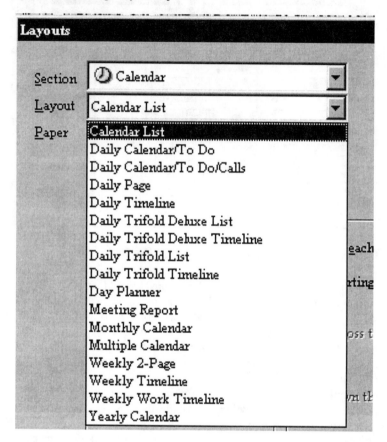

## Getting Down All the Details

A component of my job that I always used to have difficulty with was the long detailed assignment. I would run into the boss in the corridor and he would say:

I am assigning you the project that Judy was working on, the GED testing program. Now, it is pretty near the end of the fiscal year and she may have been supposed to order new tests, so find out if she was supposed to and if she did. Then, if she is supposed to have and did not, go see the budget director and ask that the money for the new tests be appropriated from either the guidance program or the community services program, whichever she (the budget director) thinks is most appropriate. Then write a memo justifying the budget amendment to the school board and have it to the superintendent two weeks before the next meeting. Be sure and attend the meeting so that you can answer any questions. Then [here he finally takes a breath] call the principal over at Ross Perot High School and find out if he has an extra room we can use for testing, about four evenings a month. Well, first call the GED office in either Washington, D.C. or the state education department and find out if we are allowed to administer the GED test anywhere other than the central administration building.

I, of course, was carrying only a felt tip pen and a brochure for the Santa Fe Opera when he stopped me, and had by now covered the brochure with letters half-an-inch high detailing as much of this as I could get down. How does all of that get into my To Do list?

No problem. Remember how you create a new task? You double click on the To Do page and the Create Task window appears with a Description space. The space looks as if it would hold four or five lines of text. But instead, as you type, the text moves upward out of the way and you can continue typing an almost unlimited amount. In fact, you can fit in all the details you have written on the Santa Fe Opera brochure. When you click OK, it all appears on your To Do page.

## Defending Your Life

At times, my job in central office administration reminded me of *Defending Your Life*, the movie with Meryl Streep and Albert Brooks. A guy dies and goes to Heaven and is told by the staff there that in order to stay he has to convince them that he has spent his time on earth well. School board elections can create similar situations for administrators. A candidate runs on a platform of saving money, preferably by cutting excess do-nothing staff from central administration. Then he wins the election. Invariably, his first action is to ask for a list of tasks performed by each central office administrator.

I always found this ironic. The administrator whose productivity was in question had to interrupt his/her productivity to document it. A factor that made such assignments especially trying for me was that I was juggling many tasks at once. Whenever I finished one, the relief was always so great that I would absolve myself from ever thinking of it again. The problem with this is that when someone asked what I had worked on, I honestly would not remember much of it. But *Lotus Organizer* can help.

See, in Lakein's original scheme to get control of your time and your life, everything is on paper. When you finish a task, you cross it off your list, and the next day when you make a new list, you simply do not write this item down anymore. You have no record to help you remember what you have done. But when you finish a task in *Organizer*, you simply go into the To Do list and click on a little box to the left of the item. The item is moved to a section of the binder called *Completed*, and a check mark appears in the little box showing that the task has been completed, as is shown in figure 3.8.

**Figure 3.8: Completed tasks *Organizer* To Do list**

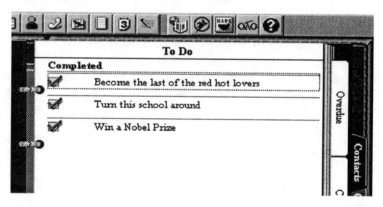

Now, when someone asks you to interrupt your work and defend your life, you can go to the Completed section of the To Do list, find a record of everything you have worked on, and quickly prepare your report for the board member.

Of course, at some point you need to clear this page. Board members do not have much interest in the study you wrote in 1988, *Cost/benefit analysis of Commodore 64 vs. Apple II-e*. To erase an old task, click on it and then use the mouse to point to the menu bar.
Click     Edit
         Clear

and the item will be erased.

## Keeping Track of Contacts

I mentioned at the beginning of this chapter that one of the great things about *Organizer* is that it lets you keep so many useful things in the same place. It is time now to talk more about that.

You probably already have a list of phone numbers and postal or e-mail addresses somewhere. The computer generation did not invent the idea of writing down ways to contact people, but what *Organizer* provides is a convenient way to maintain that information.

Click     Section
         Turn To
            Contacts.

On any page in the Contacts section, double click on a blank portion of the page. The *Create Contact* window will appear, with spaces to enter several items of information about the person. You can enter as much or as little as you wish. In figure 3.9, notice that the window contains three tabs, for work, home, and general information.

When you have entered as much information as you like, click OK. The information will be saved on the appropriate page in alphabetical order. Later, if you decide to change any information, you go to that page of the address book and double click on the address. An *Edit Address* window will appear and allow you to make changes.

Suppose you go to work in the morning and after reviewing your To Do list decide that the most important thing for you to do right now is to contact Martha Chaparro, the PTA president, about finalizing plans for the fast-approaching Halloween carnival. You simply turn to the Contacts section to find her phone number. Click the tab with the letter C. Contacts opens to the Cs. Chaparro may not be on the first page. Press the *PgDn* key to turn pages until you get to her listing (use *PgUp* to go back a page). There you will find whatever information you have entered: phone and fax numbers and e-mail addresses. There is also room for her assistant's name, any notes you need to keep on her, and other miscellaneous data (six spaces under the *Home* tab). *Organizer's* Contacts function can help you get started quickly on your #1 priority for the moment.

**Figure 3.9: Entering contact information**

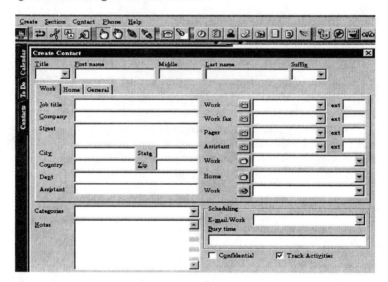

## Using Planner for Items that Take a Long Time

Only some of an administrator's responsibilities involve relatively finite items, things you can complete in a few minutes or an hour. Some of the more important responsibilities can take weeks or months, even years: implement a five-year-plan to decrease the dropout rate; carry out the board mandate that every building in the district have adequate and reliable air conditioning; bring the social studies curriculum into line with proposed national standards. It takes a long time before you get to cross such items off your To Do list.

Notice chapter 13 on tech planning by Karin Wiburg. She advises educators to complete six steps: 1) Creating the future, 2) Assessing your school or district, 3) Establishing strategic goals, 4) Building a Technology Integration Plan, 5) Making sure the plan happens, and 6) Evaluating and adjusting the plan. Now I see most or all of those steps as involving study and discussions among district educators; these steps will take time—maybe months or years. *Organizer's* list of tasks to do does not really seem to represent such responsibilities accurately. So, let us discuss the *Planner* function.

Planner lets you designate blocks of time that projects will take. So instead of putting in your To Do list an item such as, "Call budget director," you enter something like, "Meet with curriculum specialists, parents, and teachers to set priorities for instruction." You might intend to have such meetings concluded only after three or six months. For a major revamping, you may need to meet for a year or more.

Click    Section
       Go To
          Planner.

Or merely click the Planner tab on your three-ring binder. You see a rather intimidating looking form, much like wall charts that appear in corporate managers' offices (figure 3.10).

Notice what it contains: Down the left-hand side you see the months of the year; across the top are the days of the week; narrow rectangles outlined in red show the length of each month; because months are different lengths and begin on different days, these red rectangles are staggered. Thus, Planner lets you see a whole year in one view. Move your cursor across the rectangles. Notice that the date shown at the bottom of the screen changes to reflect which part of the calendar your cursor is touching. Further to the left of the names of the months are tabs for past years. On the right are tabs for future years. Click on a tab and see a different year in one view.

So how would we use Planner to carry out any part of Karin's prescription for tech planning? To begin, she suggests "Creating the future." The first step of that is "the identification of all people affected by the plan, the stakeholders, and ways for these people to provide input." Well, okay, maybe that step does not require Planner; you can sit down with a couple of colleagues and brainstorm a list of stakeholders.

But consider Step 2: "Agreement on the purpose of the plan prior to proceeding." Presumably, agreement will require time and numerous meetings. Maybe we should allocate a three-month period to achieving that, say, Friday March 15, 2002 to Friday June 14. Move your cursor to the bottom of the screen.

Click the tag that says "02."

Click     Create
                   Event.

**Figure 3.10: Opening the Planner**

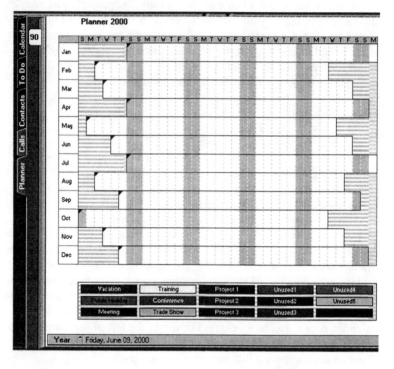

The *Create Event* box appears. For *Event type*, click the pull-down arrow and select *Meeting*. Use the *From* and *To* pull-down menus to designate beginning and ending dates for this series of meetings. In the *Notes* section, enter a description of the event. When you click OK, a blue stripe appears to show the three-month period. When you move your cursor over the blue stripe, the description that you entered in Notes appears at the bottom of the page.

Now add a second event, one that overlaps with this one, as events in school administration tend to do. Suppose that you have decided you need to devote February and March to reviewing last year's expenditures and developing a proposal for next year's budget.

Click     Create
                   Event

Select an Event type with a different color from the blue Tech planning event. Notice that there is a place to select the row. Make sure that you select a row different from the row where you have already put the blue Tech planning event. Enter whatever notes you like, set the beginning and ending dates, and click OK. Now you should have two different colored stripes on your planner, and you should be able to see where they overlap. That will be a busy two weeks! In fact, you can enter several projects to go on at the same time.

By the way, if you want to review or revise the specifics of any event, for example, suppose you selected the same row for both events, you can always double click on the colored stripe and the *Edit event* box will appear. This box looks just like the Create event box. Here, you can make changes to the specifics of an event.

Now, to see just how helpful this software can be, click the Calendar tab on your notebook. Click the arrows on the small month calendar to the left of the notebook to go to March 2002. Notice that the colored stripes appear on the page of your calendar labeled with the notes that you entered for this event. Your calendar is now reminding you that you are planning to do a major project during this time.

## Saved for Last—The Most Important Thing

Combining the ideas in Lakein's book with computer software really helped me survive my 15 years in school administration. I met many of my own goals and enough of the organization's goals to stay out of trouble. There was, however, one drawback. The computer worked so well for me that I became very dependent on it. *And then one day my hard drive crashed.* Ironically, this is both less and more dramatic than it sounds.

Hard drives crash with no noise. There is no flying debris, no skid marks, no police sirens, and no reporters on the scene. It is just as if you had a file cabinet containing years of records and projects in various states of completion, and then one day the file folders were magically removed, all the staples were pulled, and all the papers were shuffled. Next the file cabinet locked itself. That is all. Nothing more dramatic than the loss of years of effort.

Now imagine that inside the file cabinet is your To Do list, your daily decision-making tool. That is what happened to me. When I lost the contents of my hard drive, I lost my To Do list, and with it I lost control of my time and my life. For about a week I came to work each day and sat inactive and insecure. Questions without answers raced through my brain: On what was I to base my decision making? What if I was forgetting some terribly important task? What if I started to do something and it was not an A-1, but merely an A-2? The feeling of disorientation was paralyzing. After several days, of course, I made a new list and started over. I was no worse off than I had been before I ever started using the system, and I did not get fired, so apparently I had not forgotten any of the really important stuff. But I would prefer never to have gone through the ordeal.

## Doing the Most Important Thing

The good news is that you can set *Organizer* to make a backup file automatically whenever you close it down. So when you get to the end of a day of supporting students, dealing with unfunded mandates, and trying to resolve petty squabbles, there is at least one thing you won't have to worry about: You won't have to back up your *Organizer* files.

Click     File
                   User Setup
                           *Organizer* Preferences.

The *Organizer* Preferences window appears (figure 3.11). It has four tabs showing; click the one that says, *Default File*. In the bottom half of the window, where it says, *Backup*, look at the little box that says, *Create backup when closed*. If it already has a checkmark inside, leave it alone. *Organizer* will never forget to make a backup for you. If, on the other hand, the little box is empty, click inside it and a check mark will appear. Now whenever you finish working in *Organizer* and close it, it will automatically make a backup copy of current *Organizer* files.

It may be, though, that as it is currently programmed *Organizer* backs up your records to the hard drive. This does not help in case of a hard drive crash. So let us reprogram *Organizer* to back up our information to a floppy disk.

Click     File
                   User Setup
                           *Organizer* Preferences.

In the *Organizer* Preferences window, click on the *Folders* tab. You will see locations for four files, the last of which is *Backups*. As I said, it may already specify that the backup is to be written to the hard drive. But you can change that. Just replace "c:\lotus\backup\organize" with the name of your floppy drive (probably "a:"). Now, when you close *Organizer* at the end of the day, your backup will be written to the "a" drive. You can put the floppy disk in your shirt pocket or your purse, and not have to worry about what happens to the lists, calendars, and addresses on your hard drive—if, that is, you have remembered to insert a disk into your "a" drive. If you have not, you will get the message shown in figure 3.12.

**Figure 3.11: Setting preferences in *Organizer***

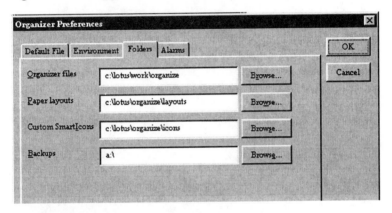

**Figure 3.12: Reminder to insert a diskette into the floppy drive**

"The device is not ready" is computer talk for "Put a disk in the disk drive." You insert the disk, click on "OK," and your backup will be successfully written to the floppy disk.

I emphasized in the preface that computers are only tools. They do not do the important work of administration, developing visions of good schools, leading people to follow your vision, and carrying out the nuts-and-bolts activities to turn a vision into reality. Nor do computers create what we sometimes feel we need, more hours in a day. But there is computer software out there that will help us manage time more efficiently and thus get around more often to doing what we really value. And for that reason, they are very good tools, indeed.

# Reference

Lakein, A. 1973. *How to Get Control of Your Time and Your Life*. New York, N.Y.: Signet Book, New American Library.

# 4

# Keeping Track of Students
# and Making Decisions

## Tom Ryan

As a high school principal and teacher, I have used electronic *database management systems* (*DBMS*) to improve efficiency, communication, and learning opportunities for students, teachers, and administrators. Integrating electronic DBMS into my school has allowed me to spend less time on the management of my school and more time on instructional leadership. The database systems described are used to help keep track of students and information in a school. The systems presented have been developed over time and through trial and error. Exploring the possibilities of database management systems has provided me with several positive insights about how schools are managed and led and about how to ensure their success.

## Database Management Systems

A database is a collection of information or data that can be organized and analyzed. Examples of simple databases might include: phone and address books, filing cabinets, bankbook registers, and inventories. Electronic database management systems save information digitally, making it easier to organize and retrieve important data.

Typically, student records are stored on cards and paper in files. The paper is stored (or lost) in offices, filing cabinets, and closets and on desks. Management of data in this fashion is extremely expensive due to the time it takes an employee to create, file, sort, and retrieve documents needed. Secure storage space for paperwork that must be maintained for several years complicates the issue even more. On the other hand, in an electronic system, an entire year of data can be easily maintained on a compact disk (CD) for a fraction of the cost of paper management systems.

Electronic databases incorporate many of the assets of other software tools such as word processing, spreadsheet, and drawing programs. Information is collected, shared, and analyzed from several points within the school or over the Internet or an Intranet. Data are easily accessed, providing the information necessary to make informed decisions and to save time in the process. Hand-held devices such as *Personal Information Managers* (*PIMs*) typically employ predesigned data management systems. PIMs store and organize phone numbers, notes, addresses, calendars and other important data. PIMs have become very popular especially since they can be connected to PCs to share information or transmit data through a direct cable, infrared, or modem connection.

Some school districts have invested in centralized computer database systems for storing information on large mainframe computers. Traditionally, these systems are difficult to access due to the need for security and the small number of terminals. Requesting unusual combinations of data from these systems can take hours of programmer time. Often, systems are limited to a select few employees. But, personal computers are now powerful enough to handle most school database needs and do it much more effectively!

## A Database to Fit Your Needs

Electronic databases can be purchased as predesigned management systems, or built from scratch using software such as *Appleworks*, *Filemaker Pro*, and *Microsoft Access*. Predesigned programs are available for schools to manage a wide range of administrative data. A school or school district can purchase attendance, discipline, and other student information programs. These predesigned programs can be effective tools for school leaders.

Many school administrators, however, do not have the resources to purchase predesigned management systems. Purchase of such programs in large districts can be very difficult, expensive, and political, making prompt change almost impossible. Furthermore, predesigned programs often require schools to modify existing systems to fit program protocols. Modifying predesigned programs can reduce effectiveness and efficiency.

The lack of flexibility and the expense of predesigned programs motivated me to explore designing an electronic DBMS that met my specific needs. I designed my first system in *Clarisworks*. Designing a database is not difficult, although it can be intimidating at first. In fact, personally designed systems have several advantages. You can tailor and modify your system to your school's specific needs. District goals, superintendents, school boards, and political issues change frequently along with expectations for school administrators. So your DBMS must be flexible. If you designed your own system, then you can modify it to adapt to those changes. Furthermore, there are indirect benefits from learning how a DBMS works. The database planning procedure forced me to look at processes throughout my school from registration to student discipline. I am now able to review, modify, and improve systems that are in place for the sole reason that it has always been done that way. I can easily modify my personally designed database to meet the ever-changing demands of running a school.

# Simplification by Database

As a principal, one of the most valuable resources I have is time. I am constantly looking for ways to reduce the time my staff and I spend on routine, noninstructional activities. If I can identify a problem early and apply an appropriate response, I save time. In reviewing the activities of my clerical staff, I found that their skills and talents were not being effectively used. They spent an inordinate amount of time filing, refiling, and searching for student information. Filling out school, district, and state required forms robbed them of precious time. Often information requested on various forms had to be researched, typed, and duplicated. A student assistant could have accomplished many of the activities consuming the time of my clerical staff. Tracking down information was also a difficult, time-exhausting function that required my secretary to engage several different data storage systems.

The student discipline-referral process is a prime example of time assassination. In conversations with other administrators, I have learned that the following scenario is not uncommon: the student misbehaves in class; a referral is written on a multicopy referral form; the referral form is sent to my office; then it is directed to the appropriate secretary. When I am available to deal with the referral, she will need to give me a history of past offenses and student information such as parent names and phone numbers.

In order to retrieve this information, my secretary would pull an 8" x 5" card from a student filing system for personal information and class assignment. She would then find and pull the student folder containing notes, past referrals, and parent communications. She would provide me with this information so that I could investigate—time permitting—attendance and grades from the district computer database system. I would then hold a conference with the student and assign appropriate consequences. Consequences would be recorded on the 8" x 5" card and on the referral form. Staff would then contact parents and perhaps record their reaction. One copy of the referral form would be placed in the student folder, another sent to the appropriate teacher, and yet a third sent home with the student. At this point, a form might be sent to another office or person, indicating times and days for suspension, detention, or community service. After all the paperwork was completed, it was sent back to my secretary to be filed in the appropriate files.

Several problems were inherent in this system. It is not uncommon for a student to have multiple referrals in a brief time period. Therefore, referrals and student information might still be scattered over several administrators' and secretaries' desks when the student broke another rule! Some folders containing student information were misfiled, never to be seen again. Students were often assigned to specific administrators based on grade level or last name. When someone other than the student's assigned administrator handled a referral, finding accurate student information became extremely difficult. The student would be sitting in someone's office waiting to be seen and not in class; secretaries were searching for the records, unable to perform their other duties; and the administrator would assign consequences to the student without complete information. Teachers and parents complained about the inconsistency of the administrative team, and information to refute the allegation was too difficult to research.

Working in this environment was extremely frustrating! Referrals were piling up on my desk, instructional responsibilities were being neglected, teachers were complaining, and above all I was losing my hair to stress. As a teacher, I had organized my record keeping using a simple electronic database to record information about my students on my laptop computer. I thought an electronic database would also help me organize my administrative life. My experience with computers was limited to simple word processing, basic spreadsheets, and elementary databases, all created in an early version of *ClarisWorks*. I pulled out the *ClarisWorks* manual and started to build a student referral database.

# Developing an Electronic Database

Databases have *fields* and *records*. A field is one item of information; a record is a collection of items about one person or event. In handling student discipline, each referral, whether written or digital, is a record. As figure 4.1 shows, each record contains fields to enter information. This is like any form you fill out. Each item of information is a field; the entire form is a record; and a file drawer full of forms is a database.

Typical fields in a student referral record would include student name, ID number, address, grade, violation, and consequences. I designed my first student database using information from the student referral form my school used. I found this to be an important first step.

Starting with a process that I was familiar with afforded me the opportunity to focus on learning about databases instead of redesigning a referral system. I made my printed referral form look as similar to the old form as possible, thereby making the process familiar to the staff and administration. Changing things through the use of new technology can create anxiety. But since I had incorporated the old forms into my new system, I was able to keep my computerized database program compatible with the paper forms the other administrators were still using.

Since information was already stored in the electronic DBMS, it made sense to print data automatically to look like existing paper forms or reports. As I developed my electronic DBMS to track information, I tried to duplicate the look of the existing paper forms provided by the district. If even the smallest detail of a form was different from the original, clerical personnel resisted. Often, I would receive a lengthy hand written letter instructing me to transfer the same data to the "official" form when the only difference between the two forms was a slight difference in font type.

# Layouts

To print out forms, I created different layouts within my database system. A layout is a presentation of specific information contained in the database. Though a database may have many fields, a particular layout shows only the ones pertinent to a particular need. Figure 4.1 (above) shows a layout that contains just nine fields of information, though the database contains many more. If information is input or modified once on one layout, it is input or modified on the underlying database, so all layouts dependent on that database will reflect the change. Layouts make electronic DBMS extremely powerful. An electronic DBMS may contain several different layouts (see figure 4.2 for another example) that can be added to or modified at any time. Each layout contains several fields of information. The electronic student database I created had several different layouts such as address labels, discipline records, locker lists, suspension reports, and new student enrollment forms.

**Figure 4 .1: Examples of fields in one record of a database**

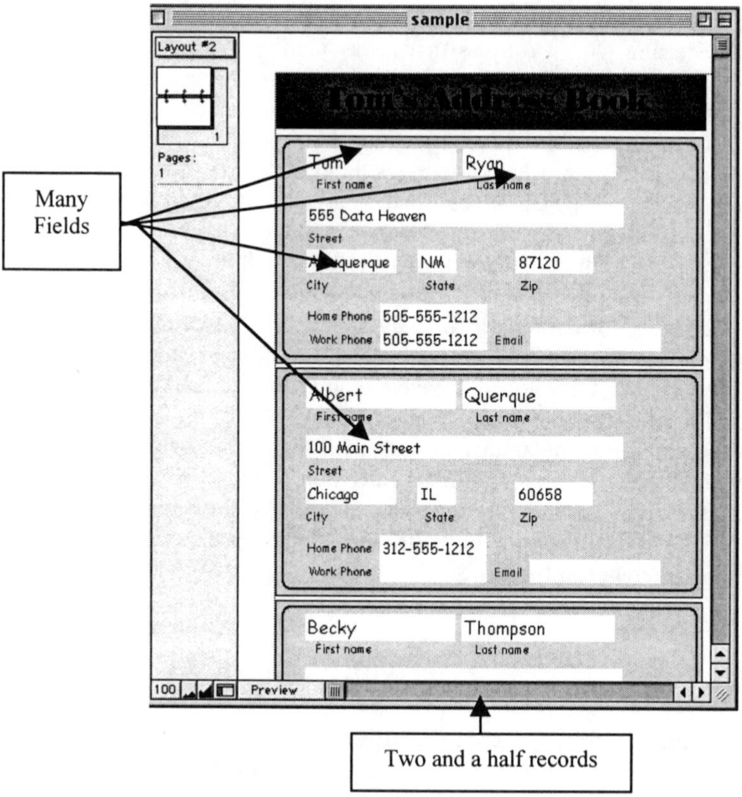

I find that proper layout design increases user understanding of the data, speed in accessing appropriate information, and presentation of material in a professional manner. Too many data can create confusion and information overload. One asset of electronic database systems is the ability to create layouts that contain just the information necessary for a task. Designing layouts is similar to using the drawing tools in *ClarisWorks* or *MS Word*. Each layout contains different font sizes and styles, colors, shapes, and graphics. Changing text and background color not only provides a more attractive presentation, but also can increase understanding of the data. I make fonts red and bold when I want to draw attention to a field. But be careful: although adding color and graphics may improve screen appearance of layouts, it slows down printing; colors and graphics may not always print well and background colors can make text difficult to read.

As I became more familiar and comfortable with database operations, my system expanded and evolved. I learned how to add graphics and color, personalize the forms, and develop different uses for the system. I included more information fields such as parent names and work phone numbers and student addresses. I also added *check boxes* for special education and regular education classifications. Check boxes allow you to quickly mark or identify a record. A check box acts as a *toggle switch* between two choices such as on/off or yes/no.

## Fine Tuning a Database Management System

Although I was impressed with my database efforts, the staff became overwhelmed with all the data presented on the forms. Feedback from staff members led me to improve my database by grouping information into three basic areas: student information on the top, referral information in the middle, and administrative response on the bottom. I placed information in boxes and increased the font size of the student's name and made it bold (figure 4.2). These changes and database design improved the system tremendously and made it much friendlier.

The discipline referral process has now changed for my secretary and me. For one thing, we no longer need carbon copy referral forms. When a student is sent to the office, the secretary attaches the paper referral to the student information card. I search the database for any prior referrals on the student. I type the reason for the referral into the electronic DBMS record while I discuss the issue with the student. By the end of the conference I have entered my disciplinary response as well as dates and documentation of parent contact. Finally, I print two copies of the form, one for the student to take home and one for the teacher that submitted the referral.

Figure 4.2: My simplified student discipline report

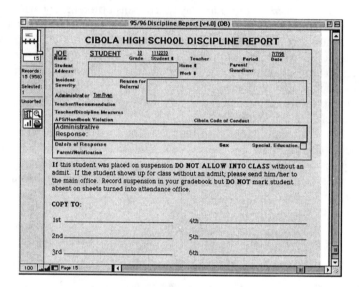

Feedback regarding the process is very positive. With the new system I am able to inform teachers very quickly regarding the discipline of their students. Furthermore, since we display accurate parent information on the return form, teachers can contact parents more easily. So they contact them more frequently. My secretary has less filing to do and we can access information more easily.

At the end of the semester I tallied my results, something else that is easier with an electronic DBMS than with a paper-based system. I was amazed to see how many student conferences I had been involved in—over 1000 in one semester! I knew I was overworked, and now I could prove it (though it did not get me a raise

But, as I tried to tally discipline referrals by infraction, I ran into some trouble. I had entered information differently from one student record to another for the same discipline infraction or response. Sometimes I would enter "profane" or "tobacco use" and on other occasions I would write "vulgarity" or "smoking." But I had to identify exactly what I was looking for when doing a search through the database. If I entered information the same way every time, it would be easier. So, I designated fields as *pull-down menus* (figure 4.4) to make sure I entered data accurately. The pull-down menu gave me a list of choices to select from, which both saved me time in typing information and ensured that entries were consistent.

I developed pull-down menus for several fields: violations, administrative responses, the administrator handling the infraction, the school code of conduct, and parent notification. Most computer databases also include options to modify fields to enter data automatically such as city, state, and zip code. With each new record, the current date was entered automatically to save time and ensure accuracy.

# Keeping Track Electronically

The referral process has been refined. Once a referral is turned in to the office, the secretary enters the data into the system. The student is sent to the administrator who calls up the referral on her machine. Consequences are determined during the conference and entered into the appropriate fields, and parent contact is documented. The teacher's original referral is the only necessary paperwork. No filing, duplication of information, or lost records ties down clerical and administrative staff. And another problem has been solved: sometimes parents contacted me by phone to complain about an assistant principal's decision to suspend their child faster than the assistant can make it to my office to give me the details. With the networked database, I have the information at my fingertips. I can now review the past discipline history of the student and talk with the parent intelligently.

The more information I included in my electronic DBMS, the greater the need to organize, sort, and find it in different ways. I can now search the database using any field or multiple fields to find information. During a parent conference, I often review all referrals for the student with the parents. I am able to call up all the student's referrals by searching the database by student ID number. Once all the referrals are located, I can sort them by date. A chronological listing of referrals helps me to communicate to parents a progressive discipline plan for their child. When I find several referrals over a short period of time, it is typically associated with a traumatic event in the child's life.

A better understanding of the causes of discipline problems has helped me make better decisions about consequences for specific infractions.

**Figure 4.3: Pull-down menu to record discipline violations**

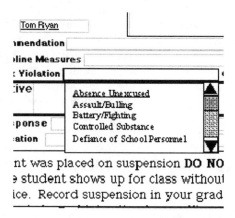

## The Evolution of a DBMS

As the uses for the database grew, the need for a more powerful database program became evident. For one thing, *ClarisWorks* was not a multi-user program. Only one person could access the student database at a time. That meant each administrator had to have his/her own DBMS and we had to manually combine the information from each administrator's database to get school totals. I needed a database program that allowed multiple users at the same time to access data over a network. I also preferred a software program that could support both *Mac* and *PC* platforms. *Filemaker Pro* was the answer. *Filemaker Pro* is a much more powerful program and it allowed all administrators and clerical staff access to the DBMS at the same time. It also provides password protection as well as different access privileges to groups or individuals.

I learned the hard way to provide different levels of access. After I had designed the DBMS and taught my team how to use it, one of the clerical staff wanted to help, and deleted several student records by mistake. My administrators now use a password so that only they can access, read, and write in the referral layout. The clerical staff cannot write in the referral section, but can read and update the student information layout. Comments made about staff members in the evaluation section of the Staff Database cannot be viewed by anyone outside of the administrative team.

Another major asset of *Filemaker Pro* is the ability to set a schedule for backing up data. Scheduling backups of data is crucial in developing a DBMS. Using the *ClarisWorks* program, I had been backing-up to floppy or zip disks because the files were not very big. Backing-up on floppy and zip disks is not the most reliable method of saving information since disks can easily be damaged, lost, or stolen. I had developed a simple system using a different disk each time I made a backup. On odd weeks, I copied to disk 1 and on even weeks, I copied to disk 2. This way, if one disk went bad I still had a relatively recent backup. Our current system backs up data to a tape drive in the server room. This system is automatic and much more reliable. Each night the electronic DBMS is copied to the server. The server is located in a different part of the building, providing greater protection against fire and theft.

My database management system has evolved over the last couple of years. Our current database imports all student personal information from a *Unisys* mainframe system the school district uses. We request a copy of student information to be saved to a floppy disk or sent through e-mail in a text file. Most computer programs can read text files. So, *Filemaker Pro* easily imports the student information into the database at the school site, saving considerable data-entry time. Our registrar enters information about new students. Since several people use the electronic DBMS, no one person is entering all the data. Some of my administrative team do not feel comfortable adding a lot of data and have their secretary enter most of the information regarding discipline referrals. The Student Activities office enters information about lockers and student parking.

Our database management system is no longer considered just a student discipline database, but also a student information system. Information about students includes discipline referrals, conferences, locker numbers, parking permits, and pictures. At our high school, we sort data in a variety of ways. For example, for our parking lot security staff, we sort information three different ways: by student name, by license plate number, and by parking permit number. This allows them to identify a student by the car s/he drives, identify a student who left the vehicle lights on, or identify the vehicle a student drives when in possession of contraband. We have developed forms that are printed with all the important information already filled in, saving time and money. We developed identification cards with pictures using a standard color printer and then laminated them for students. At the end of the semester we do a search for all students placed on long-term suspension. We generate a personalized letter from within the database inviting students back to school for the second semester. We print our own address labels using a label layout. My clerical staff no longer has to search through folders or lists, fill out form letters, and type address labels.

Because each administrator and secretary uses the database system throughout the day, we developed a menu screen to make it easier to move between layouts. This screen also provides a measure of privacy to student information, because not every person in the building has access to every layout. The various layouts represented on the menu screen are accessed through buttons. Clicking on any of the buttons will access the associated layout. Some buttons have *scripts* attached to perform several operations automatically. Clicking on the *Find Student #* button (figure 4.4) will perform a series of commands.

First, the database will *Find All* students. Next, the "Discipline Report" layout will be selected; then, the database will enter *Find Mode* and finally *Go to Field* "Student #." All of these operations are done automatically and very quickly. Besides, the buttons will allow new users to take advantage of the power of the databases very quickly without having to learn several new operations. We also added buttons and scripts to standard forms within the database. If a strong layout plan is in place, not every member of the administrative team needs to understand database design.

Besides the Menu Screen, I created a button bar across the top of several forms to allow my team to move quickly through the database. I made the button bar *nonprintable* so that it does not appear when I print a copy of the form. If a contact is required for this student, the administrator clicks on the *Contract* button. A new contract layout is accessed with student information automatically added. In the lower left-hand corner of the form, I created a *Notes* area, allowing information to be entered onto the contract, which is then printed for student and parent signatures (figure 4.5). Along with contracts, other forms can be accessed such as Saturday School, Long Term Suspension, and an Attendance Letter, all with pertinent student information already added.

My original reasons for developing the database were organizing the student referral process and saving time. Soon the database was providing information and support we had never originally planned on. For example, some members of our community perceived that the school was violent, that fights were happening on a daily basis. The staff did not feel safe. They wanted phones in every room and video surveillance systems. What people perceive can be more real than reality. To respond, we tallied all of the referrals throughout the year. With that information we developed pie charts from a spreadsheet program for the next staff meeting.

**Figure 4.4: The "Find Student #" button**

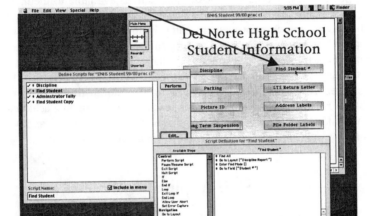

The data showed that our school was safe! The number of fights reflected in the pie chart was actually double the number of fights that had occurred since each fight generated at least 2 referrals (one for each fighter). Further analysis of the data showed that the vast majority of the fights were between ninth graders, and the majority of those were between girls. Two ninth grade girls quarreling over a boy is not exactly the picture that comes to my mind when I think of violent students on an unsafe campus.

We also charted the number of referrals for each day. The data indicated that the number of referrals rose dramatically around holidays, at the end of a grading period and after the state fair. Further analysis suggested that students did not necessarily misbehave more, but that teachers were less tolerant of disruptive behavior due to the stress of meeting grading deadlines. We turned our attention to reducing teacher stress around grading periods.

The number of referrals each teacher turned in could now be easily documented. As one would expect, some teachers never turned in a referral and others appeared to be going for world records. This led to two important improvements to the school. First, we formed a teacher committee to identify discipline options prior to sending students to the office. We publicized these options. Many of our teachers, especially the newer ones, had had no idea of alternatives available to them. The number of discipline referrals dropped 50 percent in the next semester. The second major improvement came in the form of administrative support for teachers. We became less subjective in our evaluations of staff. Instead of saying, "I think you have been turning in too many referrals," we could say, "You turned in thirty-two referrals this semester. How can I help?" Furthermore, my administrative team was able to review the types of referrals teachers turned in. We achieved a better understanding of what was happening in the classroom and were able to provide more support to teachers in classroom management.

## Staff Applications

Now that we had a software program that supported a network, we had to connect all of the administrative machines and form an interoffice network. I provided training and handouts for the administrative team to use in entering data in the system. After several weeks, I found that some administrators were using the system more than others were; those not using it were allowing the database to be incomplete.

I required the entire team to use the electronic DBMS by the end of the semester. As the end of the semester neared, the frustration of some members was increasing. I had promised them the electronic system would save them time; yet they stated that the computer increased the amount of work they had to do. It turned out that we were both correct! Instead of switching over to the electronic system, some of the team were still using the old paper system and then entering the data into the new electronic system. They had more faith in the paper system (and old habits) than they did in the electronic system. At this point, I reaffirmed my intention for everyone to switch to the electronic DBMS by semester's end. I spent extra time with my administrators who were experiencing withdrawal pain; they were allowed to continue to use the paper system if they chose to; but the electronic system was required.

**Figure 4.5: Student contract**

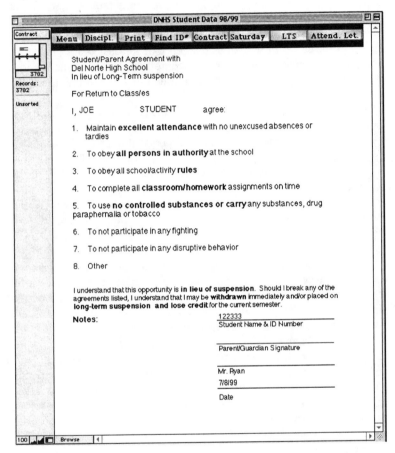

I have now developed several other databases to improve the administration of the school. An in-house work order database allows me to record work orders (figure 4.6) to be completed by the custodial staff.

Teacher comments, positive and negative, are recorded in the database along with the name of the custodian responsible. At the end of the school day, a list is automatically printed and given to the Night Lead Custodian. By next morning, the Night Lead has returned the list and signed off on each completed request. A *comment* section allows him to document why a request was not completed. The Head Custodian verifies completion in the morning and a new list is generated. The original intent of this database was to assist me in following up on in-school work orders and improve communication. The unexpected result was an evaluation tool for custodians. This tool provided documentation regarding complaints as well as kudos. Reoccurring complaints could be identified quickly and the necessary support provided to correct the situation.

In addition, I developed a teacher database using a *Filemaker Pro template* as the foundation. Templates are databases that are included as samples that can be modified to fit your personal needs. *Filemaker Pro* provides templates for business, home, and education. The templates provided with *Filemaker Pro* are wonderful! They provide a fresh approach to database design. Playing with the templates revealed new tools and uses I was able to learn by investigating how they were developed and used in the database. I used the template called *Student Information* as the foundation for the database I call *Teacher Info* (figure 4.8). I modified some of the layouts and added others.

My secretary accesses the Student Information database to record daily attendance records. After entering the data, she generates a list of teachers who are absent for the day so administrators can check on substitutes. The database even has a *picture field* where we can insert pictures. Along with the ability to issue picture identification cards, the Teacher Info database can also create business cards and staff phone and room number lists. The main layout has a button bar across the top and personal information such as name, employee number, room, and phone in the middle. The bottom half of the layout looks like four index cards. Each of the four cards has a tab that is actually a button that accesses different information on the employee. The top of the card appears to be the same; only the information on each index card changes.

This database also contains information on class schedules, administrative notes, employee cost accounts, parking, and certification areas. Any administrator can enter notes regarding classroom visits, parent-teacher conferences, and evaluation dates. I also added a layout to record information regarding each teacher's *Professional Development Plan*. Now, all my administrators can access data readily to better assess teacher performance and professional development.

**Figure 4.6: Work orders**

## In House Work Orders

| DATE OF REQUEST: | Custodial Area | REQUEST BY: | Room/ Area | DESCRIPTION OF REQUEST: | ASSIGNED PRIORITY: | DATE COMPLETE | COMPLETED BY NOTES/REMARKS |
|---|---|---|---|---|---|---|---|
| 11/12/96 | John | Nickolson | C Hall Women's Bathroom | Please clean Women's Bathroom in C Hall. | Medium | | Beth called in sick |
| 9/30/96 | John | Ford | C2 | Extremely filthy room! Please sweep. Do desks if possible. | Medium | | Malcolm - Roberts out the last week |
| 11/27/96 | John | Harrison | C4 | Sweep room and empty trash | Medium | | |
| 11/27/96 | John | Jones | C hall faculty restroom | C hall faculty restroom Men's is being neglected not paper towels this week and the furniture is in need of cleaning | Medium | | John talked with Jim |
| 11/27/96 | John | Jones | C5 | Yesterday I had to sweep my floor and empty my trash. Also, the rooms in my alley C3, 4, 5, 6 could sure use a mopping | Medium | | |

# The Future of Database Management Systems

Computer database technology continues to advance. I am currently working on developing an electronic DBMS that will allow my office to become more paper stingy. All forms will be stored digitally and printed only as needed. This spring, we hope to register all of our students for the next school year into the database to plan more accurately. I also intend to expand access to the database to all teachers from their classrooms. Enhanced communication will drive improved services for students and staff. Counseling, administration, and other support services will have access to a comprehensive student information database system that truly supports improved academic performance. Our database tools continue to evolve, improve, and reduce wasted time and money.

**Figure 4.7: Record from the Teacher Info database**

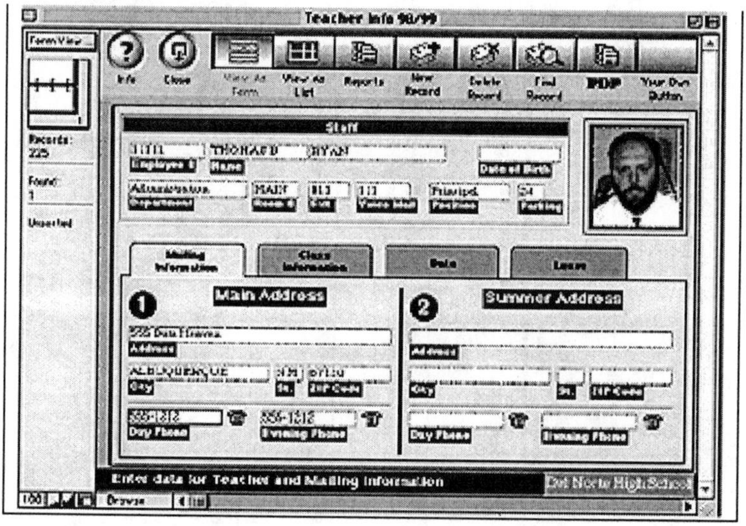

When I present at conferences on the use of electronic database tools and systems, I am often asked where I found the time it takes to master these tools and whether I took classes to learn how to do this. Most of my development ideas have been born out of need. I learned how to develop databases from reading the manual and asking questions, and through trial and error. I learn just enough to accomplish what I need at the time. As I encounter new challenges, I develop new solutions. As other administrators and staff members refine database skills, we develop a synergy and create additional possibilities, opportunities, and solutions. Not every administrator needs to learn how to build databases. I have developed DBMSs in at least three high schools and have sent copies of my database to several other administrators around the state. Some administrators learn just enough to use a specific application; others develop skills to design their own. I have taught at least one person on each campus how to manage the system. Secretaries, teachers, and even students can be trained to manage the electronic DBMS. School administrators have their hands full just running a safe environment. I feel, however, that the time I have spent learning and developing electronic database skills has been well invested.

The more I use our electronic DBMS, the more ways I find to improve how we do business. The real strength is not in the databases but in an understanding of how to create databases to meet our ever-changing needs. The ideas I have presented in this chapter really just scratch the surface of database management. Schools and administrators are being held to higher and higher levels of accountability. The need for quick, accurate information to make decisions and keep track of students is greater today than ever before. Developing the skills to create systems to meet this challenge has been a great asset to me. Saving time on the management side of my job allows me time to concentrate on being an effective educational leader.

# 5

# Successful "Library" Research Beyond the Year 2000

## Anne C. Moore

How do you find the most current information on a topic? For example, you want to prepare for an upcoming meeting by reading the latest articles on year-round schooling, school-parent cooperation, or trends in school administration. It may have been a few years since you used a library. You have tried using the Internet, but find it overflowing with so much junk. It is fun to surf, but how do you find exactly what you need in all those pages? What is an administrator to do?

Libraries and library research have changed radically in the last few years. All of our familiar paper tools, the card catalogs, the *Reader's Guide to Periodical Literature*, and the *Education Index*, have been moved online. Now it is computers instead of paper indexes that help you find references or citations to articles in magazines and journals. Those citations may be mixed in with full-text articles that you can print or e-mail to any account in the world. Today libraries often organize resources containing books, articles, and citations on a single web page. All of these are accessible to eligible patrons from any Internet-connected computer. However, you need a class, demonstration, or handout to crack the code on where these resources are located and how to use them.

Fortunately, all the databases work similarly. Once you know how to use one Internet-based subscription database, you can use any of them. At the time of publication of this handbook there are two primary places to search for information: in an *Internet-based subscription service* (an electronic database to which a library subscribes) and on the open Internet using a *search engine*. The main difference between these two are human screening, cost, consistency, and limitations on access.

Electronic databases provide citations or full-text access to data or publications that have been screened and organized by people. The materials are available only through this source, and there is a charge per search or per user. The charge covers copyright fees and the vendor's costs for producing and maintaining the database. Libraries, universities, cities, states, and companies purchase rights to use one or more databases for their constituencies. You, the end user, normally do not pay. Government databases are sometimes free and available on the open Internet. In other situations, government databases are available at public and academic libraries. The quality of the materials is high.

Internet search engines are normally free and feature the same sophisticated search techniques as electronic databases; however, the end user must carefully evaluate the results. They may include an uncontrolled variety of information sources produced by anyone from researchers at NASA to the ten-year-old living next door. Quality varies radically from high to low.

This chapter focuses on the first of these two types of sources, Internet-based subscription services. The next chapter addresses free information sources on the Internet. Let me begin by defining a few terms that will be useful as you learn about searches:

*Browser*: A software program installed on your computer that travels to the web server identified in the Location field, saves a copy of the desired web page onto your computer, and displays the web page according to its HTML coding to include text, hypertext links, images and programming language scripts. Netscape and Internet Explorer are examples of browser programs.

*Database*: An electronic resource composed of some combination of records that describe research materials and actual research materials (articles, photos, etc.). Databases are available by subscription on CD-ROM or the web.

*Field*: A section of a record. Each record is divided into numerous sections or fields to organize and identify the different types of information about the item. Title, Author, Subject, Abstract, Publisher, and Journal Title are a few examples of fields.

*Full text*: One way that articles are stored. The entire text of the item, not just a description, is included with the record (though it may not include photographs, charts and graphs). It can be printed, e-mailed, or saved to diskette for later reference and manipulation.

*Record*: The basic unit of an electronic database. Each record represents one item, such as a book, article, document, or report. It gives you all the information you need to locate the item and describe it in your bibliography or to others. It may contain the full text of the item.

*Search Engine*: Software that searches a list of web pages for the appearance of keywords, or a search strategy you type into the search box. All search engines index different portions of the web. Since no search engine can find every web page on the Internet, most web users get to know more than one. See the InfoPeople Search Engine Guide at http://www.infopeople.org/src/chart.html for a listing and comparison of free Internet Search Engines.

Here are the steps to successful research. Through the remainder of this chapter, I will elaborate on each of them.

1. Break the topic into concepts.
2. Select the "best" database to begin your search.
3. Familiarize yourself with the search techniques of the databases you plan to use.
4. Type your search strategy into the search box of the database and click the nearby Search button.
5. Evaluate the results.
6. Refine or adjust your search strategy.
7. Retrieve the items.
8. Adapt your search strategy to other databases that might contain relevant materials.

# 1. Break the Topic into Concepts

a) Until the wonderful day comes that computers will understand our everyday conversation as they do in science fiction, we must take systematic steps to make our ideas clear:

b) Write down what you are looking for in a complete sentence or magazine/newspaper style headline. For example, "I want to find articles on the current trends in K-12 school administration, particularly finance and funding."

c) Circle the best possible word to represent each aspect of your topic.

d) List alternatives for each "best possible word," since the search engine may not have your word in mind. For example, table 5.1 shows how we write out our search. Across the top of the table are the "best possible words" representing each aspect of our topic. Below each "best possible word" is one or more alternatives.

## 2. Select the "Best" Database to Begin Your Search

a) Do you have access to the Internet? Ask at local public or academic libraries about the availability of the Internet and specific databases if you do not have access at your school.

b) Are you eligible to use these databases?

c) Do you need to travel to the facility or can you access the databases remotely (from your home) with a password?

d) Is an orientation session, tutorial, or handout available to help you learn how to use these databases?

For most research in the field of education, you will need to tap some form of ERIC and multi-topic, subscription databases. ERIC is the government database that contains almost complete indexing of education journals and documents since 1966. ERIC stands for Educational Resource Information Center, and it is operated by the U.S. Department of Education. ERIC is accessible free of charge on the Internet at a number of sites. Two examples of free ERIC services are the ERIC Search Wizard at http://ericae.net/scripts/ewiz/amain2.asp and AskERIC at http://ericir.syr.edu (1989-present). ERIC is also available to libraries on CD-ROM or through several subscription services. One or more of the subscription services, such as OCLC FirstSearch or OVID, are available at most academic libraries. In the near future all ERIC resources will be available in a full-text format over the Internet. The field of education is privileged to have such excellent indexing of its materials in a free government tool. Not everything is in ERIC, but nearly every topic in education is covered in at least one document or article.

**Table 5.1: Writing out the words and synonyms for a search**

| Best possible word: | Trend(s) | K-12 | School | Administration | Finance |
|---|---|---|---|---|---|
| Alternatives: | New | Elementary | Education | Principal | Funding |
| Alternatives: | Current | Secondary | | | Budgeting |

Any form of ERIC contains indexing and abstracting for two types of items; journal articles (identified by EJ in a record's document number field) and other documents or reports (identified by an ED in the document number field) (see fig. 5.1). EJ articles have been published in scholarly education journals and may be obtained from local academic libraries that subscribe to the journal in question, through interlibrary loan, through an article reprint service (try CARL Uncover at http://uncweb.carl.org), or through one of the subscription databases listed in figure 5.1.

The documents and reports indexed in ERIC are available on microfiche in most academic libraries or can be ordered for $2.50 plus 10 cents per page from http://edrs.org/. Another resource, ERIC Digests, is made up of full-text reports from the ERIC database and is available at http://www.ed.gov/databases/ERIC_Digests/index/.

Other subscription databases are multi-topic (not just education) and contain many full-text articles you can print, e-mail, or save to your computer or diskette. The articles come from journals, magazines, and newspapers. Although database names change frequently, the most popular examples are Bell & Howell's ProQuest, EBSCOHost, and Gale's Infotrac. These databases cost thousands of dollars per year and may be provided to citizens of an entire state by the legislature (through public, school, and college libraries) or might be provided to students enrolled at a community college or university. Even though the general public may not be eligible to access these databases from their homes or offices, walk-in patrons normally may use resources on computers in academic libraries. A sample of formats of materials available in a multi-topic, subscription database (Bell & Howell's ProQuest) is illustrated in figure 5.2

## Fig. 5.1: Example of an ED document

Title: Integrating Technology in the School Environment: Through the Principal's Lens.
Author: Clark, Sharon E.; Denton, Jon J.
Note: 14p.
Publication Year: 1998
Document Type: Project Description (141)
Target Audience: Parents and Practitioners
ERIC Identifier: ED417696
Clearinghouse Identifier: IR018762
This document is available from the ERIC Document Reproduction Service.

Descriptors: Benchmarking; * Computer Uses in Education; * Educational Technology; * Elementary Secondary E
Principals; Program Evaluation; * School Administration; Staff Development; Teachers; Telecommunications; User N
[Information]

Identifiers: *Technology Integration

http://ericae.net/ericdb/ED417696.htm

## Fig. 5.2: Bell & Howell's ProQuest legend of materials formats

FORMAT LEGEND:        CITATION/ABSTRACT       FULL TEXT        TEXT+GRAPHICS        PAGE IMAGE

You must determine which database is most likely to meet your needs. All databases have limitations. They may specialize in materials on certain subjects (for example, ERIC focuses on education). They may cover a particular chronological period. Most Electronic Databases began in the mid-1980s and only a few are gradually indexing older materials. ERIC is an exception since it goes back to 1966. Some databases cover particular geographical areas. Most important, databases may include specific formats or types of materials. In addition to magazine and journal articles, electronic databases may contain newspaper articles, newswire transcripts, TV and radio transcripts, government documents, chapters from books, pamphlets, book reviews, etc.

It is an excellent idea to begin any research with a general database that contains full-text materials. These databases are easier to learn. They help you survey the literature on a given topic and use the same searching principles as the subject-specific databases (such as ERIC). In this chapter we will use ProQuest and Infotrac as our examples of multi-topic databases.

# 3. Familiarize Yourself with the Search Techniques of the Databases You Plan to Use

It is important to understand the workings of each database you plan to use, so that you can find the most relevant material and the minimum amount of irrelevant material. The concepts of precision and recall help clarify the two main types of searching. Recall searches are what doctoral students strive for when researching for a dissertation. They want to see absolutely everything even remotely related to their topic. They want to carefully evaluate each item to ensure they have missed nothing. In contrast, researchers and practitioners often prefer a precision search. They want to weed through a minimum of irrelevant material. Their objective is to locate two perfectly relevant items on the first attempt. To achieve this ideal, you must familiarize yourself with the search techniques of the databases you use.

All databases feature online assistance. Look for a question mark, "Help," "Search Help," "Search Tips," or "Help/Hints" as a hypertext link on the main search screen of the database. In addition, the library may offer a tutorial or a concise handout you can keep nearby while searching. Increasingly, these guides are available on the Internet as well. Most databases feature extremely similar search capabilities, but there are slight variations, so check the *Help* section the first time you use a new database or if your search is not producing the results you expected. As mentioned earlier, there are a few standard techniques for searching Electronic Databases.

# 4. Type Your Search Strategy into the Search Box of the Database and Click the Nearby Search Button

### Controlled-Vocabulary and Keyword Searching

Databases may support *controlled vocabulary* and *keyword* searching. A database has a controlled vocabulary when human indexers assign particular thesaurus or descriptor terms or subject headings to each record. When you type the topic into the subject search box, the thesaurus is searched. Cross-references inform us of the correct terms used in the database. A thesaurus increases your chances of finding relevant items. But beware: current jargon and issues may not appear in the controlled vocabulary because it takes time for the human indexers to catch on to new trends.

Most online databases allow you to search the thesaurus or subject guide and even let you know how many articles are indexed on a particular term. For example, the "Subject Guide" search box comes up first whenever you enter Gale's Infotrac. You enter keywords, such as school administration, and the service shows you a listing of subject terms used in the database and the number of articles listed under each one. From this listing, we determine there are 14 articles on Elementary School Administration as illustrated in fig. 5.3. We can even click on the hypertext link (View) to pull up the listing of and links to the full-text articles.

**Fig. 5.3: Subject term search in Gale's Infotrac**

**Subjects containing the words:** school administration

---

**School Administration**
See School Management and Organization
**School Administration Teachers**
View 6 articles
**Elementary School Administration**
View 14 articles
**High School Administration**
See High Schools - Management
**Utah. School and Institutional Trust Lands Administration**
View 1 article
**Cornell University. School of Hotel Administration**
View 13 articles
**France. National School of Administration**
View 5 articles

In keyword searching, you guess what words are listed in the titles, abstracts and possibly full text of the articles you want to retrieve. To prepare for keyword searching, you should be familiar with the terminology and buzzwords used in the field to describe your topic. For example, "learning logs" or "student portfolios" will pull up relevant articles in education, whereas, the terms "journal" or "diary" might apply to similar concepts in other fields. If you do not quickly find materials on your topic using the controlled vocabulary, search by keyword instead. Some databases will automatically conduct a keyword search if your subject/thesaurus search fails to retrieve any articles.

## Field Searching

Field searching allows you to limit your search to a particular field in each record in the database. For example, you could look for the appearance of the words "cooperative learning" in the title field, or the name "Sergiovanni" in the author field.

## Boolean Operators

*Boolean operators* are the most frequently used search techniques in electronic databases and Internet search engines. You insert the operators (words) *AND, OR* and *NOT* between keywords or phrases to tell the database how to combine the keywords in your search. A sample search with Boolean operators might be "multicultural and education and (middle or high or secondary)." The results would include records that contain both the words "multicultural" and "education," and one or more of the words "middle," "high," and/or "secondary." The AND operator requires the keywords on either side of it to appear in the record. For example, searching for "bacon and eggs" retrieves only records that contain both keywords. The OR operator causes the search engine to retrieve records that contain either one or both of the words on either side of the OR. For example, searching for "bacon or eggs" retrieves records that contain any of the following: the keyword "bacon," the keyword "eggs" or both keywords. Online searching is the opposite of ordering breakfast in a restaurant. "Bacon and eggs" brings you more food at a restaurant than "bacon or eggs." But in online searching, "bacon or eggs" gives you a lot more than "bacon and eggs."

The third operator, NOT (sometimes AND NOT), excludes or eliminates a keyword or concept from the search (see fig. 5.4). For example, "education not middle" will retrieve records about all aspects and levels of education, excluding any records that contain even a single instance of the word "middle." Be careful with NOT. It is easy to unintentionally eliminate relevant records with the NOT operator. In our example, records that relate to both middle and high school would be eliminated if they contained the word "middle." Valuable articles on high school could be lost. Thus, in simplest terms: AND narrows a search; OR broadens it; and NOT eliminates items from the search.

**Fig. 5.4: An advanced search using NOT in Bell and Howell's ProQuest**

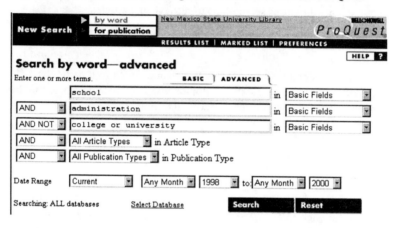

For a succinct explanation of Boolean searching, visit the University of Albany Libraries' website "Boolean Searching on the Internet" at http://www.albany.edu/library/internet/boolean.html.

## Truncation and Wildcards

In truncation or wildcard searches, a special character such as an *, ?, or ! is added to the word stem to retrieve various word endings, spelling variations, and plurals. For example, manag* will retrieve records with manage, manages, managing, manager, managers, management, and any other endings to the stem "manag." The special character can sometimes be substituted for any single letter or string of letters in the middle of a keyword to pull up variations. For example, wom*n will bring up records containing both women and woman. Since electronic databases do not all handle truncation and wildcards the same way, you must check the help information to determine which symbol(s) are used and how they are used in the particular database with which you are searching.

## Phrase Searches

Electronic databases sometimes support phrase searching using quotation marks. An article will be retrieved if the phrase appears exactly as typed somewhere in the article or abstract. "Year-round schools" and "parent participation in elementary schools" are examples of phrase searches. Most databases highlight in red or bold type each appearance of your search term or phrase in the resulting records, so each instance jumps out at you (figure 5.5). If you click on the Edit drop-down menu of your web browser and click on Find in Page, you will locate the appearances of a keyword in the text of each record retrieved as figure 5.6 demonstrates.

**Figure 5.5: Search phrase highlighted in an abstract in ProQuest. The search was "parent involvement in schools."**

Abstract:

*This paper addresses the issue of **parent involvement in school** life in the newly emerging realm of commodified education. It explores the limits of empowerment and its context-dependent nature.*

**Figure 5.6: Using the edit menu to locate the search phrase in a document**

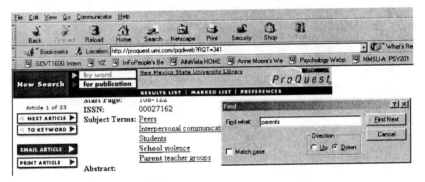

Type Your Search Strategy into the Search Box of the Database and Click the nearby Search Button. Sometimes you can press the <Enter> button to start the search. Check your browser status bar at the bottom of the screen (see figure 5.7) to see if anything is happening.

**Figure 5.7: Status Bar at the Bottom of a Netscape Screen Showing the Document Loading**

Remember to translate your search into the techniques appropriate for that particular database and take its limitations into consideration. For example, we want to find materials on trends in elementary administration from the Bell & Howell ProQuest database, a multisubject electronic database. Using a simple keyword search, we type "elementary AND school AND administration AND challenges" as is illustrated in figure 5.8. Then we click the Search button. We retrieve three citations, only one of which is full text.

**Figure 5.8: Example of a simple keyword search in ProQuest**

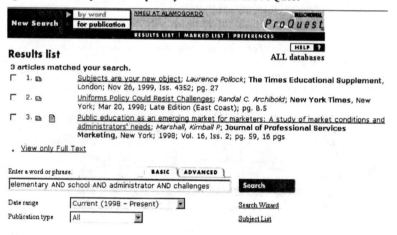

But if we search the AskERIC database, which is restricted to education items, we must use a more specific search. For example, figure 5.9 shows a search I did in AskERIC using "elementary and (finance or budgeting) and administration." I retrieved 948 items!

An AskERIC search on "elementary and trends and administration" retrieved 588 items! In the two examples from AskERIC, we would not enter the terms "school" or "schools" because a majority of the ERIC database is about schools. "School," "education," and sometimes, "teacher" are not helpful terms in a database that contains materials exclusively on education.

**Fig. 5.9: Example of a search of the ERIC database**

# 5. Evaluate the Results

Examine the items in the results listing while you ask yourself:

a)  Is this what you are looking for? Click on hypertext links to visit the citation, full text, or web page for the actual item.
b)  Does this item add to your existing knowledge of the topic?
c)  Does it provide material you can quote or paraphrase for your purposes?
d)  Did an authority in the field write it?
e)  Is it sufficiently current to meet your present needs?
f)  Does it list other sources that might provide additional useful information?

If the answer to any of these questions is "No," do not pursue the article.

# 6. Refine or Adjust Your Search Strategy

If you planned your search precisely, selected the appropriate database, and material exists on the topic, you will quickly spot the perfect article. But even when this happens, you may need two or three other relevant articles and there are still one-hundred more to be examined. A shortcut is to examine the subject or thesaurus terms applied to this perfect article. As is shown in fig. 5.10, you should see a subject or thesaurus term that matches your topic. You can now search using that term under the subject, phrase, or even keyword search to select the items that indexers determined pertained to that topic.

**Fig. 5.10: Subject terms on a relevant article on "Parent participation in schools"**

**Fostering effective parental participation in education: Lessons from a comparison of reform processes in Nicaragua and Mexico**
World Development; Oxford; Apr 1999; Alec Ian Gershberg;

| | |
|---|---|
| Volume: | 27 |
| Issue: | 4 |
| UMI Publication No.: | 01849329 |
| | 04363435 |
| Start Page: | 753-771 |
| Page Count: | 0 |
| Document Type: | Feature |
| Source Type: | PERIODICAL |
| ISSN: | 0305750X |
| Subject Terms: | School administration |
| | Education reform |
| | Parents & parenting |
| | Participation |

How many items should you retrieve in a search? This varies according to your information need. One could have retrieved as many as several hundred citations and still winnow it down to one or more excellent documents in a few minutes. The results of a database search are usually arranged chronologically (most recently published items first moving to the older items) or by relevancy (best to worst). Therefore, you begin evaluating from the top of the results and stop evaluating when the items become too old or begin to veer off the desired topic. Do not stop looking too soon, however. Unfortunately, the "perfect" items often are intermixed with other items that appear totally irrelevant.

What if you do not see what you are looking for in a cursory inspection of the results? Ask yourself these questions:

## Do You Have Too Many Items? (Need to Narrow)

a) Examine the first ten to twenty articles returned because these are normally the most relevant. Identify a few documents that look promising. Read the titles, abstracts, and subject terms of the relevant items. List subject terms and keywords that might focus more precisely on the material you seek. Rerun your search one or more times using the new terms, using AND between keywords, or conducting a subject search.

b) Sometimes it is easiest to identify one additional concept or keyword to add to the initial search with the Boolean operator AND ("AND keyword").

c) Alternatively, a more specific subject heading, controlled vocabulary, or thesaurus term may be identified through examining the subject headings applied to relevant articles.

d) Look back at the Help information in the database to identify other features provided to narrow or limit a search. Limiting features may include one or more of the following: date, geography (e.g., New Mexico), academic discipline (e.g., science), publication type, language, etc. For example, the Help section of ProQuest demonstrates date limiting techniques in this particular database with the following example, india AND PDN(>05/01/1999 AND <07/28/1999). PDN is ProQuest's code for Publication Date Numeric, which is a fancy way to tell the computer software that what follows is a date restriction. Each database has special limiting capabilities like those listed below. The techniques are described in the Help area.

The repeated appearance of articles on a particular concept unrelated to your search may indicate the Boolean operator "NOT" could help narrow the search. For example, suppose you retrieve a large percentage of hits on "discipline" in your search. You redo the search adding "NOT discipline." Again, you should use this technique with extreme care because you may eliminate an article that predominantly discusses your topic, but merely mentions discipline in passing.

## Do You Have Too Few Items? (Need to Broaden)

a)    Check your search strategy for misspellings or mistypings.

b)    Look back at your search strategy and remove one of the concepts before you run it again. Normally, there is one concept or keyword that is too specific to appear multiple times in the literature. In ProQuest the combination "trends AND elementary AND school AND administration" retrieved only one article. We can drop the "trends" concept from the search because "elementary school administration" is really the focus. Writers could have used a variety of words to represent the concept of "trends" or not even referred to it at all in relevant articles. When we redo the search, we retrieve fourteen appropriate articles.

c)    If you conducted a subject heading or controlled vocabulary search, switch to a keyword search.

d)    Add additional synonyms or truncation for one or more concepts to broaden the search. For example, replace "elementary" with "elementary or primary." Replace "management" with "manag*." Or try another database.

# 7. Retrieve the Items

The final step in working with online databases and Search Engines is to obtain the materials.

a)    *Mark.* Most electronic databases support *marking* or *selecting* of desired items as shown in fig. 5.11. This is the same concept as placing items in your shopping basket, shopping cart, or wish list at an Internet shopping site. Click a box to the left of the citation to place a "mark" next to the item. Continue marking desired items in that database. Once finished, click on the *View mark list* (fig. 5.12) or *Order Documents* to display the selected items. Fig. 5.13 shows a sample of a marked list.

b)    *Print.* If the title or Internet address is underlined and blue in color, clicking on this hypertext link brings up the desired document. You may print the item to an attached printer by clicking on the

**Fig. 5.11 Marking records in ProQuest**

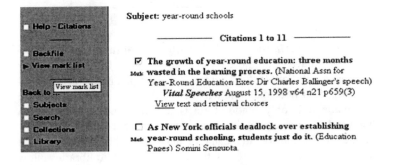

□  4. ▫  The never-ending school year; *Anonymous*; **Seventeen**, New York; Jul 1999; Vol. 58, Iss. 7; pg. 42, 2 pgs

☑  5. ▫  📄  📰  Where school's always open; *Andrea Atkins*; **Parenting**, San Francisco; Jun/Jul 1999; Vol. 13, Iss. 5; pg. 25, 1 pgs

☑  6. ▫  📄  📰  What can we learn from the data?: Toward a better understanding of the effects of multitrack year-round schooling; *Carolyn M Shields*; **Urban Education**, Thousand Oaks; May 1999; Vol. 34, Iss. 2; pg. 125, 30 pgs

☑  7. ▫  📄  📰  The effect of year-round schooling on administrators; *Louis Wildman*; **Education**, Chula Vista; Spring 1999; Vol. 119, Iss. 3; pg. 465, 8 pgs

☑  8. ▫  📄  📰  Is more school the answer?; *Anonymous*; **Canada & the World Backgrounder**, Waterloo; Dec 1998; Vol. 64, Iss. 3; pg. 11, 1 pgs

□  9. ▫  A longer school year pays off; *Anonymous*; **Parents**, Bergenfield; Oct 1998; Vol. 73, Iss. 10; pg. 156

☑ 10. ▫  📄  📰  Should students attend school year round?: Yes/No; *Daniel A Domenech*; **Spectrum**, Lexington; Fall 1998; Vol. 71, Iss. 4; pg. 24, 2 pgs

**Fig. 5.12: A marked citation and the View mark list button in Infotrac**

Subject: year-round schools

───────── Citations 1 to 11 ─────────

■ Help - Citations

■ Backfile
► View mark list

[ View mark list ]
Back to ...

■ Subjects
■ Search
■ Collections
■ Library

☑ **The growth of year-round education: three months**
Mark **wasted in the learning process.** (National Assn for Year-Round Education Exec Dir Charles Ballinger's speech) *Vital Speeches* August 15, 1998 v64 n21 p659(3)
View text and retrieval choices

□ **As New York officials deadlock over establishing**
Mark **year-round schooling, students just do it.** (Education Pages) Somini Sengupta.

*E-mail.* Select Send Page or E-mail Page from the File drop-down menu of your web browser with the page displayed to e-mail it to yourself or someone else. Fig. 5.14 shows one example of a database e-mail option. Fig. 5.15 shows an other. E-mailing is handy if you are at a computer other than your own and do not want to write down the information about the article you found. Electronic research databases often contain an icon on the page when the document is displayed that allows you to e-mail the document to any e-mail address in the world at no charge. This is a helpful feature, particularly if your topic is still unformed and you are uncertain as to whether an item will turn out to be relevant. If you later view the article in your e-mail inbox and find it to be-unhelpful, you can delete it. You will have saved the cost of-printing it.

**Fig. 5.13 A marked list in ProQuest**

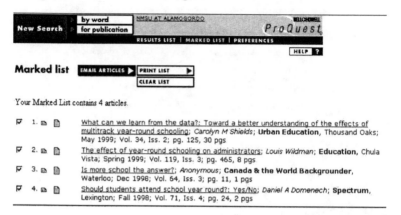

Obtain through *Interlibrary Loan*. If the item is not full text in the database, you will have to do more legwork to obtain it. If the item is only available in a *Citation/Abstract format* (for example, notice that items 4 and 9 in fig. 5.11 have only one icon before the title, indicating that the item is available in only citation format), and you really want to obtain it, then print, save or e-mail the citation. Determine if your local library subscribes to the journal, magazine or newspaper. If it does, you can drive over to make a copy of it. Otherwise, most public libraries allow you to order articles and books through interlibrary loan. Your district may also provide *Interlibrary Loan* service through its teacher resource center. This may take several weeks, so allow plenty of time.

Fig. 5.14: Print reformat and e-mail options in Gale Infotrac

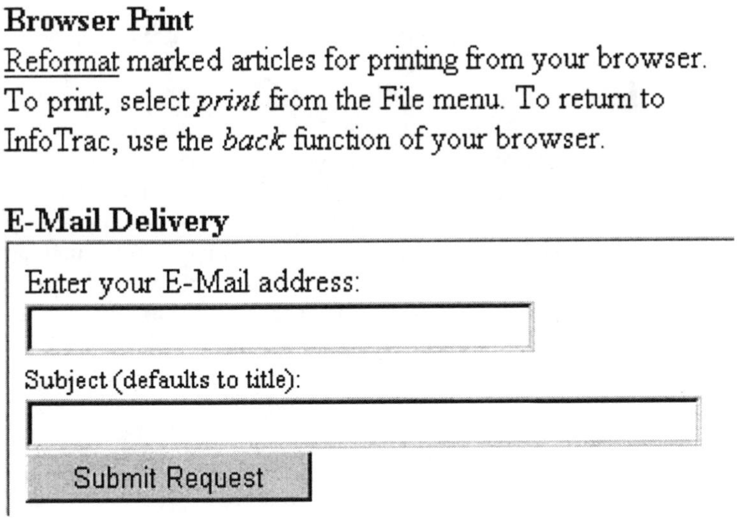

Browser Print
Reformat marked articles for printing from your browser. To print, select *print* from the File menu. To return to InfoTrac, use the *back* function of your browser.
E-Mail Delivery
Enter your E-Mail address:
Subject (defaults to title):
Submit Request

Fig. 5.15: E-mail box on Records in ProQuest

EMAIL ARTICLE
PRINT ARTICLE

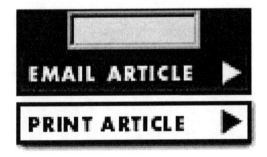

## 8. Adapt Your Search Strategy to Other Databases That Might Contain Relevant Materials.

Ask a librarian for other ideas. Use the Help instructions to discover the search techniques for this database. Follow the same procedures outlined in steps 4-7 above in each of the other databases you visit.

Electronic research can provide a wealth of information to enrich your professional and personal life. All you need, besides the searching principles outlined in this chapter, are an open, inquisitive mind, and a little time. Once you spend fifteen minutes with a single database hunting for information, you will be hooked.

# 6

# Successful Internet Research

## Anne C. Moore

There is a tremendous amount of information on the Internet. The trick is finding the information you need when you need it without having to search through heaps of irrelevant and poorly crafted websites. That is the topic of this chapter. We will discuss the types of search tools and searching techniques, and how to evaluate what you find. Evaluation is the most important aspect of interacting with information found on the Internet. That said, let us alleviate three misconceptions at the outset:

- *The Internet is the best place to find the most up-to-date informa-tion.* It is true that valuable material often appears on the Internet before it is published in books or magazines. Therefore, the Inter-net is an excellent place to discover what is new and upcoming. However, not all information is on the web. Since there is no real organization, the key to whether a given piece of information is posted is really just whether someone thought of putting it out there. The fact is that when you do not find something, it may be because it is not there.

- *The Internet is a waste of time.* It's full of advertisements, pornog-raphy, and websites designed by kids or computer geeks. There is absolutely nothing of value to be found there. The fact is that 110 million Americans were online in 1999. The implication of that number is that the Internet is full of many kinds of things. There are both rubbish and treasure. As the Internet evolves into a true communication and information storage and retrieval medium, more people are participating and investing talent, imagination, and intellect into producing and maintaining high quality websites. Each and every time I search, I uncover another gem.

- *Finding anything on the Internet is like finding the proverbial needle in a haystack.* It's next to impossible. Luck is the only answer. The truth is that there are simple, relatively standardized, and highly effective methods for locating information on the Net in a quick and efficient manner, if the desired information is there.

Rather than allowing ourselves to be seduced by the above misconceptions, it is better to think of the Internet in terms of its strengths and its weaknesses. One of its greatest strengths is its interactivity. The graphical (picture or image-based) browser programs, such as Netscape and Internet Explorer, allow surfers to click on hypertext links and visit websites all over the world in a flexible, quick, and personalized manner. Its next greatest strength is the variety of topics on Internet sites: news and current events; commercial and consumer information on health, business entertainment, and sports; government information and statistics; unpublished research (pre-print); and round-the-clock communications (e-mail, listservs, chat, and newsgroups).

The main weakness of the Internet is that the material on it may be unorganized, incomplete, unevaluated, unpredictable, unreliable, and uncensored. That is why we must develop our abilities to evaluate what we find.

# Locating Information on the Internet

There are many approaches to finding information on the web. We can divide those approaches into three categories: guessing, using subject directories, and using search engines.

## Guessing Approach

The quickest way to locate information on a common topic or originating from a particular organization is often guessing the web address for the source organization. For example, we might try to find information about Microsoft products at http://www.microsoft.com/. And rather than searching randomly for crime statistics, why not go directly to the FBI homepage? It is right where we would expect it at http://www.fbi.gov/. I will explain enough about the structure of web addresses below for you to become a good guesser, too.

A shortcut to bringing up a commercial website is to type the company name into the address field, often called the Location or Netsite box, on the upper toolbar of your web browser. Then press <enter>. This technique works for companies in the .com or commercial domain. For example, one could type "Microsoft," "booksontape" (see fig. 6.1), or "barnesandnoble" into the address field.

**Fig. 6.1: Finding "Books on Tape" by typing the name of the company**

But there are domains out there other than commercial. The term domain refers to the type of organization that sponsors the website. Here are the six most useful domains:

.com, Company involved in sales
.edu, Educational site, K-12 or higher education
.org, Organization, includes many nonprofits
.gov, Government site
.mil, Military site, often restricted to military users only
.net, Internet service or resource

Simply typing in the name of the organization does not work for domains other than .com (the default) because your browser assumes you want a site from the .com domain (if you do not specify another domain). For these other organizations, one must guess the one word name (usually an acronym or popular name) and follow it with a period plus the three-letter domain identifier. For example, if we wanted to pull up the website for the American Civil Liberties Union, we might guess that the address of its web server is http://www.aclu.org/ because it is a nonprofit organization whose name is represented by the acronym ACLU. Sometimes, this technique backfires if more than one company or organization shares the same acronym. For example, you would guess the web address for the American Medical Association would be http://www.ama.org/, but the American Marketing Association grabbed this address first. The American Medical Association was forced to settle for the unintuitive http://www.ama-assn.org/. Most people do not guess that address and thus have to use a subject directory or search engine to locate the American Medical Association site.

## Internet Subject Directories or Guides

An Internet subject directory or guide is a website that lets you search its index to the best Internet sites. *Humans* prepare its index. Later we will discuss indexes prepared by machines. A subject directory is just a set of links to these best websites. There is no actual content (other than descriptions or reviews of and links to web pages) at a subject directory site. Fig. 6.2 shows a screen capture from the Librarian's Index to the Internet (LII), a subject directory sponsored by the California State Library and the Digital Library Sunsite. You can find it at this address: <http://www.lii.org/>. At LII, professional librarians who work for the California State Library surf the web to locate the best websites on topics on which they are experts. Then they create a concise, evaluative description of each website. Descriptions and subject terms are searched for appearances of the keyword, phrase, or Boolean strategy you type in the search box.

Most directories/subject guides are collections of hyperlinks to relevant web documents or other resources arranged according to a scheme (usually by subject categories). Using subject directories is an effective way to find information on a general topic. Subject guides provide a limited number of professionally selected and evaluated web pages on specified topics. The evaluation may consist of an annotation, description, or review. Since people who are employed to surf the Net find the sites, these directories/subject guides are highly selective and helpful shortcuts to the valuable information on the Net. You may be missing lots of other websites, but at least the ones you get are important and appropriate.

Subject directories or guides can be separated into two major groups: academic or professional and commercial. Librarian's Index is an example of an academic directory because the websites indexed are selected based on their suitability for research or academic purposes.

**Figure 6.2: From the Librarian's Index to the Internet. Results from a search on "K-12 schools."**

Results for **"k 12 schools"** 1 to 20 of 46 (view all)

View: **Next 20** Jump to: Directories | Databases | Specific Resources    Results by Subject

## Best of...

American School Directory - http://www.asd.com/

A database of Web pages for each of the 108,000 K-12 schools in the U.S. Each site is loaded with pages of information, including number of students, number of homerooms, grades, phone and fax numbers, urls, school calendars, administrators, and even a local street map. You can search by several geographic limiters and limit to public, private, catholic or all. Produced with the help of IBM and Apple. - cl

Subject: K-12 schools

Classroom Connect - http://www.classroom.net/home.asp

Excellent K-12 resource. Their searchable and browsable G.R.A.D.E.S. directory contains annotated links to the best educational materials. They also have a good Guide to Searching; a Resource Station for teachers; a database of more than 4,000 schools on the Web; another of teachers (more than 4,000); and a directory of products they sell. - cl

Subject: Teaching materials

RefDesk would also be categorized an academic or professional directory because it indexes factual content, such as word definitions, news sources, famous quotations, and other information commonly found in the reference section of a library. Commercial directories or guides organize consumer information for the public on a wide variety of topics, such as travel, shopping, telephone numbers, movie reviews, and health information. Yahoo is the most popular commercial subject directory or guide. Table 6.1 identifies the major academic and commercial directories.

## Search Engines

There is currently no way to search the Internet directly. *Search Engines* are automatically produced indexes to some of the information on the Internet. Software programs called *spiders* or *robots* constantly crawl through the web and bring back a copy of each page they come across. The search engine adds every word and image in each page to its index. When you type words, phrases, or strategies into the *Search box* at the site, the index is searched and a list of the web pages with the most appearances (or some other criteria) of those search terms is retrieved.

All of this is computer-generated. There is absolutely no selectivity or evaluation taking place. The spider programs are each different and traverse the Internet at different speeds and frequencies. The search engine retrieves a listing from the current index, which is just a sample of what is available on the Internet on your topic. Each search engine uses different search techniques, and none are comprehensive. The same search entered on a different day or even a few minutes later the same day might bring up different results because the index is constantly being updated with new sites found by the spider program.

The advice I gave in chapter 5 on library searching applies here as well: for assistance in structuring your search for a specific search engine, study the search engine help screens. As an alternative, you can visit summary charts, two examples of which are Danny Sullivan's Search Engine Features Chart http://searchenginewatch.internet.com/webmasters/features.html, or Info People Search Tools Chart http://www.infopeople.org/src/chart.html. Currently, the most popular search engines are:

*Altavista*, http://www.altavista.com/
*Excite*, http://www.excite.com/
*Google*, http://www.google.com/

*Hotbot,* http://www.hotbot.com/
*InfoSeek,* http://www.infoseek.com/
*Northern Light,* http://www.northernlight.com/
*Webcrawler, http://www.webcrawler.com/*

**Table 6.1: Examples of Subject Guides (A designates academic; C designates commercial)**

| | |
|---|---|
| Galaxy, one of the first Internet subject directories, <http://www.einet.net/> | A |
| Argus Clearinghouse of Subject-Oriented Internet Resource Guides, <http://www.clearinghouse.net/> | A |
| DirectHit, <http://www.directhit.com/> | C |
| Encyclopedia Britannica E-blast, <http://www.eBLAST.com/> | A |
| INFOMINE: UC-Riverside Guide to Scholarly Internet Resources, <http://lib-www.ucr.edu/> | A |
| Infoseek, <http://infoseek.go.com/> | C |
| Librarian's Index to the Internet (my favorite), <http://www.lii.org/> | A |
| LookSmart, <http://www.looksmart.com/> | C |
| Magellan : McKinley Internet Directory, <http://www.mckinley.com/ > | A |
| Snap, <http://www.snap.com/> | C |
| RefDesk (facts), <http://www.refdesk.com/> | A |
| Yahoo, <http://www.yahoo.com/> | C |

If we want to search at *Altavista* for web pages on school vouchers, for example, we would type <+"school vouchers"> into the search box (currently identified as Find this:). As fig. 6.3 shows, on this particular occasion, the search retrieved 10,185 *hits* or links to relevant web pages.

The search engine translation software at *Altavista* and at most other search engines arranges the results by relevancy or relevancy ranking. Sites become less *relevant* as you read down the list, although the search engine (a software program) may have a different definition of "relevant" from your own. Each search engine uses its own weighting of various criteria to order the results. Your goal is to get the best sites within the first ten results. Typical weighting criteria that search engines use to rank include: greatest number of appearances of your search words or phrases in relation to the length of the document, appearance of the search words or phrases in the title or high in the page, rarity of the word or phrase in the search engine's index, currency (explained below), and proximity of search terms to one another. Each search engine weights the criteria differently according to its own algorithm.

Fig. 6.3: *Altavista* finding 10,185 sources for "school vouchers"

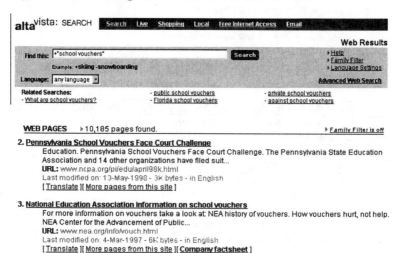

But search engine software can be tricked. Web page authors use *meta* (hidden keyword) tags and other techniques to force their pages higher in the ranking. They might repeat the major concept of the web page many times in the meta tags field, in order to trick the search engine software into ranking the page near the top in the results list. This same principle is employed by some authors of sales or illicit web pages who will add multiple repetitions of common words or phrases, such as "video games," in the meta tags field to get their web pages to bubble to the top in results lists.

As the Internet has expanded exponentially, *link popularity* has joined the list of criteria used by search engines to rank pages. This technique relies on the principle that links to a page indicate its popularity and thus value. Pages linked most frequently from other pages receive the highest rankings. *Google* implements this technique successfully. *Raging Search* by *Altavista* http://ragingsearch.altavista.com/ is a new service based on the same principle.

A typical search engine results listing provides the title of the page, the web address (URL), a hypertext link to the page, a quote from the website (usually the first few lines), last modified date, and a link to "More pages from this site." Documents are single web pages. *Altavista* also has a translate button, which will convert the text of the web page to or from German, Spanish, French, Italian, or Portuguese.

As fig. 6.4 shows, I typed the search phrase "year-round schools" into the search box at *Google*. As discussed above, *Google* uses link popularity (frequency of links from other web pages *Google* knows about) to order the 1,640 hits or results. The philosophy at *Google* is that the more web pages link to a specific page, the higher quality it is. In theory, the *Google* software uses the frequency of choices of webmasters to rank its results. This method approaches the human selection method subject directories use. The results are thus pre-evaluated, sort of like automatic peer review. Most users find excellent results in the first page of results at *Google*, but you still must make your own decisions about which sites you find most credible.

Let us review how search engines work. They are complex sites composed of four parts:

- A web interface that features the search box into which you type your search terms or strategy;
- A search translation program that manipulates what you typed into the search box and runs it across the index to extract results;
- An index to the appearances of every word the search engine knows about on the Internet; and
- A software program called a spider or robot that combs the Internet and retrieves a copy of everything it finds to be added to the index.

*Meta Search Engines* or *All-in-One Searches* allow you to run a simple search on more than one search tool with a single click of the mouse. Here are the names and locations of several:

*All-in-One,* http://www.go2net.com/search.html
*Cyber411,* http://www.cyber411.com/
*Dogpile,* http://www.dogpile.com/
*MetaFind,* http://www.metafind.com/
*Inference Find,* http://www.infind.com/
*MetaCrawler,* http://www.metacrawler.com/
*Mamma,* http://www.mamma.com/
*Profusion,* http://www.profusion.com/

These tools, a special category of search engines, help you see a snapshot of what is available on your topic at several search engines at once. The results normally include only the very highest ranked pages at selected tools or engines/directories that respond the fastest. Just like the software-produced results you retrieve from a search engine, no human evaluation is involved. Meta-search tools give you a quick overview of the most popular and highly ranked pages on a topic.

The term *portal* refers to some sophisticated websites that integrate multiple services from a single site. Yahoo, Snap, and Excite are portals that feature free e-mail, web page authoring, chat, news, search engine, and subject directory services at a one-stop web address.

**Fig. 6.4: *Google* finds 1,640 sources for "year-round schools."**

Showing results **1-10** of approximately **1,640** for **"year-round schools"**. Search took **0.18** seconds

The National Association for Year-Round Education
...education as there are **year-round schools**. The following...
...million students attend **year-round schools** in 39 states....
www.nayre.org/ - Cached: 29k - GoogleScout

Do year-round schools improve students learning?
...XII 95-EI-03 Do **year-round schools** improve student...
...Division May 1995 Do **year-round schools** improve student...
www.bctf.bc.ca/education/yrs/StudentLearning.html - Cached: 40k - GoogleScout

Year Round Schools
... **Year Round Schools** Cost-effectiveness of **Year**...
...Naylor , May 1995. Do **Year Round Schools** Improve Student...
www.bctf.bc.ca/education/yrs/ - Cached: 3k - GoogleScout

Year-Round Education: A Parent's Point of View
...achievement between **year-round** and traditional **schools**,"...
...MEMORANDUM IN OPPOSITION TO **YEAR-ROUND SCHOOLS** by Robert...
www.primenet.com/~wwalker/ - Cached: 6k - GoogleScout

Year-round Schools Gearing Up
... **Year-round Schools** Gearing Up by Robert Witt Students at a...

## Choosing a Search Tool

With such a variety of tools available to help you search the Web, the toughest challenge is often deciding which one to use. Many people get to know the search techniques and capabilities of one or two tools in depth and use them almost exclusively. A superior approach is to take advantage of the strengths of the different tools out there and use the best one for your immediate need. Table 6.2 provides a list of strengths that you might need for a particular search, and then it lists the engines that specialize in them.

Visit Laura Cohen's site at the University of Albany Library called "How to choose a search engine or directory" <http://www.albany.edu/library/internet/choose.html> to see an up-to-date list of the best tools to use for different purposes.

**Table 6.2: Strengths of some preferred search engines and their addresses**

| Strengths | Preferred Tool | Address |
|---|---|---|
| Most relevant results (uses link popularity) | Google | http://www.google.com/ |
| Best annotated subject guide | Librarian's Index | http://www.lii.org/ |
| Good to separate results into folders or concepts | Northern Light | http://www.northernlight.com/ |
| Helpful to narrow a topic with common keywords | Hotbot (Advanced Search-Word Filter)<br>FastSearch (Advanced Search-Word Filter) | http://www.hotbot.lycos.com/<br>http://www.ussc.alltheweb.com/ |
| Largest—Find information on obscure topics | Fast Search<br>Northern Light<br>Altavista<br>Excite | http://www.ussc.alltheweb.com/<br>http://www.northernlight.com/<br>http://www.altavista.com/<br>http://www.excite.com/ |
| Good information about places: Countries, States, Regions | Vive World<br>Orientation<br>Yahoo Regional | http://www.vive.net/world/countries.htm<br>http://www.orientation.com/<br>http://dir.yahoo.com/Regional/ |
| Contains maps | Mapquest | http://www.mapquest.com/ |
| Responds to natural language questions or phrases | AskJeeves | http://www.aj.com/ |

**Table 6.2: Strengths of some preferred search engines, and their addresses (continued)**

| | | |
|---|---|---|
| For kids | AskJeeves for kids | http://www.ajkids.com/ |
| Relevant to domains: .edu, .com, .net, .gov, .org, .mil | Metacrawler (Customize tab-Domain) Hotbot (Advanced Search-Location) FastSearch (Advanced Search-Domain) | http://www.metacrawler.com/customize/ http://www.hotbot.lycos.com/ http://www.ussc.alltheweb.com/ |
| Source of images, sounds, media, file extensions | Hotbot (check Image, etc. under search) Altavista (Images, etc. tabs) | http://www.hotbot.lycos.com/ http://www.altavista.com/ |
| Helpful for scientific and mathematical topics | Altavista | http://www.altavista.com/ |
| Good for facts, dictionaries, phone numbers, news pages—reference section of the library | Refdesk Internet Public Library | http://www.refdesk.com/ http://www.ipl.org/ |
| Can translate into other languages | Altavista (click Translate after each result) Go Translator | http://www.altavista.com/ http://translator.go.com/ |
| Can search in foreign languages | Altavista FastSearch | http://www.altavista.com/ http://www.ussc.alltheweb.com/ |
| To ask an expert for information or assistance | Ask the Experts list at Refdesk.com Askme.com | http://www.refdesk.com/expert.html http://www.askme.com/ |

## Searching Tips and Techniques

Finding useful information on the Internet is doable, though it is not quite as easy as many people think. Suppose we need up-to-date information on the use of technology in the classroom. We might select *Google* because it uses link frequency to show us the most commonly visited sites on our topic. We type <http://www.google.com/> (or just <google>) into the location or search box on the upper toolbar display of our web browser. Then we press [Enter]. The *Google* display appears. Next, we type our search term or phrase into the box. *Google* prefers that you type your important searchwords without any special formatting, such as + or -. *Google* assumes a Boolean "AND" between each word typed into the box. So, one way to search for our topic might be to type in the following: <technology k-12 classroom>. When I typed these words, the first source *Google* listed was this: *The Report to the President on the Use of Technology to Strengthen K-12 Education in the United States from the President's Committee of Advisor's on Science and Technology, Panel on Educational Technology.* This 1997 document is an often-quoted reference on our topic. The fact that *Google* listed it first suggests that it is an excellent resource to consult at the beginning of our search.

*Altavista* would likely be our second choice because it is one of the largest and oldest of the search tools. Furthermore, *Altavista* uses most of the sophisticated search techniques available on the Internet. We pull up the *Altavista* website by typing <http://www.altavista.com/> (or just <altavista>) into the location or search box and pressing [Enter]. Then we are ready to type a search strategy into the *Altavista* search box. Here is one way we could structure our search (other possibilities follow, and there are many ways you could try that I do not have the space to show you): <education AND technology AND classroom>.

This search uses Boolean logic (AND, OR, or NOT operators) to specify we want the search engine to return a list of web pages that *must* have *all* of the words connected by AND somewhere in the text of the page. The *Altavista* relevance programming will automatically rank pages on three criteria: 1. Frequency of appearance of our search terms, 2. The closeness of our search terms to the top of the page (or the presence in the title), and 3. The closeness of our search terms to one another.

When the OR operator (instead of AND) is placed between search words or phrases, it means you want either term or both to appear in the web pages returned. The NOT operator means you do not want the term listed after the word NOT to appear in the web pages returned. This is risky because a single appearance of the undesirable word would eliminate a page that might actually be relevant. For an excellent overview of Boolean searching, visit the University at Albany Library web page, "Boolean Searching on the Internet", at http://www.albany.edu/library/internet/boolean.html.

Another way you can structure your search is the following: <+technology+classroomdomain:govdomain:edu>. This search uses *Implied Boolean logic*, a simplification of the Boolean logic introduced above. Searchers used Boolean logic to search the first online databases. Implied Boolean searching supports faster, neater searches on the Internet. table 6.3 clarifies the translation of Boolean to Implied Boolean search techniques.

The single most important concept in web searching with Implied Boolean logic is to put a + before each search term you want to require. Thus, <+technology +classroom> will pull up web pages that contain both the word "technology" and the word "classroom." The absence of a + or – is the equivalent of a Boolean OR search. In other words, the absence of a symbol before a search element indicates the searcher desires it to appear in the resulting web pages, but does not require it to appear. Thus, "domain:edu domain:gov" means you would like to look at web pages from either government or educational sponsors or both.

Following are three other approaches:

- <+"technology in the classroom">. This search strategy requires the phrase "technology in the classroom" to appear in every web page listed in the results.
- <+technology+classroom+K-12+date>2000–domain:com>. This complex search strategy retrieves web pages published or last updated in 2000 or later that must include all three words (technology, classroom, and k-12). The pages listed in the results may not be hosted at a commercial website.
- <+title:"technology in the classroom"+"New Mexico">. The phrase "technology in the classroom" must appear in the title of the resulting web pages. The retrieved web pages must also contain the phrase "New Mexico" somewhere in the text. Treating New Mexico as a phrase is important because without the quotation marks, the results would include many websites covering the country of Mexico. As a rule of thumb, if you are looking for one or more words to appear together as phrase, include them in quotation marks.

**Table 6.3: Translation of Boolean to Implied Boolean search techniques**

| Function | Boolean | Implied Boolean |
|---|---|---|
| To require that all terms must appear for a document to be selected: | AND, as in "technology AND classroom" | +, as in "+technology +classroom" |
| To require that ANY of a group of terms must appear for a document to be selected: | OR, as in "elementary OR secondary" | absence of a symbol, as in "elementary secondary" |
| To require that a document NOT be selected if a term appears: | NOT, as in "NOT college" | -, as in "-college" |

## General Web Searching Techniques

Other techniques now expand the ways we can communicate our search needs to large, complex search engines and compilations of information. Check <http://www.infopeople.org/src/chart.html> for the most popular tools and techniques for effective searching. If you pull up peculiar results, check the help area for the tool you are using for variations or common techniques. The most common techniques appear in table 6.4.

## Evaluating Web Pages

The most important aspect of using anything obtained from the Internet is to examine it thoroughly to determine its purpose and if it meets your information needs. Experienced web searchers automatically evaluate everything they find because they know the Internet is a huge, unrestricted world. Those who are accustomed to using a library in which each book, video, and journal is carefully screened by editor, publisher, reviewer, faculty member, and librarian before it ever reaches the shelf may have limited experience evaluating information sources. Even the materials in bookstores that consist of items designed to appeal to a wide audience still have been screened more than Internet material as they had to travel through the scrutinizing eyes of the agent and the publisher before reaching the shelves. Anyone can put anything on the Net. Web pages are of high quality if they meet the basic criteria for accuracy, authority, coverage, currency, and objectivity for your particular information need at the moment (Tate and Alexander 1996). Let's discuss each criterion in turn.

**Table 6.4: The most common search techniques and their effects**

| Technique: What do you add to the search element? | Placement: Where do you put the technique in relation to the search element? | Action/Meaning: What impact does the technique have on the web pages that are returned? | Example: How might a typical search look in the search box at the search tool? |
|---|---|---|---|
| + | Before | Element must appear | +dolphin |
| - | Before | Element must not appear | -domain.com |
| Blank space | Before | Element may appear | prevention |
| " " | Around | Element must appear as specified | "gun control" |
| title: | Before | Element must appear in title of web page | title: "New Mexico" |
| domain: | Before | Web pages must be from a particular domain (org, gov, net, com, edu, mil) | domain:edu |
| host: | Before | Web pages returned must be from a specific machine (host). | host:www.microsoft.com |
| * or ? | At the end of a word root | Word root must appear, with any ending or with no ending | manag* |
| * | In place of an undetermined letter | The remainder of the word specified must appear | wom*n |

## Accuracy

According to your understanding of the subject, the information on this page appears accurate. Verify some of the information. Do books and articles found in the library present the same perspective and facts? Does the page end with references like a book or article? Is the material biased toward a particular viewpoint? Does it contain errors? Does an organization back up this perspective?

The presence of graphics or quotations indicating the site has won several awards is a positive sign although it is simple to grab graphics off other sites. Question the accuracy of the content if it contains spelling and grammatical errors and if the page does not appear professionally designed and produced.

## Authority

The alliances and purpose of a web page author offer valuable insight into the value of the page. An initial indicator is whether the page originates from a desirable domain (edu, gov, or org). Check for contact information about the author or sponsor of the page, usually provided at the bottom of each page. If the page contains an address, phone number, and e-mail address, you can trace the source. Consider whether the author or sponsor is reputable and qualified to discuss the topic covered in the pages.

In the process of evaluating web pages, it is frequently necessary to peel away the levels of the web address or URL one by one and visit each of the resulting websites to uncover proof of authority. For example, we could remove each successive level of the web address from right (specific) to left (general) to discover more information about the author or sponsor of the web site. With each successive removal of a level from the location or website field in the web browser, we leave a trailing forward slash and press <enter> to visit that site. Here is an example:

http://www.learningspace.org/instruct/lplan/rlesson.htm and press
    <enter>
http://www.learningspace.org/instruct/lplan/ and press <enter>
http://www.learningspace.org/instruct/ and press <enter>
http://www.learningspace.org/ and press <enter>

Through this exercise, we discover that the original web page we were looking at gave instructions on creating research lesson plans and was sponsored by the Learning Space Foundation, a nonprofit organization with the mission statement: "Learning Space is for teachers, created by teachers, and about teachers."

Stripping away the levels of the web address helps you discover when an author has purchased web space at an Internet Service Provider (ISP). During the stripping process, you will come upon the main page for the ISP company, which describes their services and prices. Those who purchase space for their web pages may place whatever they like on the Net within current laws.

## Coverage

Use discriminating common sense to test if the page presents sufficient detail and content on your topic. The Internet contains many teasers that promote books, journals, and products without providing the actual content. Online journal websites often feature a table of contents and a few actual articles at their website to entice. Click on links, and scroll to the bottom of each page to be certain the page contains the material you need. Is the content relevant to the specific topic you are researching? Is this the best source for this information? Watch for subscription and purchase information that indicates a sales rather than informational intent.

## Currency

Materials become outdated quickly on the Internet. Even web pages on historical and other topics that do not change often (i.e. language dictionaries) should demonstrate frequent attention by the webmaster. Most webmasters place the date of most recent update at the bottom of each page. Scrutinize pages not updated within the last six months. Maybe the author abandoned the page or replaced it with an updated version at another address. If the date is missing, the author might be hiding the age of the content. Additionally, expired or nonfunctional links to other web pages indicate the material is out of date.

## Objectivity

Evaluate the website for objectivity by checking for accurate, unbiased information with a minimum of advertising. Does the site present a balanced perspective on the issue or just one viewpoint? Sites attempting to sell products are not objective. Be suspicious. It is up to the surfer to conduct a bit of detective work to determine the intent of the author of each web page the search tool delivers. An important question is, what is the perspective of the author? I call this the *NRA* test. We know that a page at the *National Rifle Association* website is going to espouse a particular viewpoint. Many other sites on the web represent similarly strong perspectives, but they are not instantly recognizable. Always ask yourself, what is the purpose of this page? Does it answer my question? A dose of common sense and critical thinking is all it takes to evaluate a source to see if it meets your present information need. Be especially careful of the commercial sites in the .com domain because they are normally trying to sell. For most information needs, web pages in the .edu, .org, and .gov domains are the best bets because they tend to be thoroughly researched and designed to provide information.

## Summary

The major steps in searching for information on the Internet include:

1.  Clarify your information need. Write down what you need to find information on in the form of a sentence. Circle important keywords and phrases.
2.  Select one or more search tools that are likely to contain relevant information sources. Guess the addresses of organizations that might have authoritative information and visit those sites directly.
3.  Structure your search strategy according to the techniques of the selected tool.
4.  Refine your search based on the results obtained:
    a.  If you retrieve too many results, add additional search terms to narrow the topic. For example, add <–domain:com> to eliminate commercial sites or <+elementary> to narrow your search to just information on the elementary grades.
    b.  If you retrieve too few results, eliminate search terms or use more general terms to broaden the concept. For example, if the search string <+technology +classroom +chemistry> retrieves

very few pages, try the following search terms: <+technology+k12+science>

c.  Examine the best results to find other vocabulary or related concepts for additional searches. For example, the relevant pages retrieved from *Google* on the topic of <technology classroom chemistry> repeatedly mentioned lesson plans and curriculum. One could search for <technology chemistry lesson plans> as an alternative. Remember, *Google* does not require the + and − operators that *Altavista, Northern Light, Excite, Hotbot,* and other search engines expect to fine-tune the results.

d.  Try other search tools. If you must go beyond the first page or two of *Altavista* results (even after refining your search terms), try *Google* or a Meta Search tool.

e.  Check for typos and search structure errors, particularly if you believe there are more web pages on the Net than your search retrieved. Machines and software are literal. Searching involves typing the exact words and phrases into the Search box you want to find on the Internet. If you misspell a word, you will only retrieve other pages whose author misspelled it exactly the same way as you did. Use a dictionary to verify if you suspect you are misspelling a word.

f.  The misuse of the Implied Boolean operators is another common searching problem. When typing a strategy into the Search box, the + immediately precedes the search element and a space separates the search elements. For example, type <+technology +classroom> not <+ technology+ classroom>.

g.  Use the Find in Page selection under the Edit menu of your web browser to locate appearances of your search terms in long web pages.

5.  Evaluate the results according to their accuracy, objectivity, currency, coverage, and authority as they pertain to your present information need.

# Reference

Tate, M., and J. Alexander. 1996. Teaching Critical Evaluation Skills for World Wide Web Resources. *Computers in Libraries*, 16(10), 49-55.

# 7

# Administrators and Networks: How to Get Started and What to Expect

## Tom Watts

Computer networking is increasingly a fact of modern life. Most of us are now users of this innovation in computer technology. We use networks at work and for many of our daily tasks, and take our network connection for granted.

Professionals and business people now depend on network resources to collaborate on projects, to store documents, and to communicate via e-mail. We bank online; we research financial information online to make informed stock purchases and other personal finance decisions. We read newspapers and magazines in their online version (for example, *The New York Times*, a.k.a. www.nytimes.com), we purchase books and clothing from online catalogs, and we make our own airline and hotel reservations and other travel arrangements on the Web. Also, networks have revolutionized the way other critical tasks are handled, such as updating grocery lists, coordinating schedules to get sons and daughters to band and baseball practices, and checking the temperature and forecast in San Antonio for that family conference at Sea World.

In education, networks are being implemented at an increasing rate. Many corporations and businesses are offering various types of assistance to schools to get campuses wired, and the federal and state governments are making networking a central part of their educational initiatives.

The rationale for increased networking in schools generally centers on the increased availability of resources for students in a networked environment. The Internet provides expanded resources to students, in the form of online versions of books and access to international libraries, museums, universities, and other sources of information. Networks have created, in effect, virtual libraries that allow any campus to add information resources from practically every other part of the world to its own library holdings. Increased communication is another of the improvements that campuses create for their students and faculty with a networked environment. Students at networked campuses will participate enthusiastically and profitably via e-mail in discussions and forums with experts and with students in other schools, in other school districts, and even in other countries. Finally, if we ignore the importance of network skills being taught in schools, graduates will lack an important skill that colleges and the marketplace expect.

Even though networks are becoming more and more common, and we are becoming used to their presence, the task of designing a network and preparing a campus or a district for a networked environment is still daunting. As school districts and individual campuses prepare for a network, there are several important issues for administrators to consider.

Considering campus networks, several questions are important for campuses to answer for themselves, and several others are important for campuses and network specialists to agree on before the process begins. It is important to understand all the uses a network can be put to, and the differences a networked campus creates. It is important to communicate clearly with the technical experts. Finally, even though we do not need to know how to build a network in order to drive a Pentium II processor or G3 speedster down the information superhighway, it is important to know what LANs and WANs are, how Category 5 cable differs from fiber, and why we need to think about change and obsolescence even before we start to install our network.

## Planning for a Networked Campus

In most discussions of why networks do not fulfill their potential, the cause is traced back to two factors: 1) there was no exploration of the reasons why a network was needed, and 2) thus unrealistic expectations were built up and then not met by planners. The planning must ask why the campus needs (or wants) a network. If the campus can answer the question "why do we want the Internet?" it is more likely to use the Internet well. If it does not ask itself "why do we want the Internet?" then staffs are more likely to underuse or misuse it, at least for a while. The campus should also explore other reasons, besides using the network to access the Internet, why the network will be a good investment.

Tied closely to the question why do we want networking? is the more specific query, how will being part of a network change our instruction? As staffs work to answer these two questions, the unrealistic expectations will reveal themselves. If the campus expects instructional miracles once the network is up, they will probably be unpleasantly surprised. The best time to adjust expectations is in the planning stage. Positive things will probably occur and miracles may, in fact, happen. But the miracles will happen for the same reasons they always happen, because teachers, administrators, and students all work very hard and use the tools around them wisely.

## What to Ask

Questions help to establish the common ground between the campus staff and the network engineers and technical staff. In some instances, administrators are reluctant to bring up the issues and defer to the technical experts. There is certainly nothing wrong with deferring to the experts in the installation of the network, but it is important to know something about the use and purpose of a network and some of the questions to ask of the persons putting your campus network together. Most administrators, even administrators with technology backgrounds, do not have the time to get involved in the actual installation of the network. But administrators and other campus personnel should work to determine how the network will be used, and their wishes in this regard should drive installation decisions. The time to address these questions is *before* the network specialists begin their work.

Before meeting with network specialists, the campus should meet with the staff from other schools that have installed networks and are using them effectively. Those who have been through the process are a great resource for anyone about to go down the same road. The sample questions included here are a good start, but any question relating to the network and how it will transform the classrooms is important enough to ask.

- What training does the campus need?
- What are the technology levels of the campus?
- More important than the current technology level, what is the enthusiasm level for a network, and what is the resistance level of the faculty to required increased technology use?
- What district-level resources are available to pay for the installation of the network, including buying computers? What district-level resources are available to sustain the network (i.e., will the district pay for the T1 line, will the district acquire site licenses for network operating software and licenses for administrative and instructional software, will the district pay for the maintenance agreements on and repair of campus communication equipment such as servers, routers, and hubs?)

- Who will pay to maintain the campus communication equipment (servers, routers, hubs, etc.), the district or the campus?
- What does the district expect the campuses to pay out of its own budget for maintenance and ongoing support of the network?
- What is the district networking strategy for the next five years? Does the district expect to discontinue the support of any currently used software?
- What resources can the campus apply on a yearly basis to the installation and maintenance of the network?
- What should the campus expect to spend on the network annually?
- How should faculty use e-mail communication? What kind of access should students have to e-mail?
- Will the campuses be able to establish e-mail accounts for all faculty, administrators, and clerks? What e-mail system will the campus use?
- How will campus staffing be affected by the installation of the network, (i.e., can the current staff supervise the networked labs adequately; can it train users, administer the network (Internet Protocol [IP] addresses for computers, network preferences, e-mail addresses), and maintain the day-to-day operation of the network?)
- What staffing levels and what specific positions does the district suggest campuses should maintain for administration and maintenance of the network, for correction of network down time, and for troubleshooting of the network hardware and software?

The campus should include in its *Needs Assessment* a close look at any special circumstances that exist. For example, does the campus include a magnet school of some type, and if so, what purposes or special applications does that imply? Will a magnet school for prospective teachers, for example, profit from a distance-learning center and an ability to observe classrooms or to connect with a college of education? Does a campus with a large number of special education students require assistive technology to include those students fully in the technology experience? If the answer to either question is yes, then that issue should be brought up to the network specialists as a requirement of the campus network.

Other more technical questions are these:

- Will all the campus computers be able to access the Internet?
- What *browser* (i.e., Netscape or Microsoft Explorer) will the campus use to access and search the web?

- Will a *content filter* be installed? What will the campus responsibility be in the ongoing maintenance of the content filter? A content filter is a software program that prevents users from accessing certain websites, e.g., pornographic or violent sites. Normally, these filters can be updated to identify additional sites that students will be restricted from accessing.
- Will a *firewall* be installed? A firewall is a hardware barrier that prevents users from outside the district or campus from accessing the network and performing unauthorized procedures (hacking).
- Will *dial-in access* be available, i.e. will a faculty member be able to dial in from home to the network?
- Will the *bandwidth* that the campus is allocated be sufficient if fifty concurrent users access the Internet? One hundred users? One hundred-fifty?
- What level of access will substantially slow the campus's time to access Internet websites?
- What training will the campus receive from the district on administering the Internet?
- Will it be advantageous for the campus to install a *proxy server*? A proxy server is not a file server; it is an additional server that allows the campus to do specific tasks more efficiently (to add network users; to administer IP addresses; to record user browser preferences; to cache (save) Internet sites, etc.).
- Will the campus be able to use the network to access and use administrative software (e.g., student system, attendance and grade book software, etc.)?
- How, specifically, will a user access the administrative software, and have an open Internet session at the same time?
- How do the network specialists recommend adding users on the network? Should all users be set up at the same time? Should classroom computers, or the computer lab(s), or the library computers be set up first? Should a combination of machines be set up first?
- Will the campus be able to create an e-mail account for all students? Will the student accounts be individual accounts or classroom accounts?
- What limits will exist on the e-mail system; how much e-mail can be saved and for how long?
- How much student material can be saved on the server? Should students save material on diskettes?
- How will printing be done in the labs, library, and classrooms? Should the campus use networked printing rather than individual printers for classrooms?

## Uses of Networks

Some of the most important issues for administrators to understand are the uses that the network can be put to, the way the campus network connects with other networks, including a district *wide-area network* (*WAN*), and the need for flexibility in setting up the network and preparing for the future.

Perhaps the most important feature to keep in mind about computer networks, particularly in a school, is that they do much more than provide access to the Internet. This section will focus on benefits other than the Internet that a network can bring, such as connecting the students and the faculty of the school to each other. These connections can improve the daily work and communication that needs to happen on a campus every day.

For students, one of the most practical examples of this improved communication is the distribution of information and access within the campus. For example, in a networked environment that includes the library, it will no longer be necessary to take the students physically to use a machine in the library to access the electronic library resources. In fact, students can access the expanding amount of text and illustrations in journal articles and newspapers that are available at various locations (universities, libraries, and other Internet websites). Students can call up the actual text of many documents on the screen and read them, print them, or e-mail the materials to themselves. Similarly, if a computer lab is using specialized math or writing software, the lab can share the software with students in other locations without their having to be physically in the computer lab. The correct campus network will provide students with access to many different resources from many different sites.

It is probably worthwhile at this point to emphasize that the availability of materials online does not necessarily mean that all those arguments that we are approaching a paperless society are accurate. What administrators (and librarians) will find is that students who find valuable research material online will immediately print it. So a higher budget line item for paper is probably in the future for most schools.

For faculty members, the interconnection can extend beyond e-mail and communication about school activities. Those staff members that are collaborating on a project can do so in an electronic format. Grant applications, campus action plans, departmental presentations, and other projects can be shared electronically. This type of collaboration will require some adjustments in organizing and managing the contributions from various participants, but the advantages are significant to collaborators. Faculty can work together without having to be together in the same room. Sharing information, working on projects together and distributing the drafts and the final results efficiently will yield benefits to virtually any campus user working with other faculty members on a project. Teachers can share lesson plans and addresses of useful websites (department home pages, for example). No doubt that collaboration will extend across campuses as familiarity and as comfort with the technology increases.

Administrators planning a campus network should ensure that the networking technical staff knows exactly what the purpose of the network will be. The network will be most effective if it is clearly communicated to the technical experts that it is necessary for library resources (electronic indexes, catalogs, and other research tools) to be accessed by networked computers outside the library, that the writing lab software can be accessed by composition students in other classrooms and not just while they are in the lab, and that teachers can access the administrative software (gradebooks for example) while they are at the networked computer in the teacher's lab. Network specialists should understand those purposes are important to campuses and should plan to give the campus the hardware and software required for its needs.

## Communication: Talking to Network Specialists

Remember, putting networks together is fun, but it is fun in the same way that remodeling your home is fun. As you enjoy the new addition to your home, the memory of wanting to sue the general contractor out of existence fades. That feeling may recur as you work with the technical experts that come to your campus to help you—the network specialists, the cabling contractor, the hardware vendors, etc.

The first lesson to remember in conversing with technical staff is that they use a specialized vocabulary. For example, instead of saying the network will be useful, they assure you, we will give you a network with robust functionality. In fact, keep an ear out for robust. When network specialists want you to know that a piece of equipment has a lot of uses or a software product works well, but they cannot explain exactly how, they refer to the equipment and/or software as robust.

Other words that you will hear often are topology, which means arrangement of network stuff; iterative, which means something that is done over and over either by or to stuff; functional or functionality, which applies to useful stuff; integrated, which means stuff works together, which is usually better than, and usually more expensive than, non-integrated stuff; transparent, which refers to stuff that happens even though you do not actually see it happen, (transparent is often used in situations where network specialists do not actually want to say trust me); and finally redundant, which means stuff that is there in case other stuff does not work.

The stereotype of a nerdy network techie is probably justified to some degree, and in his or her defense, the technical jargon is hard to avoid, as it is in any field. But real communication with the technical staff is very important, because your work depends on their work. The most important quality in dealing with the technical staff is persistence. If their answer to your first question is too technical and jargon-laden, then ask it again; or, ask for an explanation of the part that is unclear. Do not stop until you are satisfied that you understand the answer.

Although technical experts may answer your questions with unintelligible acronyms, keep asking until you are sure they understand your question and that you understand their answer. In all cases, ask the network staff if what you want to do is possible. Then ask them if what you want to do is possible with the equipment currently in place, and if not, what are the additional equipment needs and the costs. Ask the technical staff to explain to you how they are going to make it possible for you to do what you want to do with the network.

But remember, the answer to any technical question is yes. There is almost always a qualification, though, and it is the qualifications that are important to cover. For example, do not ask will the students in the computer lab all be able to access the Internet at the same time, download information, and include the pictures and text into a report? Because the answer to that question, and any other, is yes. Instead ask whether access will be slowed down and by how much, ask whether the campus will need another server to be able to save student material, and ask if any additional equipment will be needed in the lab because of the high level of access that is planned.

Also, do not ask if the athletic trainer's office in the field house (which is about two hundred yards away from the main building) can be connected to the campus network. The answer to that question is, of course, yes. You might have to trench a path for the cable from the main building to the field house, that trenching might have to be across a parking lot or outdoor basketball courts. You may be able to use an aerial connection from the main building to the field house. You may also have to install some additional equipment in the field house to connect the trainer's office to the LAN, and the work may not be scheduled for two months. As Mario Martinez reminds us in chapter 11, the devil is in the technological details.

Use your persistence prudently though. If your network support specialists are like others in school districts, they are probably understaffed and overbooked. They may even be cranky, given the short deadlines and tight resources they have to work with. Do not call over and over, but try to consolidate questions and get answers to all of them at one time. With the research and planning that your campus does before the project, many of the questions may have already surfaced. If there is a time frame for the wiring and configuration of the campus network, plan with the network staff for status reports or updates at regular, reasonable times, and be prepared with your list of questions.

As you work more closely with the network staff, you will find some convergence in both concepts and terminology. You do not want to become a network specialist, and the technical staff does not want to become expert in instruction. What both groups (the campus staff and the technical staff) should aim for is that the campus staff acquires a more complete understanding of the technical considerations while the technical staff acquires an appreciation for what the campus staff needs. If those things happen, then everyone can be proud.

## LANs and WANs and Connections between Networks

The distinction between *local-area network (LAN)* and *wide-area network (WAN)* is a distinction that is important to understand, though the distinction is a little nebulous. Generally speaking, the LAN or WAN designation describes a network relative to other networks it is attached to. If a campus network is one of a number of campus networks connected together, then each of the campus networks is a LAN and the collection of all the campus networks and any other district connection (central offices, etc.) is a WAN.

The campus network though, can also be thought of as a larger network that is made up of smaller networks throughout the campus. The campus network can, and probably will, include several smaller networks throughout the campus. The computer lab, for example, can be configured as a network and attached to the larger campus network. Libraries often are configured as networks, and when possible are connected to the campus network. Industrial courses such as drafting and design and other commercial software applications often are taught in computer labs that are configured as networks and that are connected, in turn, to the campus's main network. All of these smaller networks can be thought of as LANs, networks that cover a limited distance and that are used generally for specific applications. So, in this example, the campus's main network can be thought of as a WAN, but the campus's main network can also be thought of a LAN, because it is one of the campus networks making up the district-wide WAN. So whether any given network should be considered a WAN or a LAN kind of depends on where you are standing, and what the specific network's relationship is to the other network(s) it connects.

In designing the district network and the component campus networks, your networking staff has the responsibility of designing the most efficient use of resources within your campus network, and the most effective connection between the campus and the other networks that make up the district WAN. You, as administrator, have the responsibility of ensuring that the campus network will be configured and equipped for the most complete and efficient distribution of services within the campus LAN, and that the campus has access to sufficient bandwidth and resources to communicate with larger networks, including the Internet, in effective ways.

## Planning for Change and Minimizing Obsolescence

One factor in the design of any network is the rate of improvement in the technology of networks, computers, and telecommunications. Establishing the physical connections for networks is expensive and time consuming. As technology improves, technicians will not want to support the system you have already installed, and you will have to upgrade. There are several options, though, that allow you to maximize the longevity of the network and minimize the effects of the changes in technology.

In planning with the technical experts, it is important to understand their perspective in the construction of the network. In the minds of the network technical staff, their task is to create a network infrastructure that can support (and withstand) a large amount of network traffic for long periods, and that will not require major renovation in its cabling for a period of years—ten to fifteen years. Because ten to fifteen years in telecommunications technology is the equivalent of several geologic eras, this is a formidable goal.

Though it is difficult to predict all the future uses of the highway, technical experts will construct an information highway for the school that is able to handle a variety of loads. In the beginning, traffic may be light such as individuals using e-mail, searching the Internet, and using word processing, spreadsheet, or presentation software. Later, there will be more activity, such as individuals downloading lots of Internet material, or a computer lab class where students save a large amount of data to a networked server and make heavy use of e-mail. And as campuses and faculties accustom themselves to technology, there will undoubtedly be even heavier loads placed on the network, such as distance learning and other video applications.

The technical experts want the information highway they create to have all the capacity required for the campus, to be able to be used with faster and more advanced hardware, and to be as efficient and effective as possible. They will create a network with the bandwidth necessary to handle the network traffic the school can reasonably expect to generate, and that is easy to maintain and administer. Accomplishing all those objectives, and at the same time knowing that changes that occur might severely disrupt any scenario, makes the work of the technical experts challenging.

The rapid changes that we have grown used to in computer and telecommunications technology will not slow any time soon; and though they can improve our lives in the long run, in the short run, they can frustrate us. Though those improvements are hard to predict, the network can be created so that it accommodates those changes without great changes having to be made to the infrastructure.

One of the critical factors in networks is the speed of data transmissions. And the speed of the networks is governed in some respects by the size, or capacity, of the cable. One of the ways that the network infrastructure can be built so that it will outlast the changes in computer technology is to cable the network so that it will be ready for the fastest speeds and highest bandwidth. Data can be transmitted at a range of speeds, from regular phone lines (the slowest rate and smallest bandwidth) to fiber optic lines (the fastest speeds and the greatest bandwidth). Not surprisingly, regular phone lines are the least expensive, while fiber optic is the most expensive. While fiber optic applications are not currently in widespread use, it is prudent to construct a network that can easily adapt to them.

## Connecting the Campus to the Network World

T1 communication lines are high speed, digital lines that are the equivalent of twenty-four regular phone lines (56K lines, the Plain Old Telephone System (POTS) lines). Because the T1 lines are larger capacity than regular phone lines, they have sufficient bandwidth for the network requirements at most schools. They are capable of delivering voice signals, data (including data from the Internet), and video. T1 lines are used to connect a campus to the central office, and in most cases they are used to connect the central office to the district's Internet service provider.

One of the critical issues in convincing teachers to incorporate technology into the classroom is reliability and performance. Networks have to be available, and the connections from classrooms to Internet sites have to be as fast as possible given the costs that schools are able to absorb. T1 lines are reliable, they are becoming more and more cost-efficient, and they eliminate the need for modems at any of the network connections. Fig. 7.1 shows connections that typically use T1 lines. An additional advantage to T1 connections between campuses and the central office is that the conversion to even faster, higher bandwidth service is easier.

**Fig. 7.1: T1 lines connecting major network sites**

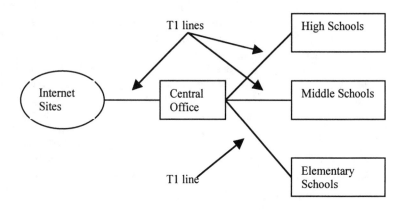

The cabling options for within schools are more varied, but if you want a campus network that will perform at high speeds, provide ample bandwidth, and be ready for changes in network processing, you do not really have a lot of choices. Schools could, for example, connect every classroom via a regular phone line and a 56 BPS (bytes per second) modem. While this would connect classrooms to the Internet, the regular phone line is a slow connection, it does not allow computers within a campus to communicate with one another, and it can get expensive.

When schools speak of networking the campus, they most often are referring to an interconnection of campus computers and high-speed connection to the Internet. This scenario calls for cabling from a communication hub on campus, the *Main Distribution Facility* (MDF), or Main Communication (MC) room, to every classroom, to all other instructional areas (libraries, computer labs, distance learning center, etc.) and to all administrators' offices. This internal campus LAN, connections from the MDF to every location where a networked computer is required are typically made, not with T1 lines or regular telephone lines, but with *Category 5 cabling* and *fiber optics*. Category 5E and 6 are the emerging cable standard.

Cabling with both Category 5 cable and fiber will allow the campus to process immediately at high speed and cost-effectively, and also prepare the campus to move to fiber optic applications when those applications are more plentiful, tested, and cost-effective. Moreover, by cabling for both Category 5 and fiber at the same time, the campus has to open the ceilings and walls only one time for both connections. Thus it incurs the bulk of the cabling labor costs only one time. If you cable the campus network with both Category 5 cable and with fiber connections during the initial cabling, then you will protect your network as much as possible against obsolescence, at a reasonable cost.

## Typical Campus Network Configuration

Typically, campus networks are configured to include an MDF, *Intermediate Distribution Facilities* (IDFs) or Intermediate Connection rooms (ICs) as necessary, and the network connections at specific workstation areas (classrooms, other instructional areas, and administrative work areas).

The MDF, as mentioned earlier, is the location on the campus where the telecommunication equipment and services that enable the campus connection to the outside world are located. Usually, this facility includes a) the telephone switch, or main telephone connection; b) the T1 line coming into the campus; and c) the communication equipment for the network connections.

The communication equipment in the MDF will include at a minimum a *Channel Service Unit/Digital Service Unit* (CSU/DSU), a campus *router*, and a campus *hub*. The CSU/DSU is, in effect, a modem for the T1 line coming into the campus. The T1 line from the central office is connected to the campus at the MDF via the CSU/DSU. The router is the piece of equipment that, logically enough, routes the traffic on the network. It sends the requests from all the campus computers to the appropriate destination—to an Internet address, to a server on the campus, or to a central office destination.

The hub is like a hub on a wheel; it is the central point to which all the spokes attach. All the hardware on the network is connected to this hub. In working with the network specialists, you should ensure that your network is configured with *switched* (sometimes referred to as *smart*) hubs. Switched hubs allow faster and more efficient signal transfers to the appropriate machine. Also, in the event that one of the computers connected to the hub fails, the smart hubs allow the other operational computers to continue to function, without bringing all machines down. Switched hubs are now less expensive than the nonswitched hubs used to be, so there is no reason not to use switched hubs throughout your network. To follow this analogy, the spokes are the cabling from the MDF to the end user locations (classrooms, library, labs, etc.). The hub and the router work in conjunction to provide a network address for each of the network computers, and to route all traffic along the network.

Any network location within 300 feet of the MDF can be directly connected via a Category 5 cable connection. Unfortunately, most campuses (especially secondary campuses) exceed the 300 feet limitation by a significant margin. That is where the IDF comes into play. The IDFs are like boosters for the network signal, and ensure that the cabling can support the distribution of the signal at a fast enough speed and a high enough quality. The IDFs typically include switches that are used for the connections of the computers beyond the 300 feet mark from the MDF. The IDF is then connected back to the MDF, the campus router, and campus main hub. The connection between the MDF and the IDF is a fiber optic connection, referred to as the *network backbone*. The fiber connections ensure that along the backbone of the network the network traffic travels at the fastest speed and cleanest quality possible.

The IDF will support network machines for another 300 feet. If the campus requires additional IDFs, and most high schools and middle schools do, these IDFs are located at 300-foot (approximate) intervals until the network connects machines at the farthest distance from the MDF.

## Category 5 Characteristics

As mentioned earlier, network cabling is most often done from the MDF (or IDF) to the classroom with Category 5 cable (or 5E, and soon, Category 6), a cable that will support voice, data, and video communication. This is especially important if the network connections are made to every classroom, as a Category 5 cable will support a data connection (for Internet and other software applications), a voice connection (for a telephone in the classroom), and a video connection. Also, Category 5 is widely used and very reliable.

Most networks using Category 5 cable will transmit at 10 Mbs (megabytes per second) to the network computers. The next advancements in network speeds for Category 5 will be to 100 and 1000 Mbs. As more and more schools incorporate Internet access and other networked software into the curriculum, the speed of the network becomes more and more important. As you talk with the network specialists and technical team about your network, they should plan for a network that will, in the near future, use 100 Mbs speeds, and that will be ready to move to higher speeds (*Fast Ethernet* is one of the next steps in network speed) when that conversion is cost efficient and the technology is fully tested and reliable. Category 5 cable will support those network speeds, with changes in the communication equipment necessary to support the higher speeds of information transmission.

## Fiber Optic Connections

Fiber is fast and has enormous capacity. Fiber optics use light signals along special fibers, as opposed to electric signals transmitted across copper wires. The advantages of fiber include immunity to electromagnetic interference, higher bandwidth, and greater distances of transmission.

Fiber applications unfortunately have a single, very large disadvantage: they are very expensive. The expectation is, as with most technology, that the costs will decrease in the future as more fiber applications are available. But network connections for fiber are expensive, and in general, the cost of fiber applications is prohibitive at this point.

As noted above, one application where fiber is used is in the backbone of a campus LAN, that is the connections between the equipment in the MDF and the equipment in the IDFs. These fiber connections ensure that the signals along the backbone of the LAN travel at the fastest speed possible.

## Network Cabling for the Future, and Today

Though the active network connections to the individual work stations (whether in an instructional area or an administrative location) are usually cabled with Category 5 cable, in the future fiber will be used for those connections, because of fiber's greater speed, higher capacity, and greater reliability. Though fiber should be installed at the same time the Category 5 cable is installed, the fiber connections are not used at this time because it is simply too expensive to connect machines to fiber and because applications are not ready for it. It does make sense, though, to install the Catagory 5 and the fiber at the same time.

As mentioned earlier, cabling to the campus classrooms with both Category 5 cable and fiber at the same time will result in significant labor savings and minimized disruption. At the same time, it also extends the life of the network, as all indications point to fiber-based applications in the future.

Cabling for a fiber connection everywhere a Category 5 network connection is made, at the same time that the building is being cabled for Category 5 connections, is the most effective plan for districts to avoid some of the problems with obsolete network connections, or the possibility of obsolescence after only a short life span. Some campuses include a Category 5 and a fiber connection at every instructional location (classroom, library, labs, etc.), and only a Category 5 connection at administrative locations (principals, assistant principals, counselors, clerks, etc.). The rationale for that is that the administrative applications (usually student information systems and finance systems) require less bandwidth than the instructional software, which might include Internet sites, graphics, animations, or other high-bandwidth requirements. Districts cabling with both Category 5 and fiber can obtain warranties on the network connections for up to fifteen years, ensuring that the network will be useful for an extended period of time.

## Care and Feeding of the Campus Network

The best approach that a campus can take in preparation for a network is to allocate enough physical space for network facilities. This includes a room approximately fifteen feet by fifteen feet for the MDF. This room will have to house the communication equipment mentioned earlier: T1 line interface and CSU/DSU, the telephone switch, the campus router, and the campus hub. Additionally, the MDF is the termination point for the network cabling for the computers directly connected to the MDF and the cabling for the IDF connections. Campuses as a rule lack physical space to give away, but this facility is absolutely a must for the network. In addition, it should have environmental controls to ensure air conditioning. The equipment in the room will generate significant heat and a lack of conditioned air will definitely harm the equipment.

The IDFs require far less space, but there will have to be room for at least a switch and some panels for network wiring. Some campuses locate IDFs in closets or supply cabinets, and those locations are generally sufficient. Like the MDF, the IDF should have at least some air conditioning, and if the campus locates the IDF in a multipurpose room (custodian room, for example) it is important to ensure that the communication equipment is protected from dust, heat, and rough treatment. Some telephone technicians and network specialists joke that they cannot recognize hubs or telephone switches unless there is a mop leaning against the equipment. Not all campuses are that lax in treatment of network equipment, but there is a tendency to let the equipment occupy shared space. If the equipment is neglected in a shared facility, then damage will result, sometimes sufficient to disrupt the network. While space in every school is at a premium, it is critical that the network equipment be given protection from dust, heat, and rough treatment.

The other issues dealing with the care and feeding of a network have to do with its use and sustainability. These are issues that should occur to you early in the network creation process, and they will be issues that others will be only too happy to let you address. Lucky you! The crucial issues are how to pay for this addition to your campus, how to make sure the equipment lasts a long time, and how to make sure that you get the best use out of it.

As an administrator, remember that you and your district will be making a two-stage investment: there will be an initial outlay that puts the network into place and gets you going, and then there will be the recurring costs that keep the network operational at the optimum level. There will be recurring costs, for equipment maintenance, equipment replacement, and additional equipment. No matter how well you plan, do not be surprised if someone wants a change—a different location for a network connection, an additional connection, etc.—that requires you to call back the cabling contractor for more work.

As noted earlier, it is important at the outset, in the discussion with the technical experts that you understand what costs your campus will be expected to bear for the ongoing, recurring costs of the network. The district central office will be, in most cases, the lead player in the development of the district WAN, and it will be in the district's best interest to standardize the LAN equipment on all campuses. If the costs for the campus LANs are included in the district's central office technology budget, it is easier for the district to obtain a better price on equipment and cabling services. It is also easier to establish and sustain a policy on standardized campus LANs. Finally, it is easier to track the overall costs for the installation of the network.

Having the costs located in a centralized budget, and not in your campus budget, is probably preferable to you. However, two important issues must be made clear: 1) the fact that the network budget is centralized should not result in your having to accept a network that does not meet your instructional needs, nor should it preclude your input with the district's network specialists, and 2) should the recurring costs (maintenance, etc.) be shifted to the campus, the campus budget has to be adjusted to cover these costs. The second point is especially important if the campus network cabling is done in stages. For example, if the first stage covers cabling in the main building only, and a second (or third) stage of the cabling covers the outlying buildings and portables, be sure that all stages of cabling are funded, whether the budget is in the central office or funds are allocated to your campus budget to cover the costs.

The E-rate program covers much of the cost of the telecommunications infrastructure, and your district must take advantage of that program. There are several procedural issues that must be met in applying for E-rate funding, so your district must comply with those requirements. In addition, several states are also taking an active role in establishing educational networks for K-12 schools; those resources are important in sustaining the network. Though the federal and state programs are very helpful in defraying costs, the best approach is the long-term plan of your district for the funding of the educational network. A campus administrator would probably be best served by understanding the long-term plan of the district for technology, and understanding how the funding of technology is structured. In the event such a plan does not exist, the best course of action is to address the lack of a long-term plan and funding approach with the central office staff and all the campuses in the district.

Also, this *will* be a heavily used network. You will probably need *someone at your campus* to make sure that everything is running, and running well. This does not have to be a network specialist, but it does need to be someone who can work with the technical staff and who understands what the teachers and you need from the network. If you rely on the network in the instructional areas, then you will find that a day without the network can be devastating to instructional goals. When the network resources are integrated into the instructional day, then the network is as important as electricity, water, textbooks, or any other necessity. It will no longer be a luxury, but one of the fixtures in the classroom that must work on a day-to-day basis. The daily use of the network will be the best compliment you and your staff can receive on your ability to create a useful network, but that daily use will also be your greatest challenge. It is a challenge best met by an ally right there on your campus, i.e., a full- or half-time network-savvy employee.

You also need to make sure that training for all this new equipment is available for everyone who will be utilizing the network, including refresher courses throughout the school year. You will know if you are talking to someone who does not understand the value of good training, or someone who has forgotten to add training into the calculus for a well-used network, if that person tells you that using the network is intuitive. Do not listen to persons like that. Insist on training that is multitiered—that is, the training addresses those on your staff that love computers, those that hate them, those who are still on the fence, those who tolerate them, those who ignore them, and those that are terrified by them.

## Network Magic

It is tempting to believe that a computer network is an information panacea. Networks are important and they are useful, but they come without the magic. The magic is in the creativity and the hard work that teachers, students, and administrators employ in the use of the network resources.

Networks connect students and teachers to virtually unlimited resources, but in embarking on the use of a campus network, some campuses have found the unlimited resources to be as daunting as limited resources. It is important to allow the network to achieve its potential via use by intelligent teachers and students. It probably will not happen overnight, and there may be some frustration in the first tries at Internet research, sharing resources, or collaborative projects.

The good news is that there are a lot of sources for help, and a tremendous camaraderie among network users, particularly Internet users. A good first step is to look at places like *The New York Times* on the web (www.nytimes.com), or PBS Online (www.pbs.org), or National Public Radio Online (www.npr.com). These sources all have a portion of the website devoted to educational activities and suggestions. Journals (such as *Technology and Learning*) have reviews of websites and suggestions on incorporating network resources into the classroom. And other teachers are perhaps the best resources, for they know the difficulties in using these resources and how best to incorporate them. With careful attention in the design of the network, realistic expectations for its use, and an optimistic outlook for the network potential, schools can make the best of the computer environment as an educational tool.

# 8

# A Network Connection: Now What?

## Tom Watts

At a recent planning meeting on technology and its uses, one of the mentor teachers attending asked if we could frame the issue from the point of view of a classroom teacher. Specifically, the mentor wanted to know if anyone could help provide an answer to the question that she said was most often posed to her: Now that I have a network connection in my room, how is the classroom different from before?

The mentor is a mathematics teacher, and in her work she most often dealt with math and science teachers at the middle school level. She was dismayed at the lack of enthusiasm she found among teachers for the incorporation of technology into the daily curriculum, and she wanted some ideas to help her turn that disinterest into enthusiasm.

And so some of the participants in that seminar began to pursue the answer to the question that the mentor had posed. Certainly the classroom is different; that was, after all, the intent behind the planning, the wiring, and the placement of technology resources in the classroom. But the question helped to frame some of the tasks that a district faces once the wiring is complete. The teacher's question deserves an answer, and the best phrasing of the answer is not just that the classroom is, in fact, different because of the connection to the network, but also that the difference is a positive one—that the classroom is better and more flexible than it is without the connection to the network.

The question is a good one because it framed the question from an interesting perspective. Teachers are looking at the networks from a very basic perspective—what are the benefits to the classroom, and specifically, what are the benefits to the students? The participants explored the differences, though they knew in large measure what the differences would be. The question also was useful because it presented the group with a task not only to answer the question, i.e., what was it exactly that the network added to the classroom, but also to explore how best to present this new tool to the district's teachers.

Too often we hear the question paraphrased by persons with a commitment and belief in the efficacy of technology in the classroom. When these persons repeat the question, they often do it in a tone of amazement that there are still persons in the universe who question the value of technology. But most teachers and administrators ask the question in absolutely good faith, wanting to know how in fact the classroom is changed and what is necessary on their part to make use of the resources. They could be skeptical, but even if they are, they can be convinced that the networked classroom does make a positive difference to students, teachers, and administrators.

Everyone thought the question was a good one, forcing the proponents of the networked campus to define its importance without assuming simply that technology is good and without assuming that everyone already agreed on the usefulness of technology.

# A Connected Classroom

The easy portion of the answer is that the classroom is different because it has been connected, via the network, to the other classrooms and instructional areas on the campus, and to networks outside the campus, most notably the Internet. Then the question becomes, obviously, what does that connection to other classrooms and instructional sites and the Internet do for my classroom?

The answer really depends on what the teacher wants to do in the classroom and how the teacher wants to use the network to complement his/her strengths. One of the misconceptions of network configurations is that a network limits the way that classroom teachers can use the computers in their rooms. The misconceptions arise, perhaps, from initiatives that have stressed a computer in every classroom, without really addressing the purpose of the computer or confronting the idea that only prepackaged material can be used. Undoubtedly, some of the misconception is the product of technology initiatives that have been forced on teachers without sufficient explanation as to purpose or objectives, without enough (or any) input from teachers, and too often without the required training or follow-up. Too many of those initiatives have been introduced amidst a great deal of promised benefits. The reality has been that the training in the use of the systems or software has not allowed teachers to incorporate the technology into the classroom as a complement to the strengths that already exist there. Perhaps teachers view network connectivity as one more technology program that, despite the current enthusiasm and promise, will over time receive decreasing emphasis and support and then just go away. We must show teachers, especially the reluctant ones, the network's value as a classroom tool.

Now I must move on to a second critical question. While teachers are asking, "How will networks change what I do with students," administrators might well ask, "To what extent should I force teachers to include network resources in their curricula?" Though I cannot give you a simple answer for your situation, I will provide suggestions for configuring and using computers in the classroom. I hope these suggestions help both parties make up their minds.

The network design explained in the previous chapter calls for the connection of every classroom and instructional area to the network with a cable connection that supports voice, data, and video. Classroom connections are linked back to the main campus communication room (the Main Distribution Facility, or MDF), and from there to a central network connection that supports all network services such as Internet access, e-mail, and routing (which means sending data packets along the network to their correct destination; for example, sending a request from a student computer to access the New Mexico State University website so that the request does, in fact, reach the NMSU website). By employing this type of network configuration, you provide users a great deal of flexibility in the way that they use the network.

## Classroom Network Options: Making Sure that the Network Complements Teacher Strengths

Computer technology is similar to other areas of information systems in that there is controversy over the advantages and disadvantages of competing solutions to problems. Because the debate is ultimately unresolvable, organizations cycle back and forth between the competing solutions. For example, the issue of in-house programming versus third-party software development was debated by application managers who had to weigh continuity, customized processes, and speedy implementations in deciding which route to take. Though third-party development seems to have become the favorite path in the last decade, that doesn't mean that the issue has been settled decisively. Similarly, the data entry function moved back and forth between centralized and distributed data entry, and companies regularly move from one approach to the other, depending on how management views the advantages and disadvantages of each system.

In educational settings, one of the cyclical issues that has been debated recently is the best deployment of computer technology for instruction. The two main camps are those that see a need for computer labs (centers where thirty to fifty machines are grouped with access to a variety of applications), and those that prefer to see machines distributed to many classrooms. At the inception of the use of computer technology in schools, computer labs were easily the most popular way of using technology. As more computers became available for schools, more staff opted not just to locate computers in classrooms to use them to support the classroom curriculum, but to minimize the use of computer labs. Labs, they argued, meant students got the idea that the computers were used in the lab room only and that they were not tools that could be used in virtually every discipline.

This is an issue that educators will continue to discuss. Most recently, there has been something of a compromise. Schools have labs (provided they can free up a classroom and get enough computers to equip it). But they are also beginning to distribute computers throughout individual classrooms, networked to other computers in other places. The benefit of a networked campus is that the campus can have more of the best of both worlds. Individual classrooms can be configured in many different ways to complement the course material being taught and the teaching strengths of individual teachers; and computer labs can continue to be effectively used. A single machine, or multiple machines, can be connected in a classroom, depending on the preferences of the campus or teacher, and, of course, depending on the availability of resources.

## Connection of a Single Machine

The connection of a single machine in the classroom is illustrated in figure 8.1.

Category 5, or Cat5, is the cable that is used to make the connections from the Main Distribution Facility (MDF) to the classroom. Cat5 will support voice, data, and video signals at a minimum speed of 10 megabits per second, up to 100 megabits per second, or at even faster speeds.

If only one machine is connected in a classroom, there are still several options for its use. Increasingly, teachers are using the network connection to connect their computer to the networked administrative systems (student information, grading, attendance, etc.), in order to key in data directly to the systems and to analyze data that have been entered (later in this chapter, I provide more information about the use of administrative systems). The machine can also connect to networked instructional resources (library resources, Internet access, computer labs, etc.). If the school or district supports e-mail, then that service will also be available to the teacher on the networked machine.

**Figure 8.1: One networked computer in a classroom**

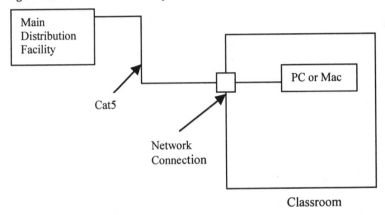

The single machine is not as limited as one might think either. Though only one machine is connected, the computer can be connected to a large screen TV screen, and if the teacher wanted, he or she could connect to websites relevant to the classroom work and display the site via the large monitor to the entire class. A teacher who wanted to incorporate specific websites, and who wanted to maintain control over the website could use this type of computer setup and bring a wide array of resources into the classroom without worrying over any of the issues related to Internet access by students.

Furthermore, teachers can allow students to do specific tasks, such as checking e-mail, using a specific instructional software program, or researching a topic on the Internet. One machine in a classroom is perhaps not the best use of the network, but that scenario can still be used effectively.

# Connecting Multiple Computers
# in the Classroom

In other cases, campuses or teachers can also choose to connect more than one machine. In these configurations, multiple machines are connected to a switch and the switch is then attached to the network connection in the classroom as seen in figure 8.2.

**Figure 8.2: More than one networked computer in a classroom**

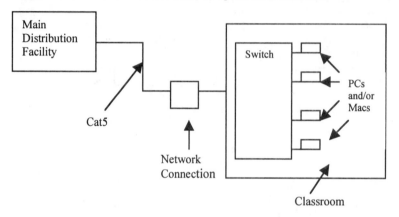

This type of configuration offers a great deal of flexibility. Switches will generally connect multiple machines (usually in multiples of four and usually up to about twenty to twenty–five machines in a room). In most cases where twenty or more machines in a room are connected to the network, an IDF is created in the classroom so the computers are cabled directly to the LAN backbone. Teachers can have a cluster of four machines, or multiples of four, in their classroom. These configurations allow students to use the machines in the classroom, either for specific software or to access any of the network resources available in the classroom. Teachers have found these arrangements effective, as students can use the machines when it is appropriate in the course of the curriculum, and the classroom machines decrease scheduling problems in using computer labs for specific computer projects.

For example, a teacher in an English class could decide that eight machines in the room are enough for students to research essay assignments or term papers, or to find information on a specific question, say, what dramas are scheduled for the summer in New York City. The methods for incorporation of the machines and the network resources into the class day are really only limited by the imaginations of the teacher and the students. A student question can be researched immediately. Students can work in groups on the machines, either looking up material or putting together a presentation, either in hard copy, in a slide presentation, or in some other type of multimedia format. When a current event becomes the focus of the class, the event can be researched to obtain an overview of the topic, or the most recent commentary or reporting on the event. The recent shootings in Colorado and Georgia are perfect examples of events that are vitally important to high school students in every part of the country. There are many different types of sources that are available on the Internet to research and gain a broader view of such a topic: e.g., newspaper and other reports; editorials and other commentaries; and student forums on violence in schools.

Teachers tend to be receptive to these classroom options, as they are able to integrate the computer technology in the fashion that they think is most productive for the curriculum and their teaching style. The networked campus also accommodates the newer, emerging technologies and the directions that schools are going in the uses of technology, such as electronic textbooks, laptops for students, wireless networking (both infrared and radio frequency) that allows students to move their computers around in classrooms or libraries, and some of the advances in distance education and video applications.

# Integrating Technology into the Curriculum: Networks and Access

Integrating technology into the curriculum is one of the tenets of most technology plans, and it is one of the most elusive of the goals. People forget that the technology is not the point; the curriculum is. But technology can be implemented well or poorly to support the curriculum. The advantages of networks are that they offer more access to computers for students, and that they connect those computers to an amazing array of resources. Networks also offer consistency in the access to the resources, making computer systems a little easier for networking specialists and technology support staffs to keep working. Networks also offer flexibility in the use of the computer technology, allowing campuses to incorporate the technology with the strengths and the goals of the campus.

Incorporating networks into the definition of integration of technology into the curriculum addresses the issue of equity of access. One of the most important issues in the use of technology is the "digital divide," the differences in access to technology between privileged and disadvantaged groups of children. One of the ways that a robust campus network can help address that divide is in sheer numbers. Integration of technology into the curriculum has a sheer quantitative element, in that if there are not adequate resources (i.e., enough computers) for all students to have meaningful time on a computer, then there is no real integration possibility. Networks can help provide more access and thus make it possible for access to be equitable, either from a lab or a classroom scenario. Rather than gearing software to stand-alone machines, or to machines that exist on a "stand-alone network" (a network that does not connect to a *local area network* (a LAN) or a *wide area network* (a WAN) but only connects multiple machines for the shared use of specific software), networked machines allow more students to use a broader range of software and access a far wider variety of resources than any other configuration of computer equipment.

The central issue is the use of the network as a tool to strengthen and improve schools. The arguments for and against increased computer use in the schools will continue; and dedicated, innovative, interested, and interesting teachers will offer the best arguments on those issues. Computer technology is not—has never been—a panacea, but it has become important as one of a modern student's educational tools. Though students will learn in various ways, in some cases using a great deal of technology and in some cases not, students do need to be familiar with technology and to be able to use computers and to understand their best use. Students need to be able to negotiate networks, to use the Internet, and to work with others on computer projects. They should also, in general, be prepared to explore, learn, work, and flourish in academic environments where electronic resources are integral components and where network skills are among the basic academic requirements.

# Classroom Management Tools: The Administrative Side of the Classroom

The greatest amount of attention, justifiably so, has been on the potential of computers to improve or complement teaching. A real opportunity exists in another realm of any teacher's reality, and that is in the use of the network for administrative tasks. Teachers, administrators, and counselors rely heavily on administrative systems, the student information systems that address attendance and grading, and that store the increasing amount of data that schools are required to report (demographics, special programs, free and reduced lunch participation, health and immunization, etc.).

In the past, student information was entered into the system either by clerks or from the scanner sheets that teachers had to bubble for attendance and grades. Bubbling grade sheets and attendance rosters has callused the fingers (and the psyches) of more than one teacher. In addition, organizing the staff for data entry (getting information to the clerks) and then verifying that the information was entered correctly into the system have given headaches to administrators across the board. Schools have found that the administrative tasks can be streamlined and made more accurate by the direct input of information from the information source, which in the vast majority of cases is either a teacher or a counselor.

With computers in every classroom connected to a networked student system, teachers can record daily or period attendance directly into the attendance portion of the student system. That data entry scheme is less time-consuming for the teacher, as the computer entry is quicker than the scan sheet bubbling. The data entry format is also less cumbersome, as it eliminates some of the paperwork and the hands that are required to process the paperwork. The same holds true for grading cycle data requirements, and for the data that counselors, nurses, assistant principals, and other administrators are required to work with.

School districts are implementing grade book software that is either part of a larger student information system, or that interfaces with that system. Using such a system, the teacher will have the class schedule already loaded into the grade book, without having to type or write in the students' names. The teachers can then enter the grades directly into the electronic grade book. The data from the teachers' grade books are then used to create the grade reports and progress reports that the campus uses (report cards, progress reports, at-risk reports, etc.). In some cases, the grade books also allow the teachers to type lesson plans into the system, and then match the lessons with assignments and curriculum goals.

A single electronic grade book software package will never satisfy every teacher on the campus. Those that have never used a computerized grade book may be reluctant to start, and those that already have a preference for a particular computer grade book will not enjoy changing over to one selected for the entire school to use. But, in the long run, the advantage is less time and energy in recording grades, better control of the process, and a more uniform grading process.

For the sake of the person or persons who must maintain the grade book software, it is important to limit the software choices or even to decide on a single grade book system. Trying to maintain multiple packages and incorporate them all into one standard set of reports (report cards, progress reports, parent notices, etc.) will be a daunting task for even the best organized support group.

The student system that accounts for attendance, grades, scheduling and other student information may be the best way to convince teachers, especially skeptical teachers, of the value of computers, networks, and electronic information. Giving teachers input into the selection of systems will help ensure that you select one that meets their needs. In addition, once teachers become comfortable in the use of the software for attendance and grading, they become the best advocates for additional use of the network in the classroom, for both instructional and administrative purposes. They also become a tremendous, informal support staff of their own, offering help to their colleagues and suggestions for enhancements of the software products.

## A Better Classroom

The answer to the original question, "Now that I have a network connection, how is my classroom different?" is not easy or short. A lot of the answer depends on the preferences of the questioner and the willingness of the questioner to adapt to the "different" classroom. In many respects, the classroom is simply enlarged, allowing for additional resources and more opportunity to use them. The classroom should retain the strengths that the teacher brings to it in the first place; the network will not automatically improve any aspect of the classroom without the direction of the teacher. But the classroom will have an additional tool that can be used in a variety of ways to complement the work of the teacher and realize the goals that the campus has for students.

# 9

# New Tools for Strategic Decision Making: Systems Thinking Applied with ITHINK

## Bruce D. Baker

"The most dangerous, hideously misused and thought-annihilating piece of technology invented in the past fifteen years has to be the electronic spreadsheet" (Schrage, cited in Richmond and Peterson 1997, vii).

## But What About the Process?

As a researcher and instructor who lives day to day by his most current version of *Microsoft Excel*, I initially found this quote quite disturbing and perhaps even intimidating. Hey, I love my spreadsheets and I use them for just about everything: data management, budget planning, statistical analyses, teaching simulations, grade recording, and tracking our family finances. The remainder of Schrage's article continues in a similar tone, leaving someone like myself to seriously question what I have accomplished in all my years of teaching my students, both K-12 and at the graduate level, how to manage and analyze data to make informed decisions. It was only recently, after finally getting familiar with the alternative I will discuss in this chapter, that I began to understand more fully the shortcomings of spreadsheet methods and the endless possibilities that exist elsewhere. As a side note, however, I do not intend to uninstall (nor do I recommend you uninstalling) *Excel*, or ignoring chapter 2 of this book.

Whatever the kind of data or analyses—student achievement gains, financial data, or statistical relationships between school performance and population demographics—each of our traditional spreadsheet approaches typically yields a limited set of information that focuses primarily on what I will refer to as the *symptoms* of the system. This is not to suggest that symptoms are not important. In fact, symptoms of schools and school systems, like symptoms of physical ailments, are important *indicators* of potential problems in some underlying *process*. Thus, it is important that we continue to use our traditional tools (spreadsheets) continuously to monitor those symptoms.

Well then, what are we missing that is so important? As in treating our ailments, we have two choices in trying to resolve problems in our institutions: (1) we can treat the symptoms or (2) we can try to affect the underlying process. We generally understand the second method to be more effective for achieving long-term success. Unfortunately, our current symptom-analysis "tool-kit" does little to help us understand underlying processes and even less to help us understand our own role in strategic management in affecting those processes. Given these shortcomings of our current tool-kit, are there reasonable alternatives?

This chapter introduces one alternative tool-kit, a microcomputer-based (Windows or Macintosh) software package called *ITHINK*, developed by High Performance Systems of Hanover, NH. An interesting side note is that the developers of *ITHINK* began their software endeavors in the mid-1980s as developers of environmental modeling software known as *STELLA*. At that time, the field of *systems thinking* and *dynamic systems modeling*, founded in the 1960s by J. W. Forrester (1968) of MIT, became popular for studying vastly interconnected complex systems such as ecosystems. Some began promoting the usefulness of this new paradigm to organizational management, and a few even extended the paradigm to the management of educational institutions (Clauset 1982; Clauset and Gaynor 1982; Gaynor and Clauset 1983). Since the popularization of Peter Senge's *Fifth Discipline* (1990) and *Fifth Discipline Fieldbook* (1994), systems thinking as a mental discipline and as a theoretical framework for organizational management has been making another comeback. I strongly recommend that you take some time to read Senge's (1990) *Fifth Discipline*, if you have not already, before embarking on the use of *ITHINK* so that you may begin to adopt the mind-set behind the software.

The widespread availability of microcomputers, coupled with the user-friendliness of applications like *STELLA* and *ITHINK*, presents new possibilities for the growth of the systems-thinking paradigm that did not exist when its popularity peaked in the early 1980s. The developers of these two programs, in response to the renewed interest in systems thinking in management, have branched out into developing software and demonstration models specifically focused on management decision making. Beyond broadening our conceptual understanding of complex systems, these applications allow us to develop simple and practical process-simulation models for strategic analysis and planning.

Unfortunately, as this is only a single chapter of a two-chapter sequence in this book, and I am introducing both a new thought paradigm and a very different software approach to problem solving in management, we must set rather modest goals. Though by no means thorough, this chapter begins with an introduction to some of the basic tools in *ITHINK*, and a description of how one goes about constructing a simple model in *ITHINK*. By necessity, this section also includes some basic discussion of systems-thinking concepts such as feedback loops. Chapter 10 displays two types of school problems that may be addressed with *ITHINK* tools: (1) an operations management problem relating to enrollments, staffing, and budgeting and (2) a social systems problem related to educational standards, student motivation, and effective schools.

## Feedback Cycles and Systems Thinking

One major advantage of process modeling with *ITHINK* over traditional spreadsheet methods is the relative ease in studying *feedback structures*, or *closed-loop systems*. Feedback exists where some measure, X, affects another measure, Y, but then Y in turn affects X. Unless you are particularly creative with the structure of a spreadsheet, this type of relationship typically leads you down a road toward the dreaded message: "*ERROR-CIRCULAR REFERENCE.*"

The two most basic types of feedback cycles are *positive* (or *reinforcing*) *feedback* and *negative* (or *balancing*) *feedback*. Reinforcing feedback exists where some action, X causes an increasing reaction, Y, which in turn causes an increasing reaction of X. Balancing feedback generally exists where there is some external constraint on the system. It would be unreasonable, for example, to assume that the amplification of reactions between X and Y in a reinforcing feedback loop could continue endlessly. In balancing feedback, the external constraint could be the availability of natural resources, or an imposed *desired state*, like a desired temperature. Thus, the system will not show continual amplification but will converge toward equilibrium with respect to consumption and production of natural resources or to achieving the desired state.

Consider fig. 9.1, which by Peter Senge's (1990) typology of feedback cycles would be a reinforcing cycle. In the case of competitive admissions to private schools or colleges, the perceived quality of the schools affects the applicant pool for those schools positively. The improved quality of the applicant pool in turn affects the quality of the actual students at the school, which then more than likely affects the perceived quality of the school. Each effect is *positive*, amplifying the level of each variable with each turn of the cycle, yielding the response curve of perceived quality (or any of the other measures in the cycle) presented. Hence, the positive, or reinforcing, feedback cycle.

**Figure 9.1: Example of a positive or reinforcing feedback cycle**

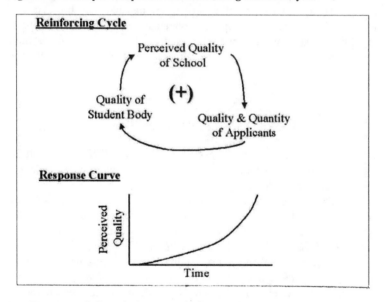

Because of the relative complexity in the design of social or biological systems, growth patterns as would be generated by this process do not tend to continue forever unfettered. Generally, there are constraints on the system that eventually temper or balance the growth of any particular component of the system. Our perceived quality cycle might, for example, continue endlessly if there were an endless supply of better and better students and if there were no other institutions competing for these students, ratcheting up their own performance to remain competitive. But we know that is not the case, and ultimately the quality of our student body will begin to stabilize—we hope at a very high level.

The scenario of competing for a limited population of students is analogous to an ecosystem in which several species are competing for natural resources. Ultimately, as a result of different species competing for some of the same, and some different resources (varied levels of consumption), the system comes to a balance where there are appropriate numbers of organisms of each species and appropriate levels of production and consumption for the system to be sustained. This is one example of naturally occurring balancing feedback.

Another simpler biological example involving a defined external constraint is the hormonal regulation of our blood sugar levels. For example, when we eat a food containing sugar or carbohydrates (which are broken down into sugars), the sugars are absorbed into our bloodstream through our intestines, and our blood sugar level goes up. Assuming we are not quickly burning off those sugars (we are just lounging around), a hormone, insulin, is released into the bloodstream to stimulate the uptake of those sugars to our liver where they are converted to glycogen and stored. Thus, insulin plays a balancing or negative feedback role in that as blood sugar level increases, insulin is produced, decreasing blood sugar level and in turn reducing the need to produce more insulin. This example is perhaps more analogous to two examples that follow: a shower and hiring for growth.

An example commonly used to relate negative feedback to daily life is that of getting the right shower temperature. Figure 9.2 displays a feedback loop representation of the shower temperature problem. Here the externally imposed constraint is the desired temperature. Current temperature is compared against desired temperature to determine the *gap*. Appropriate adjustments are made, that is, if you are being scalded you probably either increase the cold water flow or decrease the hot, or if you are still chilled you will turn up the heat a bit. As seen in the response curve, the balancing nature of these actions eventually guides us toward a solution.

Experience, at least our experience with unfamiliar showers in older buildings, tells us that life is not always as simple as figure 9.2 would suggest. Impatient beings that we are, we actually tend to expect an immediate or nearly immediate response in change in water temperature as a result of our action. We act; it responds. Typically, however, there is a time delay before the system can respond, perhaps the time it takes for the hot water to make it from the heater on the bottom floor up to the third floor shower. Thus, we act; we get impatient that there has been no response; and we act again. Within moments, we find that we have overacted and must respond by reacting in the opposite direction. The point is that a simple time delay within this relatively simple systems archetype can create a situation that is much more difficult for us to manage intuitively. This is where systems modeling becomes a particularly useful tool for both developing our understanding of such systems and practicing our skills in managing them. So let us get on with it!

**Figure 9.2: Example of a negative or balancing feedback cycle**

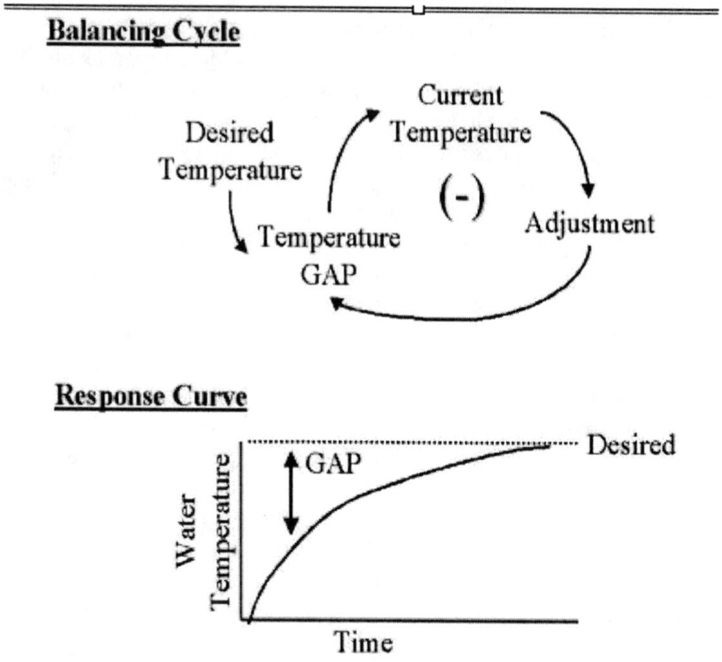

### Balancing Cycle

### Response Curve

# Drawing Pictures of the Way Things Work

*ITHINK* models, like the preceding systems models, consist of pictorial representations of processes. *ITHINK* models consist of three layers (like sheets in a pad): (1) An underlying layer of *code*, (2) A *model* layer that displays the structure of the systems model, and (3) The *user interface* and major model components layer, referred to formally as the *high-level map*, which is often constructed as a *control panel* with controls for operating the model as an interactive learning environment. Moving back and forth between the layers involves clicking the "up" or "down" arrows in the upper left-hand corner of the model window. There is little if any necessity to ever access or work within the code layer of the software, unless you are among the few, like me, who derive a twisted joy from that kind of thing. It can be interesting, once you have constructed and tested your model, to see how the program has converted your pictorial representation into relatively simple equations.

Models are generally constructed within the model layer of the software, with the exception of the addition of controls and model output or creation of a model map presented in the user interface. The model layer allows the model developer(s) to generate a systems model through a pictorial/icon-driven interface. That is, you draw a picture of how you think a particular system works, assign some basic assumptions, and then try it out.

Note that this pictorial approach to model building may feel quite counterintuitive to many of you at first, especially if you have become accustomed to spreadsheets and other "standard" software. Also, the software itself takes some getting used to if you are among those like me who have been subliminally conditioned by Bill Gates to interpret all icons and mouse actions as they relate to *Microsoft* products. My favorite example of how things differ in *ITHINK* is that you do not remove an element from your model simply by clicking on it and pressing "Delete." Rather you click on the little stick of dynamite on the toolbar and then click the item you wish to remove, symbolically blowing it up.

# *ITHINK* Models of Feedback Structures—
# Let's Go!

figure 9.3 below uses *ITHINK* tools to display the shower-water temperature (balancing) feedback loop. These tools relate back to the various components of the feedback cycles we addressed earlier. The model includes four basic components: (1) A *stock*. A stock is like a container, a bucket or box, of some "tangible, countable, physical accumulations" (Soderquist, Peck, and Johnston 1997, 15). A stock can, however, be used to represent something less tangible like accumulated knowledge as we will see later. (2) A *flow*. Flows in general are actions, primarily used to change quantities within stocks, like pipes into or out of a tank, where the tank is the stock. Recall in the shower temperature feedback example that we controlled the flow. A less tangible flow might be "learning" which affects accumulated knowledge as a stock. (3) A series of *connectors*, or links between related components of the system, and (4) *Converters*. As we will see, converters play a variety of roles in *ITHINK* models.

**Figure 9.3: Example of an *ITHINK* representation of controlling temperature in the shower**

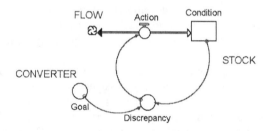

Note with regard to flows and stocks that you cannot have one without the other. Why? Well, a flow, like a water pipe, must flow somewhere or it will serve little purpose. A stock can indeed exist in isolation, but it too will do little good unless you simply wish to have a bucket of ten (whatever) sitting somewhere, randomly placed in your model.

Let us begin with the stock (rectangle), which represents the measure of the initial condition, which in this example can be the initial water temperature. The desired temperature is stored in the converter identified as *Goal*. Thus, the current value of the *Discrepancy Converter* is *Goal minus* current *Condition*. To close this gap, we must alter the flow, just as we turn the knob in the shower. For this model, we can design a user interface such that the user controls the rate of flow (of hot water), labeled *Action* in figure 9.3. With our (almost) completed model we can test an individual's skill and patience in converging on an optimum temperature.

There is one small, but certainly not inconsequential, converter missing in our diagram above. To complete the diagram we must add a time delay converter, which could be attached to our action flow. The time delay could be set such that it takes two, three, or more cycles for the condition to respond 100 percent to our action. As noted earlier, the time delay is what most often tends to confuse us in dealing with a feedback loop. Our mental model of the discrepancy at the moment immediately following our action is this:  Previous-Water-Temperature *minus* Action-I-Just-Took. But the reality of the discrepancy may be Previous-Water-Temperature *minus* (Action-I-Just-Took *divided by* twenty-Second-Delay) meaning that in that first second, only one-twentieth of your action has actually occurred. So, as discussed earlier, we become impatient that we have not immediately resolved the discrepancy and tend to overact. Typically, over time, through a series of decreasing overactions and overreactions, we converge on our solution as seen below in figure 9.4, basking in the glory of achieving that ideal water temperature.

**Figure 9.4: Goal achievement after overactions and overreactions**

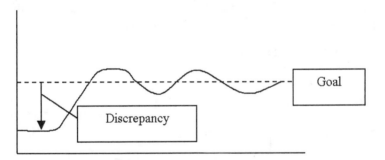

But to more effectively manage this system we need to be able to anticipate the delay and make our assessment of the discrepancy not by checking what the water temperature *is now*, but by anticipating what the water temperature *will be*, after the expected delay, subsequent to our actions. To use a more appropriate example of this, let us get out of the shower and head for the school.

# Out of the Shower and Into the School

The next example is one of a feedback loop quite similar to the shower example, but applied to personnel decisions in a school district. The central problem is one of how to make hiring decisions for a dynamic organization, one that is changing in size and does not necessarily have a stable workforce. The goal, like shower temperature, is a form of equilibrium, managed by hiring for growth. The case involves a mid-size city in NJ in the early 1990s, where enrollment growth necessitated increasing the total staff of the district, but over time there had been dramatic increases in staff attrition.

Figure 9.5 represents one cycle of the hiring/attrition feedback loop that had developed in the district at the time. Total staff vacancies of 125 had been posted in 1992-93. Plans were made to fill posted vacancies. By the time the interviewing and hiring process came around, vacancies had increased to 731. Given the pool of applicants at the time, only 233 offers could be made, and eventually only 197 were hired, leaving a new deficit, only a year later of 534, or nearly 25 percent of the total staff. Continuation of such a cycle would no doubt create significant problems for a district already experiencing a variety of other problems.

**Figure 9.5: Effect of hiring for present vacancies rather than anticipating future attrition**

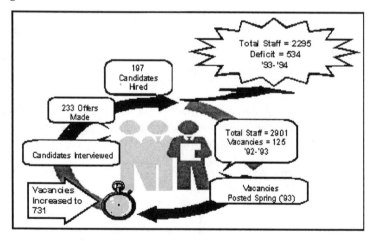

The growth in discrepancy between actual and desired staffing resulted primarily from neglecting the time dimension of this particular problem, thus ignoring whatever events might be occurring during that time. The personnel department was *planning for now* so to speak. An important mental skill under such circumstances is to understand how to *plan for then*. But planning for then involves intuitively understanding the time dimension of the problem to anticipate future needs and attempt to respond to those needs, rather than simply responding to current needs (as if they were future needs). Modeling systems processes in *ITHINK*, even processes as seemingly simple as this one, provides opportunities to test a variety of changing scenarios and to make and learn from mistakes in crucial decisions without facing real world ramifications. Thus, modeling systems processes can enhance our intuitive understanding of the role of time in systems problems.

Before we move on, allow me to clarify a few things about this particular example. For one, I have chosen to isolate one particular part of a much larger and more complex system. I have chosen to focus on the fact that the district's rate of hiring, slowed by a lag in the hiring process, is falling behind the district's rate of growth, creating an increasing and potentially insurmountable gap over time. This is a classic, but simplified outcome of "planning for now." While it may seem absurd that any administrator would be this shortsighted in personnel planning, when faced with the additional complexities that affect acceptance rates (e.g., changes in the available labor pool and competition for applicants), outcomes like those in this example become more common.

Let us begin by looking at a basic Human Resource Infrastructure that is included as a sample model with the ITHINK software (figure 9.6). This model can be used to anticipate personnel needs for a growing business. You can construct this model yourself in the *Run-Time* version of *ITHINK*, which may be downloaded from http://www.hps-inc.com/products/ithink/runtime.html. The limitation on the Run-Time version is that you cannot save your models.

Components (stocks, flows, etc.) are added to the model by pulling objects from the toolbar and drawing the picture in figure 9.6 on the palette in the model layer. Let us begin with the stock of the diagram: Headcount, or the number of employees (teachers) needed in the school/district at a given point in time ($t$). The stock is created in the model by clicking on the stock tool (figure 9.7) then clicking on the blank area below the toolbars that will become your new model (model layer).

You can now name your stock (in this case, "Headcount") by typing the name while the stock is highlighted. Double clicking the stock icon will reveal the upper left-hand window of figure 9.8. In this window you may specify an initial headcount. For purposes of this illustration, please set it at fourteen as shown in figure 9.8.

This stock of teachers is affected by two flows, one inflow (hiring) and one outflow (attrition). Flows may be added to your diagram by clicking the flow tool (figure 9.9) and dragging the flow either to (if it is an inflow) or from (if it is an outflow) your stock.

The outflow (attrition) is a function of the attrition fraction converter and the total headcount. Add converters to your model just as you added the original stock. Connectors may be added by selecting the connector tool (as shown in figure 9.10), then dragging connectors (in the appropriate direction) from, and to, the appropriate icons (Refer back to figure 9.6 for the structure of the model).

Once the model components are added, they must each be defined, just as we defined the initial headcount for the stock. Let us begin with the assumptions. In this case we assume attrition to be proportional, rather than absolute. This assumption is important in that as the organization grows, the same attrition fraction will necessitate a greater number of absolute hires simply to hold the system at equilibrium. That is, if in 1997 you have 1,000 teachers and a 10 percent attrition rate, you will expect to need 100 new teachers for the following year. But assuming that the organization itself is changing in size, you cannot expect that the same number, 100, will be true of the following year.

**Figure 9.6: ITHINK representation of a basic human resource infrastructure**

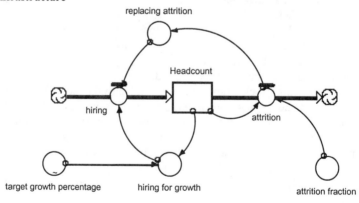

**Figure 9.7: The stock tool**

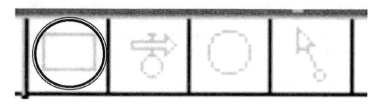

If the organization is growing at a rate of 10 percent per year, you will have 1,100 teachers and your attrition that year (at 10 percent) will be 110, not 100. Typically, such values are selected in two ways (1) based on historical patterns in the district, or (2) for purposes of testing plausible alternative scenarios, because history is not always the best indicator of the future.

**Figure 9.8: Window to define stocks and flows**

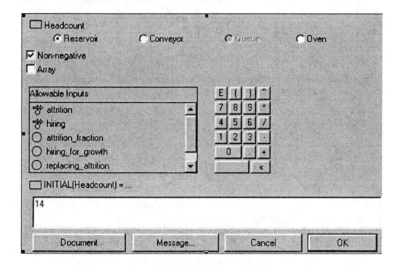

Before we begin assigning the assumptions, we must first make sure the model is set to the *function definition* mode. Immediately below the Up/Down arrows in the upper left-hand portion of your model window is an icon. It probably currently appears as a globe (this should be the default, *Global* setting). Clicking the globe once changes it to a chi-square icon, indicating that the model is in definition mode. Now you can begin creating the mathematical definitions of your stocks and converters. The stock and flow definition screen is shown back in figure 9.8, while the converter definition screen is shown in figure 9.11. We will move back and forth between these figures/screens in defining the various components of our model.

**Figure 9.9: The flow tool**

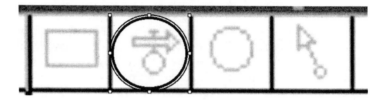

**Figure 9.10: Converters and connectors**

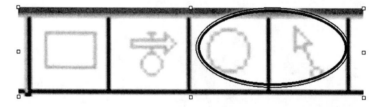

We set the attrition fraction by double-clicking the attrition fraction converter and entering the value we wish the attrition fraction to assume (figure 9.11). Initially this factor may or should be based on some historical knowledge of attrition from the organization. For purposes of this example, try setting the attrition fraction to 0.25. Now, given the stock of current headcount and our attrition fraction, we can define the attrition flow, which is labeled "attrition." When we double click the flow, we see the window in figure 9.12.

The section *required inputs* in figure 9.12 lists the various model components that are connected to the attrition flow. We use these components to specify the attrition flow, which in this case equals the Headcount times the Attrition Fraction. Note: we need not write out the equations entirely ourselves. We can simply click on an input and it will appear in the equation window. Our role is to specify the mathematical nature of the relationship.

**Figure 9.11:  Window to define converters**

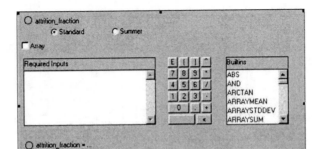

A key *exogenous factor* or *imposed constraint* we must define is the growth rate of our organization. Exogenous factors are factors that are determined external to the system itself, or pre-set at the arbitrary boundaries of the model. For example, the desired temperature in the shower model is an exogenous factor. If we were working in a private corporation (and most *ITHINK* examples were constructed for these purposes) we would likely establish a desired growth rate—just as we established a desired shower temperature. Like the attrition rate, the growth rate would likely be proportional, though it does not really have to. In public education, growth rate is still exogenous—imposed from the outside. We do not usually get to pick and choose how quickly we grow. Rather, growth rate is imposed on us by our environment.

As with attrition rate, in this model we can use historical information to set growth rates and then test alternate scenarios. We can extrapolate probable scenarios on our own, as we will do here, or eventually learn how to use the software at more advanced levels to generate extrapolated data. *ITHINK* allows us to use either numerical or graphic input for converters. Specifically, for information like our growth rates we can either (1) assign a single number to indicate a constant growth rate for each cycle, or (2) under the *builtins* list (figure 9.12) we can select the *time* mode and either enter a series of changing growth rates as numbers or, draw a picture (as figure 9.13 shows) of the pattern of growth we desire or expect. For demonstration purposes, I have chosen to use the *graphic interface* to map the desired growth percent of our organization. With our growth rates defined, we can define the hiring-for-growth converter as a function of the desired growth percent and the current headcount (figure 9.14).

**Figure 9.12: Window to define flows**

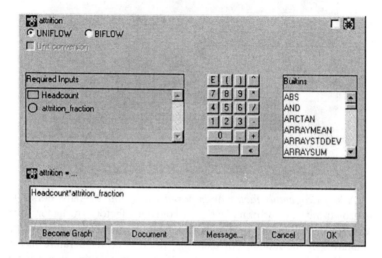

In this model, given the example of the New Jersey school district, our variable of interest is our necessary rate of hiring, or the hiring flow. Our hiring flow is a function of two other factors, hiring to balance the attrition rate, and additional hiring to meet target growth rates. The two variables, *Replacing Attrition* and *Hiring for Growth,* cumulatively affect the variable *Hiring.* Intuitively estimating proportionally growing needs in a proportionally growing organization can be a rather difficult task without a model like the one we have just constructed. The mathematical definition of the flow (hiring for growth + replacing attrition) can be seen in figure 9.15.

At this point, you may have noticed that before you define a model component, it appears with a question mark on it, and after it is defined the question mark is gone. All question marks (on your model at least) should be gone at this point. Now, we could run our model, because it is fully defined. But it would be a less than fulfilling experience in that we would not see anything happen, as we have yet to create any output tables or graphs.

**Figure 9.13: Using the graphic interface**

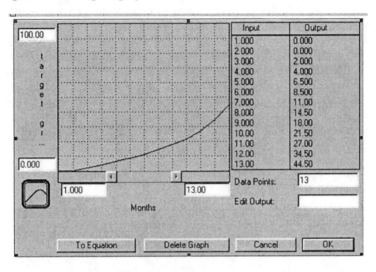

**Figure 9.14: Window to define hiring for growth**

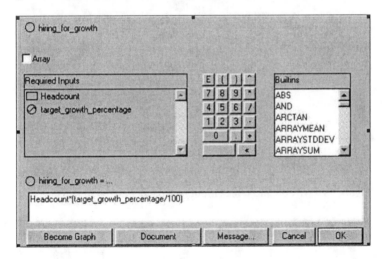

The next step in creating a user-friendly model for testing scenarios is to create a *user-interface layer* with some output tables. To begin creating this layer, click the up arrow in the upper left-hand corner of the model window to bring you to the top, or interface layer (to return to the model layer, click the down arrow). An interface typically consists of output tables and graphs and some controls to manipulate in order to test different possible outcomes. In this case, we will present only ways to create output tables and graphs. You begin this process by selecting the table or graph tool from the toolbar, as shown in fig. 9.16.

Place the new table or new graph on the blank sheet for the interface layer. Table or graph output can also be added directly to the model layer if you wish to quickly test whether your model is working as expected. After placing your table or graph onto the palette, you need to define which variables you wish to display numerically or graphically. This is done as seen in the windows in figs 9.17, 9.18, 9.19, and 9.20 (I will go through these one at a time for you). Here, for example, the graph in figure 9.17 is set to display headcount, attrition, and hiring.

**Figure 9.15: Window showing the relationship among three variables**

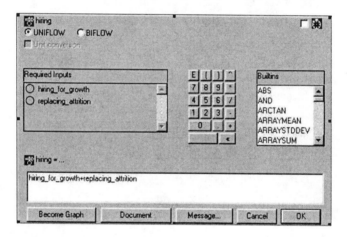

Figure 9.16: Graph and table output tools

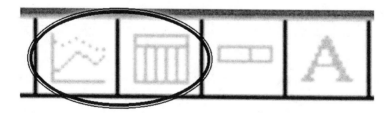

When you drag and drop the graph onto the palette and double click on the graph, the window shown in figure 9.18 appears. You might, for example, wish to track (a) your total headcount (stock) (b) your attrition (flow) and (c) your hiring (flow). To graph these three variables, select them from the *allowable* list (one at a time) and click the arrow to put them into the *selected* list.

**Figure 9.17: Outcome from the simulation: headcount, attrition, and hiring**

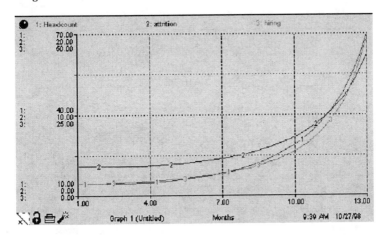

There are a number of other features that may be set on your graph. You may set the number of periods/cycles you wish to be displayed (from one to thirteen—assuming each time period is one year here with our data). You may also title your graph. And you may make *comparative* graphs. A comparative graph can be used to compare the output on a single variable under multiple scenarios. We will try this in the next chapter (figure 10.3). After clicking OK for your graph settings, you will *pin* your graph to your pallete by clicking the pin in the upper left-hand corner. If you do not do this, when you click back to the palette, your graph will be hidden (behind the palette).

The graphics themselves are unconventional and can be confusing. Note that a key of the variables plotted generally appears at the top. The key is color-coded on your computer screen though it is not in this book. What can be confusing is that multiple scales are presented on the same Y-axis, and keyed to their respective variables; this makes it difficult to discriminate between variables intended to be on the same scale at different levels. A rather simple solution is to use the table output in *ITHINK* (figure 9.19) rather than a graph. Then copy the data from the table and paste it into *MS Excel*. In *Excel*, you can graph the data however you like.

**Figure 9.18: Window for specifying output in a graph**

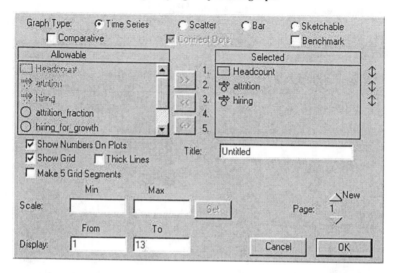

Figure 9.20 shows the window for specifying table output with the same three variables presented in the graph in figure 9.17. It is created similarly by double clicking the table on the palette and then assigning the variables to be listed. Again you have the *comparative* option for making multiple comparisons of the same variable under different conditions. Also, like multilayered *MS Excel* spreadsheets, you can if you wish create multiple layers of graphs with just one graphic. This is done with the *page-setting* arrows just above the cancel and OK buttons. Each new page can be a new table of new variables. The same can be done with graphs. You can access pages after pinning the graph or table to the palette by clicking the folded corner in the lower left-hand corner of the table or graph.

At this point, you would no doubt like to try to run your model. In its usual clever way, High Performance Systems has included the small running-man icon in the lower left-hand corner of the palette as the tool for running the model. Clicking the running man brings up a small toolbar reminiscent of the buttons on a tape or CD player. You have a forward arrow for *Play*, two lines for *Pause,* and a square for *Stop*.

You also have a drop-down menu, to be discussed in the next chapter, that allows you to adjust a variety of time and run settings. For now, click play, and see what happens.

**Figure 9.19: Table output from an ITHINK simulation**

| Months | Headcount | attrition | hiring |
|---|---|---|---|
| Initial | 14.00 | | |
| 1 | 14.00 | 3.50 | 3.50 |
| 2 | 14.11 | 3.50 | 3.61 |
| 3 | 14.50 | 3.56 | 3.95 |
| 4 | 15.23 | 3.68 | 4.41 |
| 5 | 16.36 | 3.91 | 5.04 |
| 6 | 17.96 | 4.23 | 5.83 |
| 7 | 20.28 | 4.69 | 7.00 |
| 8 | 23.68 | 5.36 | 8.76 |
| 9 | 28.59 | 6.34 | 11.26 |
| 10 | 35.94 | 7.77 | 15.13 |
| 11 | 47.92 | 9.98 | 21.96 |
| 12 | 69.04 | 13.71 | 34.83 |

(Window title bar: 9:39 AM  10/27/98    Table 1 (Untitled T)

# Summary

In this chapter, we have covered substantial ground both conceptually and technically. On a personal note, I found that for several months, this stuff simply did not click with me—I could not grasp the time dimension of the models, even having had extensive statistical training in formal econometric time series modeling (perhaps that was actually a hindrance). Being so bound to my spreadsheets and matrix mind-set, I also found the pictorial representations confusing. So I set it down for a while, but it never really left my mind. One day, not too long ago now,

**Figure 9.20: Window for specifying output in a table**

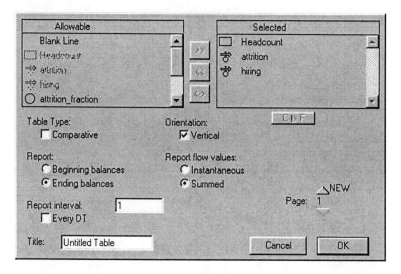

I came back to it having read a few additional articles on the topic and played around on some systems-thinking websites (e.g., for information on STELLA and ITHINK, visit http://www.hps-inc.com. For VENSIM, go to http://www.vensim.com.) Quite simply, after this incubation period it began to click, and I found myself sitting at my computer one afternoon just modeling whatever I could think of. The chapter that follows actually presents some of the outcomes of that day. I tell this story, however, not so much as a lead-in to the next chapter as encouragement to let this stuff incubate in your minds for a while if at first it seems, well, less than intuitive.

# References

Clauset, K. H., Jr. 1982. Effective Schooling: A Systems Dynamics Policy Study. Ph.D. diss., Boston University.

Clauset, K. H., Jr., and A. K. Gaynor. 1982. A Systems Perspective on Effective Schools. *Educational Leadership,* 40 (3), 54-59.

Forrester, J. W. 1968. *Principles of Systems.* Cambridge, Mass: MIT Press.

Gaynor, A. K., and K. H. Clauset, Jr. 1983. Organizations and Their Environments: A Systems Dynamics Perspective. American Educational Research Association. (ERIC Document Reproduction Service No. ED 231 049).

Richmond, B. and S. Peterson. 1997. *An Introduction to Systems Thinking.* High Performance Systems, Inc. Hanover, N.H.

Senge, P. 1990. *The Fifth Discipline: The Art and Practice of the Learning Organization.* New York: Doubleday.

Senge, P., A. Kleiner, C. Roberts, R. Ross, and B. Smith. 1994. *The Fifth Discipline Fieldbook: Strategies and Tools for Building a Learning Organization.* New York: Doubleday.

Soderquist, C., C. Peck, and D. Johnston. 1997. *Getting Started with the ITHINK Software: A Hands-On Experience.* Hanover, N.H.: High Performance Systems, Inc.

# 10

# Back to School: Systems Models and the Educational Setting

## Bruce D. Baker

There are numerous opportunities for process modeling in school management. In some cases, simple models can be constructed for problems we would have previously addressed using spreadsheet applications. Many of these models may be *hard data* models, like the example of hiring for growth presented in the last chapter. Hard data models are those for which the stocks and flows represent accumulations of and changes in quantities of tangible objects. We can also, however, construct models based on *soft data* or *soft assumptions*. These models may address stocks such as student learning or student motivation or, as mentioned in the previous chapter, the perceived quality of an institution.

In this chapter, we will discuss one hard data example and one soft data example. The hard data example involves studying the relationships among enrollments, staffing, and budgetary demands. I chose this example because it is the type of situation commonly dealt with in a spreadsheet environment. My hope is that this example will help you make a smooth transition from the spreadsheet environment to the systems model environment. The soft data example is borrowed from Clauset (1982, see also Clauset and Gaynor 1982, and Gaynor 1998) and was first presented as part of a project at Boston University referred to as the "Effective Schools Project." In particular, the soft data example explores the relationships among external standards, teacher expectations and student motivation to learn. That said, it is time to boot up again and go back to school.

# A Structural Model of Enrollment
# & Budget Impact

The basic structure of this model was originally presented to me by Chris and Jane Soderquist of High Performance Systems, Inc. (personal communication). I then added features (primarily graphic output) to the model described in this chapter. This is just one indication of the type of business that High Performance Systems, Inc. runs and the level of user support they provide.

Now that we're familiar with the tools of ITHINK, let us jump right into the pictorial representation of the model. Fig. 10.1 shows a simplified process model of the relationship between enrollment, staffing and total payroll (I have provided the actual code in appendix A). We assume four basic stocks of students in the model: Preschool, Elementary, Middle, and High School Students. Then we assume there to be a directional flow from one stock to the next, with a pre-set number of years defining the rate of each flow (ELEM = 5, MID = 4, HS = 4). We assume the initial flow to be a function of the birthing rate, which we have set as a graphic/manipulable flow. That is, the flowrate can be changed by double clicking the flow icon and either (1) altering the shape of a general graph or (2) entering data. In this model we have added a dropout fraction at the high school level as an additional outflow with a user-adjustable dropout rate. In this case the dropout rates on the model can be adjusted by using the sliding lever on the control panel.

Finally, the model includes a simple link to another model (not shown) that consists of only three converters (Teachers Needed, Average Salary, Total Payroll) for calculating teachers needed and total payroll. In that model, teachers needed is a function of a desired pupil/teacher ratio and the total number of students in the system (PRE + ELEM + MID + HS = TOTAL). Then, total payroll is a function of the teachers needed times the average salary. The basic structure of this model can easily be extended to represent the greater complexity of real world situations. But, it is generally best to begin with relatively simple models and test how well the models function before they become too complex.

Figure 10.2 displays a user interface for the enrollment model. This particular interface includes both manipulable control levers and graphic output. Two types of. Simulation controls are used in this model. Single bar controls are used for setting dropout rates and desired pupil teacher ratios. Each lever can be set for adjustment within defined

**Figure 10.1: Sample school-based decision-making model: Enrollment/staffing (Framework developed by Chris Soderquist of High Performance Systems, Hanover, N.H. Modified by Bruce D. Baker)**

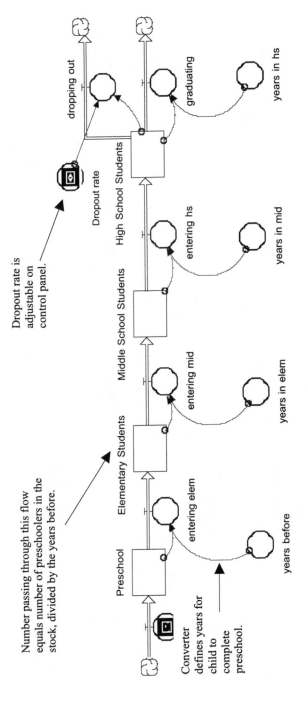

ranges across either discrete (for example, allowing only whole number increments) or continuous (allowing for the complete sliding scale of values) scales. Creating these tools is very similar to creating the graphs and tables. You simply pull them down to your palette from the toolbar; then double click them to assign the variables to be manipulated by the given tool. The graph of birthing rates is currently set to a wavelike pattern. Typically, this graph would be based on historical birthing data for the district. If you desired a different pattern, you could change this graph by double clicking and inputting the desired data.

The model provides outputs showing enrollments and payroll in both graphic and table form. Fig. 10.3 displays the output for payroll of five trials of the model using incrementally different pupil to teacher ratios. Our intuition should tell us that lowering pupil-teacher ratios will (1) require more teachers at that given point in time and (2) cost more at that given point in time. ITHINK, however, allows us to see how these variables interact to create not just "absolute" cost differences through time, but converging and diverging cost differences (as seen in the total payroll chart) that yield very high peaks at times when applying the lowest ratio option.

A comparative analysis of this type, where an "input" measure is incrementally adjusted to see its effect on outcomes, would commonly be referred to as a sensitivity analysis. The goal in this case was to test the sensitivity of long-run cost and personnel demands to varying policy decisions regarding pupil to teacher ratios. The graphs and table have been set to Comparative mode so that subsequent trials all appear on the same graph. Note the long-run differences in total payroll both as seen in the graph and the data table. Sensitivity analyses can be run manually by adjusting settings after each trial and rerunning the simulation, or the simulation can be set to run a series of analyses through the "sensi-specs" option where inputs are incrementally adjusted within specified ranges. To use this option, you would select "sensi-specs" from the RUN menu. In the window that appears, you would select (1) the variable to be manipulated, (2) the number of scenarios (runs) to test and (3) the highest and lowest values of the range to be tested. ITHINK will calculate the incremental values in between. You can decide whether you want them incrementally distributed or perhaps normally distributed.

**Figure 10.2: Manipulable control levers and graphic output for the enrollment/staffing model**

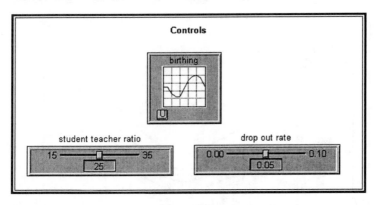

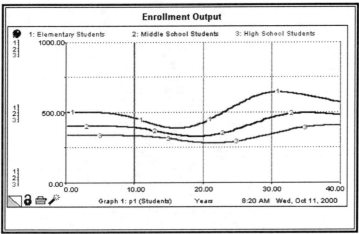

**Figure 10.3 Output from the enrollment/staffing/salary model**

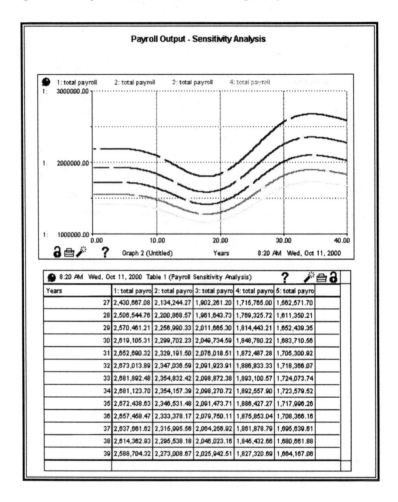

# A Soft Data Example:
# The Effective Schooling Project

This systems model was originally discussed by Clauset (1982) and
Clauset and Gaynor (1982). Gaynor (1998, 113) discusses a project in
which he and his colleagues addressed the expected dynamic
relationships between teacher expectations and student performance.

Fig. 10.4 shows Gaynor's initial representation of the "multiplier dynamics of schooling" system. Gaynor apparently chose to refer to this archetype as a "multiplier dynamics" model because of its underlying positive feedback structure. The assumption underlying the model is that student academic performance is increased by higher teacher expectations, by way of more intense instruction affecting student motivation and achievement. In turn, higher academic performance among students tends to yield even higher expectations among teachers, creating embedded, reinforcing, or positive feedback loops that drive the system. If you recall the original positive feedback loop presented in the previous chapter, the typical outcome of such a loop is a multiplying (exponentially) growing dynamic with respect to each stock in the cycle. Such a pattern is also sometimes referred to as an explosive "dynamic." Fig. 10.5 shows how Gaynor's initial model of "multiplier dynamics of schooling" can be structured in ITHINK. (I have provided the actual code in appendix B).

**Fig. 10.4: Gaynor's "multiplier dynamics of schooling" model**

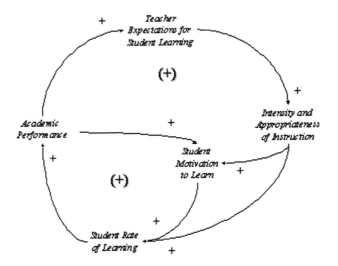

There are perhaps a plethora of ways to represent this system with ITHINK tools. For this example, I have chosen a structure in which the model represents Teacher Expectations, Academic Performance, and Motivation to Learn as stocks. Each of these stocks may be increased or decreased (bi-directional flow) by a set of change factors, or converters that help to define the flows mathematically. This model indicates that

**Figure 10.5: ITHINK representation of Gaynor's "multiplier dynamics of schooling" model**

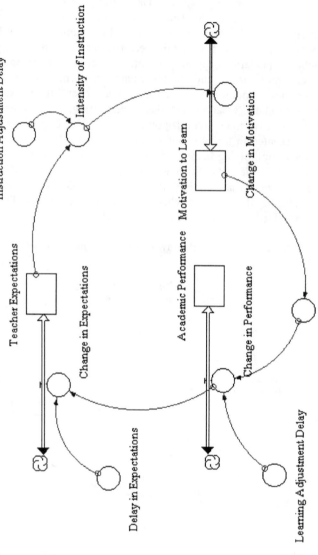

a change in the stock of student performance has a direct and positive effect on change in teacher expectations (but with a slight delay; i.e., teacher expectations do not change immediately). Without the delay, the relationship would be simply represented: Change in Expectations = Change in Academic Performance. With the delay, the value of change in academic performance is divided by the delay, such that if delay = 3, only 1/3 of the change in expectations occurs in the first period. After three periods, the change in expectations has met the level that matches the academic performance level—three periods earlier. But of course, by this time, performance has continued changing, continuing to drive the cycle. An alternate interpretation to connecting the change in performance to the change in expectations might be to connect the change in teacher expectations with the level of the academic performance stock.

The overall response pattern of the major stocks in the model can be seen in the ITHINK output chart in Fig. 10.6. For this example, I have chosen to create my own graphic in MS Excel by saving the output from a table in ITHINK as a text file, then opening it in Excel. I find this approach easier when I need to make a meaningful, clear presentation of ITHINK output.

**Figure 10.6: Output from "Multiplier Dynamics" Model**

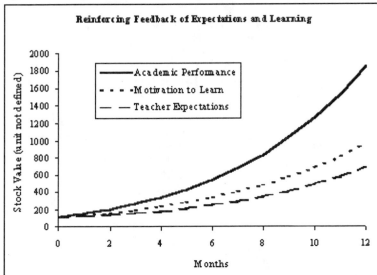

As it turns out, it was not simply Gaynor's or Clauset's intent to validate this pattern of reinforcing feedback. Rather, the authors of this conceptual model had concerns as to how this cycle worked when external conditions were

changed—the introduction of externally imposed (state mandated) standards—and how those conditions might affect different students differently. The
assumption they employed was that external performance standards create mandated teacher expectations, which for some students might actually create a
negative explosive response. Consider Fig. 10.7, where our emphasis is now on
weak and/or at-risk students. The assumption of the new model is that externally
imposed standards that are "too high" may, in fact, negatively affect the appropriateness of the intensity of instruction. The relationship between "intensity
appropriateness" and student motivation remains direct (positive), but in this
case, higher standards reduce the appropriateness, which in turn reduces student
motivation and subsequently student academic performance. At this point, we
can either continue the cycle to include a reduction in expectations, or hold those
expectations to the external criteria. These, perhaps, are some scenarios you can
test on your own, by adding to the model started for you here.

**Fig. 10.7: Gaynor's model applied to "weak" students**

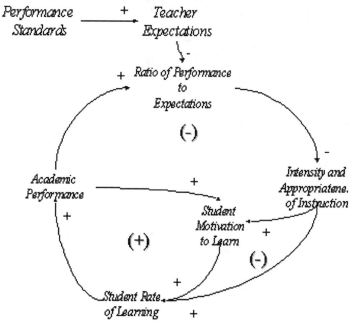

# Closing Thoughts and the Road From Here

It is important to remember that embarking on dynamic systems modeling and using systems-modeling software requires many people both to adopt a new mind-set about problem solving and to develop a new set of computer skills. Therefore, I highly recommend the following two books as a starting point:

- Richardson, P. 1991. *Feedback Thought in Social Science and Systems Theory*. Philadelphia, PA: University of Pennsylvania Press.
- Senge, P. 1990. *The Fifth Discipline: The Art and Practice of the Learning Organization*. New York: Doubleday.

Should you choose to go beyond this chapter in your systems-modeling endeavors (and I certainly hope you do), your next step will be to choose the software you wish to use. I have presented only ITHINK in this chapter. I was first exposed to systems-modeling software while teaching biology and coordinating student environmental research projects in the late 1980s. At the time, STELLA, High Performance Systems' original systems-modeling software for the Macintosh was first becoming popular, and had begun to make its way into classrooms as a teaching tool. As with STELLA, an advantage of ITHINK continues to be the quality of instructional resources that accompany the software. But other alternatives do exist for dynamic systems modeling. George P. Richardson of SUNY at Albany, editor of Systems Dynamics review and winner of the J. W. Forrester award for his 1992 book *Feedback Thought in Social Science and Systems Theory*, has suggested a software package called VENSIM, which may be obtained from: <www.vensim.com> (including free copies of a demo version). Richardson's recent work with Vensim includes models of foster care caseloads in New York state and Medicaid reform in Vermont (Richardson and Anderson 1995).

While dynamic systems modeling has existed now for decades, its frequent use has been restricted to a relative few fields until recently. As one indication of the potential future popularity and importance of these methods, the Harvard Business School has recently begun distributing ITHINK *Learning Environment* Simulations as part of its well-known case materials collection. Information and links may be found through the High Performance Systems website.

Bromley and Jacobson (1998) call attention to a "pervasive concern that computers tend to isolate learners and therefore are antithetical to collaborative learning" (144). But it seems to me that the greatest value of the systems thinking paradigm and dynamic systems modeling can be derived from the model development process itself, and group interaction over the process, rather than running simulations and observing the graphic and numerical output of the models. Much recent research has focused on the group process of model building in the public policy setting (Anderson and Richardson 1994; Richardson and Anderson 1995). Given the proliferation of site teams in school-based decision making, ITHINK or other systems-modeling software provides a novel opportunity for creative strategic problem solving that brings together rather than isolates constituents, thereby stimulating collaborative learning.

# Appendix A: Code Layer
# for Enrollment Staffing Model

Elementary_Students(t) = Elementary_Students(t - dt) + (entering_elem - entering_mid)
    * dt

INIT Elementary_Students = 500

INFLOWS:
entering_elem = Preschool/years_before

OUTFLOWS:
entering_mid = Elementary_Students/years_in_elem
High_School_Students(t) = High_School_Students(t - dt) + (entering_hs - graduating -
    dropping_out) * dt

INIT High_School_Students = 334

INFLOWS:
entering_hs = Middle_School_Students/years_in_mid

OUTFLOWS:
graduating = High_School_Students/years_in_hs
dropping_out = High_School_Students*drop_out_rate
Middle_School_Students(t) = Middle_School_Students(t - dt) + (entering_mid - enter-
    ing_hs) * dt

INIT Middle_School_Students = 400

INFLOWS:
entering_mid = Elementary_Students/years_in_elem

OUTFLOWS:
entering_hs = Middle_School_Students/years_in_mid
Preschool(t) = Preschool(t - dt) + (birthing - entering_elem) * dt

INIT Preschool = 600

INFLOWS:
birthing = GRAPH(time)
(0.00, 100), (3.00, 100), (6.00, 100), (9.00, 100), (12.0, 100), (15.0, 100), (18.0, 100),
    (21.0, 100), (24.0, 100), (27.0, 100), (30.0, 100)

OUTFLOWS:
entering_elem = Preschool/years_before

avg_salary = 32000
drop_out_rate = .05
student_teacher_ratio = 25
teachers_needed = Total_Students/student_teacher_ratio
total_payroll = avg_salary*teachers_needed
Total_Students = Elementary_Students + High_School_Students + Middle_School_Students
years_before = 6
years_in_elem = 5
years_in_hs = 4
years_in_mid = 4

# Appendix B: Code Layer for Effective Schools Model

Academic_Performance(t) = Academic_Performance(t - dt) + (Change_in_Performance)
    * dt

INIT Academic_Performance = 100

INFLOWS:
Change_in_Performance = Student_Learning_Rate/Learning_Adjustment_Delay
Motivation_to_Learn(t) = Motivation_to_Learn(t - dt) + (Change_in_Motivation) * dt

INIT Motivation_to_Learn = 100

INFLOWS:
Change_in_Motivation = Intensity_of_Instruction
Teacher_Expectations(t) = Teacher_Expectations(t - dt) + (Change_in_Expectations) * dt

INIT Teacher_Expectations = 100

INFLOWS:
Change_in_Expectations = Change_in_Performance/Delay_in_Expectations
Delay_in_Expectations = 3
Instruction_Adjustment_Delay = 4
Intensity_of_Instruction = Teacher_Expectations/Instruction_Adjustment_Delay
Learning_Adjustment_Delay = 2
Student_Learning_Rate = .75*Motivation_to_Learn


Note: All assignments of effect magnitudes and delay times in this particular
    model are arbitrary.

# References

Anderson, D. F., and G. P. Richardson. 1994 – July. Scripts in Group Model Building. 1994 International Systems Dynamics Conference. Stirling, Scotland.

Bromley, H., and S. Jacobson. 1998. Technology and Change in School Administrator Preparation. In *Technology and the Educational Workplace.* Thousand Oaks, Calif.: Sage Publications, 127-149.

Clauset, K. H. 1982. Effective Schooling: A Systems Dynamics Policy Study. Ph.D. diss., Boston University.

Clauset, K. H., and A. K. Gaynor 1982. A Systems Perspective on Effective Schools. *Educational Leadership,* 40 (3), 54-59.

Forrester, Jay W. 1968. *Principles of Systems.* Cambridge, Mass.: MIT Press.

Gaynor, A. K., and K. H. Clauset., Jr. 1983. Organizations and Their Environments: A Systems Dynamics Perspective. American Educational Research Association. (ERIC Document Reproduction Service No. ED 231 049)

Gaynor, A. K. 1998. *Analyzing Problems in Schools and School Systems.* Mahwah, N.J.: Lawrence Earlbaum Associates.

Richards, C. E. 1989. *Microcomputer Applications for Strategic Management in Education: A Case Study Approach.* New York: Longman.

Richardson, G. P. 1991. *Feedback Thought in Social Science and Systems Theory.* Philadelphia: University of Pennsylvania Press.

Richardson, G. P., and D. F. Anderson. 1995. Teamwork in Group Model Building. *Systems Dynamics Review,* 11(2), 113-125.

Senge, P. 1990. *The Fifth Discipline: The Art and Practice of the Learning Organization.* New York: Doubleday.

Soderquist, C., C. Peck, and D. Johnston. 1997. *Getting Started with the ITHINK Software: A Hands-on Experience.* Hanover, N.H.: High Performance Systems, Inc.

# Software and Other Web Resources

STELLA & ITHINK. High Performance Systems Inc. Hanover, NH.
  http://www.hps-inc.com

VENSIM: Downloadable modeling software at:
  http://www.vensim.com

Bellinger, Gene. Homepage on Systems Modeling.
  http://www.radix.net/~crbnblu/musings.htm

Richmond, B. 1994. Systems Dynamics/Systems Thinking: Let's Just Get On
      With It.
  http://www.hps-inc.com/st/paper.html

# 11

# The Consultant Decision

## Mario Martinez

As a consultant, I'm overpaid even if I do bad work.
—Dogbert, from the comic strip *Dilbert*

## Introduction

Consultants are very much like plumbers; they perform jobs that we don't know how to do, don't want to do, or don't have the time to do. And exactly for these reasons, there will be many times when you will be faced with the question, "Should we hire a consultant?" But there are other questions that surface when you are considering whether or not to hire a consultant. For example, consultants are appropriate for some situations and not others. But which are which? Consultants are convenient because you can hire expertise only when you need it, but when should you solve your own problems as opposed to having somebody solve them for you?

Imagine for a moment that summer is finally here and you have just completed your sixth year as the principal of one of ten schools in your district. Over fifteen years of teaching and six as a principal, you have pretty much seen and done every job there is to do at the school. Now, as an administrator, you have just enough time at the beginning of the summer to come up for one breath of fresh air before planning for the coming school year!

You have many ideas for improving your school, and the Superintendent has also asked you to lead a committee of administrators in studying the technology associated with the upcoming plan to implement site-based decision making. Since technology will be a central theme in your committee work, she also has asked that the committee keep its eyes open for processes that could be enhanced by technology—be it improvement in administrative or teaching tasks. Your main concern is the administrative systems, like finance and accounting, which are now designed for a very centralized type operation. With site-based decision making, every principal will be responsible for managing his/her own budget, but this will be difficult to do with tools designed for central oversight. In addition, principals will now have to prepare their own budgets and then send the requests to central office. Can technology help with the transition to systems that are friendlier to site-based decision making? Can technology help district principals in preparing and understanding budgets?

Certainly, some of your investigations will require you to decide whether a consultant should be used. Technology may help improve certain administrative or teaching tasks. How do you recognize whether either one can be improved by technology? Would a consultant help? If you decide you do need a consultant, what type of consultant? How do you avoid a consultant who is overpaid but underworked? All good questions, and perhaps ones you have not thought about in a systematic way. Since you do not consider yourself a technology guru, properly deciding whether to obtain outside help will be a particularly relevant concern. As you try to gather your thoughts about technology, consultants, and the like, it might help to consider two scenarios that are very different in complexity and scope. Scenario 1, finding a way to reduce paperwork, is an example of a *technical solution*. Scenario 2, making the transition to site-based decision making, is more complex. I consider it to involve more of a *systems approach*.

## Scenario 1: Moving Beyond the Age of the Abacus

As you begin to think about this whole technology business, you decide to start off with a familiar unthreatening area that will also be the easiest to improve: using technology to reduce teacher paperwork by automating parts of the grading process. In fact, making the grading process more efficient might free up some faculty time to work on the more difficult scenario 2.

The tedious process of calculating and recording grades has been around since your grandfather's grandfather was in school, and so are many of the instruments that were used back then: paper, pencil, and abacus. The majority of your teachers still use the same pencil and paper, though some have graduated to using a solar-powered calculator. This concerns you because the district's student population is growing and faculty has already taken on increased workloads as a result. Although the process of grading is fairly simple, it is time consuming. As a former teacher, you are well aware of how stressful it is at the end of each semester. The tasks of grading, handling student problems, and dealing with testy parents all seem to collapse on you at once. Administrative staff feels related stress as well, because they must record and archive grades and other student information as required by central office. So far you feel like you have considered many of the issues surrounding grading and technology, and you hope the details that will inevitably surface will not be too insurmountable to implement a new process.

For example, with computers, every teacher should be able to maintain some of his/her personal grading preferences, but the actual calculation and subsequent recording should be automatic and efficient. And it would be nice if all the grades were automatically transferred to your office once teachers had entered them into their computers. You suspect that automating the process will require some standardization, and you think that spreadsheet software could probably help, but that is about the extent of your knowledge.

## Scenario 2: The Devil is in the Technological Details

Your more complex problem is to deal with the move to site-based decision making. The District's plan to decentralize is a good one, and the Superintendent asked you to chair the committee on technological needs because you were the one who voiced a concern in this area when the plan was announced (s/he who speaks inherits the work). You remember a colleague at a conference several years ago who told you that his district had not anticipated the technological details, and that attention to some of those details would have made the transition to site-based decision making much easier. The devil was in the technological details.

# Do You Need a Consultant?

Both of the scenarios above identify problems without specific solutions. You can describe the problem but do not know what details would solve it. When you can broadly describe a problem or need, but know little of the solution or how to implement it, a consultant may be in order.

There are many variables to consider when assessing whether or not to use a consultant: time, money, urgency, political situation, willingness of faculty to change, etc. Money may be the central factor for you. This chapter will take you through steps that will help you justify to your superiors your need for money to hire a consultant.

Below are some questions and considerations that comprise your *Consultant Guide*. This guide can help you assess whether you should secure a consultant to help you implement a technical installation. Each problem or issue will be different, so the items are meant to serve only as a guide. Rate each item from one to ten. One indicates a strong "no"; ten indicates a strong " yes."

1.  Is there pressure to resolve an issue?

Considerations: Urgency may be due to employee stress, dysfunctional processes, dissatisfaction with current communications or processes, etc. Urgency does not necessarily imply that there is a defined timeline in which a solution must be provided, but it does mean that there is a pressing need to resolve a problem.

2.  Is there a deadline?

Considerations: Sometimes a naturally occurring event (such as the start of a school year) creates an obvious deadline. Sometimes authorities impose a deadline.

3.  Is this an issue that people within the organization do not know much about?

Considerations: Sometimes almost no one within an organization has the understanding or expertise to help implement a solution. It is always important to determine the knowledge your staff and faculty have regarding any issue that may require outside help.

4.  Are you unable to provide incentives for organization members with expertise to share it?

Considerations: People are often overextended. The internal knowledge to implement the solution may exist, but there must be incentives for those staff who have expertise to share it. This is a question of employee priorities, incentives, and motivation to complete new or additional tasks.

5.   Will there be resources for follow-up support and training?

Considerations: You would not feel comfortable buying a state-of-the-art personal computer for each teacher, loaded with the latest software—and then not providing training on how to use it. We know that it discourages people to see a program implemented without sufficient follow-up training. If you will not be able to provide follow-up training to implement a consultant's recommendations it may be better not to seek a consultant in the first place.

6.   Is it important to obtain an "outsider's" perspective on this problem?

Considerations: Sometimes a leader needs to seem to distance him/herself (or a particular solution) from political considerations. Calling on internal sources may be inappropriate, even if the knowledge does exist, because of sensitive political realities. It can be advantageous to gain an outsider's input. It is sometimes politically savvy to have someone other than the organization provide a solution, or at least a different perspective.

7.   Is it important to standardize and/or automate tasks?

Considerations: Technology should help with routine jobs so that staff can concentrate on other projects that are not so routine. Routine tasks should be automated and standardized to the fullest extent possible. A consultant may know how to help take advantage of technology's capabilities in this area.

8.   Can a consultant help increase productivity in an observable way?

Considerations: Leaders may need to produce evidence that their innovations have paid off. Increased productivity is often hard, or even impossible, to measure. But today's public policymakers and top administrators often ask for evidence to demonstrate the value of an investment. So we should search for evidence, either qualitative or quantitative, that productivity has increased. For example, reducing the number of days to process paychecks or grades is easily measured. You may plan to formally ask each principal in the district whether the process of budgeting has improved. A consultant should be able to suggest other indicators.

If you score a 50 percent (forty out of eighty possible points) or above on this test, then you should at least talk to a consultant. It is possible that one of these issues, or some other (e.g. a politically sensitive concern), will carry more weight than the other questions, so you must consider your score in light of what you know about your organization. Now let us consider each of the two scenarios.

# Moving Beyond the Age of the Abacus— Ratings

You are convinced that grading and recording can be done more efficiently, so the major question you now face is whether you need a consultant's help. Let us go back through the consultant's guide and rate each question from one to ten:

1. *Is there pressure to resolve an issue?* Burnout and stress levels are high among your teachers. You have a solution in mind and are excited about it, so would like to investigate the reality of this solution as soon as possible. A more efficient grading process would not only increase efficiency but also ease the end-of-the-semester crunch. Score: 7

2. *Is there a deadline?* You have to be honest; this is something you and the math teacher think would be a good thing. No one else is pressing you to get it done. From your proactive perspective, it would be a ten; from everyone else's, probably a one. You split the difference. Score: 5.

3. *Is this an issue that people within the organization do not know much about?* Though you know little about implementing a solution, you do have faculty members who are knowledgeable about databases and spreadsheets. Score: 4

4. *Are you unable to provide incentives for organization members with expertise to share it?* Although you do have some knowledgeable faculty members, their time is limited and there is no real incentive for them to work on an extra project such as this. Score: 9

5. *Will there be resources for follow-up support and training?* You do believe that your in-house computer buffs will embrace the solution quickly and be willing to train other teachers. You may also be able to negotiate with a consultant to provide two or three training sessions during in-service. Score: 8

6. *Is it important to obtain an "outsider's" perspective on this problem?* This is a technical problem that is not very controversial, so it does not matter if the solution comes from the outside or the inside. Score: 1

7. *Is it important to standardize and/or automate tasks?* You believe that some aspects of grading should be individualized depending on the teacher and the subject; but you also believe that standardization and automation are needed, and you stand ready to argue the point with anyone who disagrees. Score: 10

8. *Can a consultant help increase productivity in an observable way?* Teachers now have five days to get their grades in after students complete their last assignment. Administrative staff at each school then has two days to send the information to Central Office. Based on conversations you have had with administrators from other states, you believe the total process could be reduced from seven days to five. Score: 10

**Total score: 54 (67.5 percent)**

It seems like hiring a consultant is a good idea, but consider some other factors not mentioned in the checklist before you make your final decision. What is your personal intuition as a leader? Will you be able to convince your faculty to change the way they have been doing something for years and years? Questions such as these will help you finalize your decision.

The thing you should be able to do, should you hire a consultant, is to describe the issue and the need. In the case of automating the grading process, the solution provides for automatic calculation, storage, and transmission of student grade information. In addition, your math teacher has already told you that a spreadsheet application (see chapter 2 for examples of how spreadsheets work) is the likely answer. One thing that is a mystery is how grade information on each teacher's computer can automatically be transferred to the computers at your office. Your initial goal will be to find a consultant who can honestly give you an assessment of what you have (in terms of computer power and software availability) and what you need for the solution.

## The Devil is in the Technological Details— Ratings

1. *Is there pressure to resolve an issue?* Your superintendent says, "Rain, sleet, or snow, site-based decision making is coming." As committee chair, it is up to you to anticipate any technological wrinkles that may arise along the way. You know that the finance and accounting systems were programmed to produce reports that are compatible with a centralized organizational structure and decision making process. These systems will definitely have to change, but you are not sure exactly how. Score: 10

2. *Is there a deadline?* Like many things that start with a new school year, so will site-based decision making. It is critical to start figuring out the technical problems that need to be addressed. Score: 10.

3. *Is this an issue that people within the organization do not know much about?* You are in the business of hiring people who can teach kids, so you do not have a lot of management information systems specialists. The faculty and staff who know the most about computers and technology have learned it on their own, so they have not specifically been trained to conceive of solutions demanded by this issue. Score: 10.

4. *Are you unable to provide incentives for organization members with expertise to share it?* This question is not applicable since you have no internal expertise and therefore no significant staff time will be required.

5. *Will there be resources for follow-up support and training?* Honestly, you do not know, but you will emphasize to the district's leadership the importance of training staff members on any new system that might be implemented. Score: 5.

6. *Is it important to obtain an "outsider's" perspective on this problem?* In this case an outsider's perspective is of great importance since decentralization will surely create some polarization within the organization. It is always credible to have outside experts whom people may consider neutral. Score: 10.

7. *Is it important to standardize and/or automate tasks?* Standardization and automation would be nice, but the most important thing is to make sure that your computer systems are aligned with the coming organizational structure. Score: 5.

8. *Can a consultant help increase productivity in an observable way?* If staff is busy doing things manually because your computer systems are not compatible with site-based decision making, they will be wasting unnecessary time.

Total score: 60 (85.7 percent of seven questions, since question 4 was not applicable).

It definitely looks like a consultant is in order, and since this is a district-wide concern, you are confident that the School Board will front the money to at least get some assessments and estimates of what will be required.

## Expectations of the Consultant

There are many things you can reasonably expect from a consultant, while other expectations may be unrealistic, unreasonable, or impossible for the consultant to fulfill. First, you should expect a consultant initially to assess your situation at little or no cost, depending on the magnitude of the problem. In scenario 1, you already know the general solution (a spreadsheet), but the consultant still needs for you to describe the problem and your software and hardware capabilities. The consultant should have the expertise to recommend a likely solution and provide time and cost estimates. But s/he cannot suggest an exact solution until s/he becomes more familiar with your technological infrastructure (what type of software is on your computers, the power of your computers, etc.). The consultant may find, for example, that you have licensed permission to use Lotus software when s/he thinks Microsoft software would provide a better solution. In any event, you should reasonably expect a proposal to scenario 1 within a few days.

In scenario 2, the initial assessment may be more complex. It is unreasonable to think that a consultant can give you a proposal in two days. If the consultant spends considerable time assessing your situation, a nominal fee may be appropriate (it varies depending on the consultant). Suppose the consultant has to look at your accounting and finance systems and talk to staff members who work with these systems. He estimates this will take three full working days, or twenty-four hours. It is not unreasonable for consultants to charge over $100 an hour, but do not rush to offer this amount. You hold the cards in this case because the consultant wants the work and knows you have a choice to look for somebody else. You can come up with different creative suggestions, but let me give you two: First, it is common for clients to ask a consultant for an initial assessment. If the initial assessment is not going to take an inordinate amount of time, it is reasonable to ask the consultant to do it for free. If, on the other hand, there is going to be considerable time involved in assessing your situation, you can negotiate what the assessment is worth. As a consultant, I have often invested six to ten hours, free of charge, writing a proposal or assessing a client's environment. I have been willing to do this because I wanted the work and I needed the client as much as they needed me.

If an initial fee for assessment is appropriate, the amount you negotiate does not have to be the consultant's regular, hourly rate (e.g. twenty-four hours x $100/hour). Some of the factors to consider in your negotiation are these: How comfortable are you negotiating? How much do you think the consultant wants the job? How much can you afford? Another option is to tell the consultant you do not want to talk about hourly rates until you are ready to sign a contract, and that you are willing to pay a fixed amount for his initial assessment.

As you can see, when you deal with consultants you have to be a good business person because you will likely be dealing with people who are in business to make money. Always remember that before you sign a formal agreement your consultant should provide a reasonable estimate of time and money needed to implement the new solution. In sum, a consultant's initial proposal to you should contain three elements:

1.  An assessment of what you have now. This is important because the consultant cannot give you a true time- and cost-estimate without knowing your current technological capabilities.

2. An assessment of what you need in order to get where you want to go (the solution): You will have to describe where you want to go in general terms. The consultant might be able to make suggestions or provide alternatives but, by and large, the consultant's solution is dependent on how you describe the problem. If you have described the problem accurately, the consultant's solution should be able to describe timelines and checkpoints.

3. An assessment of time and cost: It is important to remember that this is only an estimate, unless you can reach a specific total contract amount. If you are satisfied with the consultant's apparent capability and the other portions of the proposal, you may indeed be ready to agree on a specific timeline and contract amount.

## Contract Considerations

Some consultants will ask for time flexibility but are willing to agree on a specific contract amount, or a fixed price contract. Others will confidently tell you that the job will be done by a certain date, but the cost may vary depending on the number of days or hours that are spent implementing the solution. In a situation like this, you may want to set a maximum amount that you are willing to pay, just so that you protect yourself against any possible disagreements as the contract nears completion. Finally, it is possible that both time and money will only be estimates at the time the contract is signed. In such a case, make sure that you are comfortable with the estimates, or again try to reach an agreement based on the maximum time and cost you are willing to tolerate.

As a rule of thumb, the more unknowns there are to a contract (e.g. the consultant cannot specify an exact finish date or you cannot provide information that would help the consultant give you a complete initial assessment) the higher level of trust you need to have with a consultant. Also, the complexity of your consulting needs will vary and, as you might guess, the more complex the job the more credibility and trust you should be looking for. Variability and complexity in a contract require higher levels of trust because you probably know less about solving the problem so you will have to trust that the consultant is doing the right things. It is like when I take my automobile to a mechanic. I know absolutely nothing about fixing vehicles, so I have to look for a mechanic that I trust—especially if there seems to be a major problem with my vehicle.

An established consulting firm may have your trust simply because it is reputable, whereas an individual that you have only heard about may not carry the same credibility. Do not hesitate to hire an independent consultant who was referred to you by word-of-mouth, especially if you trust the reference. Fortunately, I have a good friend who knows a few mechanics around town, and his referral guided me to an auto shop that I feel comfortable with.

## The Consultant's Caveat

So far we have talked about things that a consultant can offer you, but there are many things that the consultant cannot do. First and most important, the consultant cannot change the attitudes and behaviors of your faculty and staff. For example, suppose a consultant has implemented a software solution to automate the grading process, but you have several faculty members who insist on doing things the old way. The consultant has provided the solution, and maybe given some training, but it is your management responsibility to persuade and help others see the value of the solution. It is not the consultant's job to get everyone to buy in.

Second, it will be important for you to allow your consultant some flexibility in implementing technological solutions. It is likely that unforeseen circumstances are going to emerge, so be flexible if some setbacks occur. For example, a consultant may update a specific software application on your computers, but the data (say, student records) from the old application cannot be automatically transferred to the new application. There legitimately may be extra time involved in figuring out how to transfer the information.

## Consultant Possibilities

Through our scenarios of automating the grading process and altering financial and accounting systems to accommodate decentralization, I have tried to give you some practical examples of situations that might occur and why you might consider a consultant. Now, I would like to cover two other areas that will be of use to you. First, what other types of technological situations might warrant a consultant? Second, where would you find a consultant? In addition to our two scenarios, here are examples of other tasks that a consultant may be able to help you with:

- Designing Web pages
- Installing E-mail systems
- Installing computers, office equipment, and other technical components into your school
- Designing systems to automate accounting and finance processes
- Designing databases to track students, analyze data, or create reports
- Setting up technology labs or installing computers throughout a school

So, where do you find a consultant? Many who have been downsized or fired, or just plain do not fit into public, private, or educational culture are sure to tell you they are consultants (as a consultant, I am allowed to say that). Consultants can be people who work independently and out of their home, graduate students or university faculty members, small companies, or large consulting firms. The wide range of people who might claim to be consultants is a reason to rely on references and word-of-mouth from people you trust.

The size and complexity of your job will help you determine whom you should consider hiring. You probably would not contact a consulting firm to help you with Web page design. This is a fairly low-risk job in which many college students have expertise. In addition, there are a variety of individuals, small companies, and university resources available to help you with this sort of thing. It would be advantageous to talk with colleagues and friends to see if they have any local recommendations.

Larger jobs, such as implementing an automated accounting system that will keep an historical account of revenues and expenditures would require a more established source. For a job of this sort, it may be wise to contact an established consulting firm. Many such firms have departments that specifically serve the public and educational sectors.

Word-of-mouth remains one of the best ways to find outside help for your school's needs. You will undoubtedly find people who have used consultants if you start asking your colleagues. You can also find consultant services by searching the Internet or looking through a business directory from your local library.

# Conclusion

Many times administrative leadership will perceive that a problem exists or that a new technology will "fix" something or provide benefits. Indeed, in the first scenario we discussed in the chapter, the principal perceived a need, detected a problem, did an assessment, and then took further steps to consider whether a consultant was needed. This was certainly a unilateral type of decision-making process. Many authors would call this type of decision making "top-down." The fact is that top-down decisions are often effective, efficient, and necessary. In relation to making a decision about consulting, top-down decisions may be effective for low-cost, low-risk, simple jobs. The more extensive your technology needs, however, the more sense it makes to be more comprehensive in your decision making process. And, as discussed, the more complex your technological needs, the more sophisticated and reputable must be your consultant. Table 11.1 describes the decision-making process for different types of change, along with the likely complexity of the problem.

**Table 11.1: Relationships among types of changes, solutions, and decision-making approaches**

| Type of Change | Solution Complexity | Decision-Making Approach |
| --- | --- | --- |
| Technical Installation | Simple | Top-management makes decision to find consultant and implement a solution. |
| Systems Approach | Simple-Complex | Management analyses inputs and outputs of the school; involves employees in the process. |
| Gap analysis | Complex | Management formulates teams to assess the current state of the organization and possible needs. |

(Adapted from: Thach and Woodman 1995)

Drawing back on our scenarios, the "Age of the Abacus" would fit under the *technical installation* process of decision making. For a job of this scope and complexity, management decision making is not likely to cause a lot of problems, though it may be useful to consult with staff and gather their opinions if time permits. Tasks such as installing computers throughout a school or designing new accounting systems are more complex. For such decisions, you should consider forming a committee, like the one you were chairing in the "Devil is in the Technological Details" of scenario 2. It is risky and unwise for a single individual to unilaterally make multiple decisions that have wide-reaching ramifications for the entire organization. A systems approach or *gap analysis* (as shown in table 11.1) will help you garner input from different knowledgeable insiders in your school to ensure that you are pursuing the right course of action. The last two decision-making methods in table 11.1 also help mitigate the negative political perceptions and opinions that usually accompany a change that is instigated by the organization's leadership.

One thing is certain in today's day and age as technology continues to flow into our organizations: the demand for consultants will increase. I have provided the consultant guide questionnaire, the scenarios and the decision-making method table as tools to help you think systematically about whether or not you need a consultant. You will still have to make judgment calls and use your intuition to make your final decision.

# Reference

Thach, L., and R. W. Woodman. 1995. Organizational change and information technology: Managing on the edge of cyberspace. *Managing Organizational Change*. Ed. W. W. Burke. New York:
American Management Association.

# 12

# How Administrators Become Technology Leaders

## Carmen L. Gonzales, Ph.D.

## Introduction

"The trouble with the future is that it usually arrives before we're ready for it" (Glasow cited in Bailey, Lumley, & Dunbar 1995, 22).

The world is in the midst of a communication revolution that will rival the industrial revolution in terms of impact and importance. Emerging technologies such as the computer, telecommunications, CD-ROMs, and videodisc are examples of tools that power this revolution. These technologies impact learning and education by providing numerous sources of information and communication. They present teachers, administrators, and policymakers with unprecedented opportunities and challenges.

As technology becomes more prevalent in schools, expectations for improvements in education grow as well. Although technology is not a panacea for the challenges facing today's schools, when used appropriately it can be an effective tool for promoting practices shown to improve teaching and learning. Technology can be a powerful ally for education, but only under the direction of knowledgeable educators and citizens. An engaging curriculum, enhanced by technology, and taught by well-prepared teachers familiar with the modern workplace, is crucial for students since schools are the primary places in many students' lives where they will have access to technology.

A major challenge in the path of bringing schools into the Communication Age is the lack of vision on the part of school leaders. Research supports the notion that school administrators are catalysts who shape the vision, set direction, and model changes that current educational reform efforts reflect (Hawkins, Panush, and Spielvogel 1996;

Fullan 1991; Norton and Gonzales 1998). Administrators play a key role in shaping their school's environments; however, they often lack the in-depth understanding of the value of technology for learning and the importance of tying these new tools to culturally responsive and problem-based learning approaches. Administrators also underestimate the amount of change required to redesign schools and curricula to be able to use the potential of technology for teaching and learning (Wiburg 1997). In order for technology to be successfully integrated in the schools, someone must lead the efforts.

As I stated earlier, the school administrator is central to key decisions about technology access and use, especially when those decisions involve changes in the culture of the school. So, what should a profile of an administrator knowledgeable about technology include? Coughlin and Lemke (1999) suggest the following skills and characteristics:

- Administrators at the building and district level model the effective use of technology in support of learning and administrative functions.
- Administrators are able to initiate and support professional development processes that reflect attention to principles of adult learning.
- Administrators are competent in leading and managing systemic change processes at the classroom, school and/or district levels.
- Administrators maintain a solid knowledge of the applications of technology to student learning (37).

Despite the importance of technology to all constituents in the educational system, school districts often move into a technology project without a clear plan. This chapter will provide administrators with questions and places to find answers that will enable them to plan and lead a technology effort that leverages and maximizes resources to meet their greatest educational needs. If America's schools are to succeed in meeting educational goals in the twenty-first century, it is crucial that policy makers and school administrators understand the impact of technology on teaching and learning. Educators must create programs that capture the opportunities promised by emerging technologies in ways that are affordable and sustainable, and that allow for future growth and expansion. Learning technologies are effective only when they appear within a larger context of educational reform. In that context, it is important to consider equity, professional development, student learning, and assessment/evaluation as they relate to learning technologies.

# Equity

While technology is often thought of as a solution to many of today's education problems, it can also extend existing ones. Data show that in the last three years an increasing number of American homes have become connected to the Internet; about fifty percent of classrooms are now connected; and the number of students for every computer in U.S. schools has dipped below six for the first time (McConnaughey and Lader 1999; Jerald and Orlofsky 1999). While computers in homes can expand students' opportunities for learning, increase their access to educational resources, and promote parental support of schools and learning, unequal distribution of those computers in homes can widen the "digital divide." Since technology plays such a large role in modern society, those who do not use computers at home effectively are likely to be at an educational, economic, and social disadvantage.

Warren-Sams (1997) reveals that inequities in technology exist in the following areas:

*Access.* Physical access to available educational technologies varies greatly across districts and within schools. Funding differences between rich and poor school districts are substantial and result in less access to educational technology for lower-income and ethnic minority students.

*Type of Use.* Unconscious stereotyping on the part of educators keeps them from challenging ethnic minority, lower-income, differently abled, and female students academically. Within schools, research shows that different groups of students use the computer in different ways. This indicates that school staff may play a role in perpetuating inequities.

*Curriculum.* Often computer software contains gender or ethnic bias or both. Schools must make available to students a variety of software that meets the needs and interests of all students and makes them feel they belong in the world of computing (4).

Administrators must inform themselves about issues related to equity in educational technology. To help you determine what you can do to ensure equity in your schools and/or districts, ask yourself the following questions:

- What processes or policies would you establish to ensure *all* students have equitable access to technology in your school and/or district?

- How will you work to overcome existing access inequalities among schools and among districts?
- What benefits and/or disadvantages might the use of technology present to the students and/or teachers?
- How should schools/districts set minimum standards for technology to ensure that *all* students have adequate access?
- How can access to technology at school narrow the gap between the " haves" and "have nots?"
- How can we convince policymakers to become advocates for equity in educational technology?

As you consider these questions, you may want to refer to the following online resources:

- Closing the Equity Gap in Technology Access and Use: A Practical Guide for K-12 Educators http://www.netc.org/equity/
- Ensuring Equity <http://www.nap.edu/readingroom/books/tech-gap/equity.html>
- Falling Through the Net II: New Data on the Digital Divide <http://www.ntia.doc.gov/ntiahome/net2/>

# Professional Development

Recent trends show that "teachers must become technologically literate" (Ely, Blair, Lichvar, Tyksinski, and Martinez 1996, 33). The United States Office of Technology Assessment (OTA) stated that in the process of acquiring hardware and software for students to use, the most valuable part of the education equation, the teacher, is often left out of the loop. Only 20 percent of teachers feel "very prepared" to integrate technology into their teaching (1995). OTA recommends that funding of professional development activities should be at least 30 percent of a district/school budget. Most districts/schools spend far less than that. Unfortunately, the structure of most schools works against successfully providing the much-needed training for teachers. Besides the funding obstacle, teachers are isolated in classrooms, with little time for collaboration and reflection.

Professional development in the use of technology in the classroom is also very complex because the focus of attention should not be on the technology, but on improving student learning through improvements in instructional practice. According to *Education Week*,  "Teachers are more likely to feel better prepared to use technology in their classrooms if they receive curriculum-integration training than if they receive basic-skills training [in technology]. And the biggest benefits have come to teachers who had both kinds of training" (Jerald and Orlofsky 1999, 60).

Designing professional development for the Communications Age requires us to move away from the traditional model of a "one-shot in-service presentation," where there is inadequate opportunity to practice new skills and little ongoing support. Research in the field of professional development suggests that teachers learn best and are more likely to incorporate new approaches into their teaching when they can experiment and reflect in a nonthreatening setting. Teachers, like their students, must have ample opportunity to discuss and collaborate with their peers and instructors (Fulton 1996; Grant 1996). According to Grant, professional development must help teachers to "move beyond 'mechanical use' of curriculum and technology to become facilitators of inquiry" (1).

A highly effective model of professional development is using teachers to train other teachers. Teachers-teaching-teachers is particularly effective in establishing good rapport among peers. Building communities of learners and allowing teachers to network and share ideas with their peers provides the opportunity for opening the isolated classroom and bringing in new resources to support new models of teaching (Reil and Fulton 1998). Because they are familiar with the regular classroom setting, teacher/presenters can help participants see how technologies can enrich and support learning. Since teacher/presenters understand classroom culture and the demands of teaching, their guidance is often more relevant and credible to other teachers.

Given the potential of technology to transform learning and teaching, and given the challenges of implementing technology within established classroom traditions, school leaders must look for the most effective way to provide professional development along with ongoing support. Weekend and/or after school workshops offered in different areas seem to be the best way to provide access to technology for working teachers. The workshops should be designed to provide opportunities for teachers to (1) experience excellent models of technology integration; and (2) think systematically about the translation of those models into their own classrooms. Teachers do not need to be "done to" or "told what to do"; they need examples of good practice and support in the form of collaboration with strategies for integrating technology.

Technology has been found to be a powerful tool to support learning where:

- The curriculum emphasizes reasoning and problem solving,
- The curriculum moves students to apply discipline-based knowledge to solve problems,
- Both students and teachers are learners,
- Students and teachers are motivated and engaged,
- The learning environment is responsive to students' prior knowledge and experience, and
- Authentic assessment practices are used.

In order to involve students in real-world problem-solving tasks, teachers themselves need to experience those kinds of tasks. The only way that educators can internalize these new approaches is to experience such learning situations for themselves. Teachers and/or administrators need ongoing support and sustained learning opportunities to develop their skills and confidence in using technology effectively in instructional environments.

Administrators must inform themselves about issues related to professional development in the use of educational technology. To help you define your professional development needs, consider the following questions:

- What do you want as the main focus of professional development sessions (learning computer applications or working with curriculum)?
- How can schools/districts plan for ongoing and sustained professional development in technology integration?
- How can teachers/administrators get access to technology to practice their newly acquired skills?
- How can schools/districts build time for educators to reflect on how to change their practice using technology?
- How can they build-in funding to provide incentives (i.e. substitutes, stipends, release time, etc.)?
- What does research say about the impacts of reform-based technology use with teachers and administrators?

As you consider these questions, you may want to refer to the following online resources:

- Professional Skills for the Digital Age Classroom <http://www.milkenexchange.org>
- Professional Development: A Link to Better Learning <http://www.ceoforum.org>

- Plugging In: Choosing and Using Educational Technology <http://www.ncrel.org/ncrel/sdrs/edtalk/toc.htm>

# Student Learning

"Research suggests that deep and sustained access to technology has the potential to have a positive impact on both students' learning and on the school community's views of their students' capabilities" (Honey, McMillan Culp, and Carrigg 1999, online document).

Students in schools today have been weaned on multidimensional, interactive media sources that are very different from anything in the experience of the generations preceding them. If we are to give these students the education necessary to succeed in our technologically intense future, a new form of educational practice must replace our existing methods.

According to the SCANS Report (Whetzel 1992), "Good jobs will increasingly depend on people who can put knowledge to work" (1). Two main conditions have changed in the last quarter century in the world of work: the globalization of commerce and industry and the explosive growth of technology. The SCANS Report identified five competencies as being necessary for preparation of all students, both for those going to work directly out of high school and for those planning higher education.

*Resources:* Identifies, organizes, plans, and allocates resources (allocates time, money, materials, space, and staff)

*Interpersonal:* Works with others (works on teams, teaches others, serves customers, leads, negotiates, works well with people from culturally diverse backgrounds)

*Information:* Acquires and uses information (acquires and evaluates data, organizes and maintains files, interprets and communicates, uses computers to process information)

*Systems:* Understands complex interrelationships (understands social, organizational, and technological systems, monitors and corrects performance, and designs or improves systems)

*Technology:* Works with a variety of technologies (selects equipment and tools, applies appropriate technology to specific tasks, and maintains and troubleshoots technologies)

If we are to prepare students with the above competencies, the traditional models of learning need to be expanded to include learning that promotes all of the following (Jones, Valdez, Nowakowski, and Rasmussen 1995):

- Engaged, meaningful learning
- Collaboration involving challenging and authentic tasks
- Technology as a tool for learning, communication, and collaboration

We know that students learn best when they play an active role in their learning, rather than a passive role of recipient of information transmitted by a teacher or textbook. Students given an active role in their learning use higher-order thinking and act as problem solvers in their learning process. The teacher becomes a "guide on the side" rather than a "sage on the stage." We can no longer expect students to memorize and absorb a static set of facts, because those facts soon become obsolete. The sheer amount of information available grows ever more rapidly, and what students need to know changes as quickly as the world around them. Students "construct" their own knowledge as they come across various information resources. This means they must learn how to investigate, classify, evaluate, and communicate information. Technology can be a tool to facilitate these processes. Computers, along with other technology, allow the creation of incredibly rich multimedia environments and allow instant access to databases and online information sources. We now have the opportunity with these tools to reshape the nature of inquiry and exploration.

As the world of work becomes increasingly globalized, and interaction across cultures becomes more common, people will need to develop skills that will enable them to work together effectively. Working in small groups, in class or online, helps students develop the social interaction skills that will make them successful and productive workers in the future. Through collaborative learning, students may experience more ownership of their learning, which results in increased motivation and achievement. Technology enhances collaborative learning by facilitating the sharing of resources—between classrooms as well as individual students—and the management of group tasks.

Technology can be a powerful tool for students' learning. The traditional classroom tools—pencils, paper, and books—are still necessary. But for students to construct and revise their ideas and to access and study information, the traditional tools alone are not adequate. Computers, video, and other technologies engage students with the immediacy they are used to in their everyday lives and extend it to a new purpose. Technology must be thought of as an integral part of the curriculum. Really, it is not *what* technology is used for in the classroom that will make the difference, but *how* it is used.

Administrators must inform themselves about how perspectives on learning are changing because of student technology use. What are the implications of how technology may be changing learning?

- How are schools/teachers going to teach students to be critical information users? How do you know the information that students are accessing on the Internet or CDs is accurate or credible?
- How are you going to address the learning needs of all students?
- What kind of learning can occur with technology use that could not occur before?
- How might technology help to improve student performance?
- What kinds of learning experiences leverage the power of technology to involve students in tasks that require higher order thinking skills as well as mastery of basic concepts and skills?
- What are effects of reform-based technology use on students and classroom practices?

To help you develop responses, refer to the following online resources:

- Rural New Mexico Students Gain Access to the Global Village with Technology
  <http://www.edvancenet.org/res_toolkit_stories_roy.html>
- Reasons for Bringing Technology into Schools
  <http://www.ed.gov/pubs/EdReformStudies/EdTech/reasons.htm>
- Reinventing Schools: The Nintendo Generation
  <http://search.nap.edu/html/techgap/nintendo.html>
- Meaningful, Engaged Learning
  <http://www.ncrel.org/sdrs/engaged.html>

## Assessment and Evaluation

Assessment of technology's success and evaluation of its potential uses in education is not simple. This is mainly because schools are unevenly equipped with technology and teacher training to use it appropriately in their curriculum. First of all, on average, teachers take five to seven years to become comfortable, confident users of educational technology. Apple Classrooms of Tomorrow devised a series of stages that occur during the process of integrating technology to transform the learning environment. Teachers begin in the *entry* level, where they struggle to learn the basics of using technology. Then comes *adoption*, where they use technology at a basic level using drill, practice, and tutorial software. Next is *adaptation*, where they move from basic use to discovery of its potential for increased productivity, such as using word processing for student writing. Fourth is *appropriation*, where they have achieved mastery over the technology, and now use it as a tool to accomplish a variety of instructional and management goals. Last is the *invention* stage, where teachers are able to develop entirely new learning environments that utilize technology as a flexible tool. Learning becomes more collaborative, interactive, and customized.

Furthermore, evaluation is difficult because we know that it takes three to five years to see a substantial achievement gains from traditional ways of assessing students, namely standardized tests. As a result, most studies on technology's effectiveness are formative and summative evaluations of various existing technology applications in education. There has been little funding spent on in-depth research and development (R&D) for K-12 education. So far the emphasis has been more on qualitative research and evaluation, and less on development and validation. Many believe that before technology can have a long-term impact on education, it is necessary to have a strong R&D agenda that promotes development combined with the needed research to inform the education community and stakeholders about effective practices and products. The research should help to determine the extent to which these new practices and products related to technology promote needed education reform.

The following questions, adapted from the "12 Keys for Success" in EDvancenet's *Leader's Guide to Education Technology* (Bigham 1999), may help you as you consider issues related to assessment and evaluation:

- How are we integrating technology into long-range education improvement plans? Have old beliefs and behaviors about teaching and learning been altered?
- Have criteria been established to prioritize spending and provide funding for technology?
- Do we have evidence of community involvement and support?
- How are we addressing equity issues when planning for technology acquisition?
- What is the role of technology in the institution's overall educational goals and programs? Is student information literacy valued as highly as traditional literacy?
- Does our professional development plan involve technology?
- How do we develop quality content based on standards?

- What do we do to involve the community in technology decisions? Has an electronic connection been established between home and school?
- How do we nurture partnerships with other organizations to support change? Are we developing a "learning community" for all learners?
- What are our measures of success for technology use? Do we use multiple measures emphasizing student excellence?
- What commitments have we made to reassess and revise our school improvement plans regularly?
- How do we celebrate the accomplishments of technology in our schools?

As you consider these questions, you may want to refer to the following online resources:

- Technology: How Do We Know It Works? <http://www.ed.gov/Technology/TechConf/1999/whitepapers/paper5.html>
- Learning with Technology: A Presenter's Toolkit for Leaders <http://www.edvancenet.org>
- Professional Development: A Link to Better Learning <http:// www.ceoforum.org>

# Conclusion

Many educators who understand and appreciate technology's potential to help schools and learners are convinced that schools must change, but the learning curve is steep. It takes time to equip schools with computers and to staff schools with teachers who understand how to integrate technology meaningfully into their curriculum. There are three factors that foster progress: teachers' motivation and commitment to students' learning and to their own personal development as teachers; support and collaboration in schools and districts; and sufficient access to and support of technology.

In order to address the concerns uncovered by evaluation and research, change must occur systemically. As with other substantial education change efforts, research has shown that successful districts had strong leadership that focused on the integration of technologies for teaching and learning (Hawkins, Panush, and Spielvogel 1996). However, administrators are often left out of the loop when it comes to professional development opportunities. Educational leaders such as principals, assistant principals, superintendents, assistant superintendents, and coordinators need to share struggles and solutions and investigate new theories and practices together.

# References

Apple Classrooms of Tomorrow. *Teacher Centered Staff Develoment.* [Oline document]. www.apple.com/education/professionaldevelop ment/ tchrcenterstaff.html 22 March 01.

Bailey, G. D., D. Lumley,, and D. Dunbar. 1995. *Leadership and Technology: What Schools Board Members Need to Know.* Alexandria, Va.: National School Boards Association.

Bigham, V. S. 1999. *Learning with Technology: A Presenter's Toolkit for Leaders.* [Online document]. www.edvancenet.org 22 March 01.

Coughlin, E. C., and C. Lemke. 1999. Professional Competency Continuum: Professional Skills for the Digital Age Classroom. Santa Monica, Calif.: Milken Family Foundation.

Ely, D., P. Blair, P. Lichvar, D. Tyksinski, and M. Martinez. 1996. *Trends in Educational Technology 1995.* Syracuse, N.Y.: ERIC Clearinghouse on Information and Technology.

Fullan, M. G. 1991. *The New Meaning of Educational Change.* New York: Teachers College Press.

Fulton, K. 1996. Moving from Boxes and Wires to 21st Century Teaching. *T.H.E. Journal,* 24(40), 76-82.

Grant, C. M. 1996. *Professional Development in a Technological Age: New Definitions, Old Challenges, New Resources.* [Online docment]<http://ra.terc.edu/alliance/TEMPLATE/alliance_resource s/reform/tech-infusion/prof_dev/prof_dev_frame.html.> 22 March 01

Hawkins, J., Panush, E. M., and R. Spielvogel. 1996. *National Study Tour of District Technology Integration: Summary Report.* From Center for Children & Technology, CCT Reports, Issue No. 14. New York: Education Development Center.

Honey, M., McMillan Culp, K., and F. Carrigg. 1999. Perspectives on Technology and Education Research: Lessons from the Past and Present. [Online..document}.<http://www.ed.gov/Technology/ TechConf/1999/whitepapers/paper1.html> 22 March 01.

Jerald, C. D., and G. F. Orlofsky. 1999. Across the Nation: Raising the Bar on School Technology. *Education Week* 19(4), 58-108.

Jones, B. F., G. Valdez, J. Nowakowski, and C. Rasmussen. 1995. *Plugging In: Choosing and Using Educational Technology.* Washington, D.C.: Council for Educational Development and Research.

McConnaughey, J. W., and W. Lader. 1999. *Falling Through the Net II: New Data on the Digital Divide.* [Online document]. <http://www.ntia.doc.gov/ntiahome/net2/falling.html> 22 March 01

Norton, P., and C. Gonzales. 1998. Regional Educational Technology Assistance—Phase II: Evaluating a model for statewide professional development. *Journal of Research on Computing in Education,* 31(1), 25-48.

Office of Technology Assessment. 1995. *Teachers and Technology: Making the Connection.* Publication No. OTA-EHR-616. Washington, D.C.: U.S. Government Printing Office.

Reil, M., and K. Fulton. 1998-April. Technology in the Classroom: Tools for Doing Things Differently or Doing Different Things. Presented at American Educational Research Association. San Diego, Calif.

Warren-Sams, B. 1997. *Closing the Equity Gap in Technology Access and Use: A Practical Guide for K-12 Educators.* Portland, Ore.: Northwest Regional Educational Laboratory—Equity Center.

Whetzel, D. 1992. *The Secretary of Labor's Commission on Achieving Necessary Skills.* ERIC Digest. [Online document]. <www.ed.gov/database/ERIC_Digests/ed339749.html> 22 March 01.

Wiburg, K. 1997. Dance of change; Integrating Technology in Classrooms. In *Using Technology in the Classroom,* eds. D. L. Johnson, C. D. Maddux, and L. Liu, 171-184. New York: Haworth Press.

# 13

# Effective Planning for Technology

## Karin M. Wiburg

Over the last seven years and across two different states, I have worked with superintendents and principals who needed advice on how to get technology into their schools or districts. Their first questions usually have to do with the kind of hardware or software they should buy. When I am lucky enough to have a chance to sit down with these administrators, I ask them to *stop thinking about technology* for a minute and tell me about their school or district. What would they like their teachers and students to be able to do that they cannot do now? What processes do they use for program improvement? How would technology contribute to those processes? What can it do for learning, teaching, and administration? In general, administrators have not had many opportunities to develop a vision of how technology might enhance the teaching and learning process. So let us begin there. First we will talk a bit about visions, good ones and bad ones, and what we know about how schools end up there. Later I will walk you through six planning steps to help you reach the place *you* want to be.

## Bad Scenes and What We Know About How People Got There

In a fourth grade classroom, the computers are seldom turned on and when they are, they are used as rewards for students who complete their "regular" work. In a high school the teachers joke that the computers are there to impress the parents and catch dust. Surely no administrator would want to preside over such scenes. We would much rather our actions foster good scenes. So let us consider factors that prevent good scenes from happening. Historically, a number of factors can be shown to have limited the power of technology when used in instructional settings. These factors include:

- Those most knowledgeable about technology are not usually in instructional leadership positions in school districts.

- At the same time, those most knowledgeable about curriculum and instruction do not know enough about technology to feel comfortable making decisions about purchasing and using it. They have too often turned to vendors who promised "magic boxes" and unrealistic solutions.

- Most staff development has focused on the technology itself, e.g., how to do word-processing or e-mail, and not how to integrate technology with teaching strategies in the content areas.

- Technology planning has not been well integrated with other planning for school and program improvement.

- Reliable access to multimedia-capable computers and Internet resources has been severely limited for teachers, students, and administrators. While many schools have computers, they may not be capable of running current programs and may not be in locations easily accessible to teachers, students, and administrators. Limited access to quality uses of technology is especially a problem in poorer districts where the *digital divide* between rich and poor continues to grow (Tapscott 1998).

- And that concern brings us to our final factor: Educators have misunderstood "equity" to mean providing equal access to computers for every teacher and student in the building. This has at times resulted in everyone getting his/her twenty-minutes-per-week of computer time and *no one* getting the full benefit that effective technology use can provide.

# Good Scenes and What We Know About How People Got There

## Bay Park Elementary

Bay Park Elementary on the West Coast is an example of an old, traditional school building being transformed into a modern learning environment. Tables have been pulled out into the halls and small computer learning stations set up between and in the backs of classrooms. Supported by several grants, this school has been actively involved in restructuring, and has spent significant time in self-assessment and deciding how technology might help improve things. The school has a strong background in the arts and the use of video for learning. It also has had some specific weaknesses in the development of higher-level thinking skills in the language arts and social studies curricula.

The school goals include: (1) integration of curriculum across grade levels and subject areas, (2) use of real-world experiences and a variety of media and methods to meet the diverse student learning needs in the community, (3) development and implementation of alternative measures for evaluation of student progress, and (4) use of the whole community, including the student, as a learning resource. A clear look at the school's long-term goals, strengths, and weaknesses provided the direction for the technology plan for the school. Creative, student-centered technologies, including word processing, desktop publishing, and multimedia authoring tools were logical choices based on the school's mission. During the next two steps, staff articulated goals in terms of student outcomes, teacher and staff outcomes, and a process for managing technology integration. The planning team rated staff development in the appropriate teaching strategies for the use of these student-centered tools just as important as the technology tools themselves.

## Star Middle School

Star Middle School, on the border with Mexico, set out to restructure a school in a very poor neighborhood with a history of student problems. The principal who took on this challenge included technology as part of the effort to restructure learning experiences at this school. Decisions about technology were made in the context of teacher teams engaged in interdisciplinary curriculum development and the need for both in-school and after-school programs to serve the community. Early on, the staff decided to use a *distributive model* so that eventually four computers would be available in every classroom, beginning with all language arts classrooms. Since students needed help with the writing process, the school acquired software to provide it. Staff developed additional computer labs to meet other specific needs of the middle school and the community. For example, students can use a technology-education lab to learn to use new technologies such as computer-assisted drafting, and manufacturing and multimedia technologies. Students who need to acquire English quickly can take advantage of the fifteen computers placed in the "Newcomer Center." The school also benefited from a two-year grant effort with a nearby university that assisted teachers in reorganizing their classrooms and teaching strategies to take better advantage of the technology resources in the classroom. The teachers now maintain a web page and have developed technology-integrated units and web-based units for use within their teamed classrooms.

## Eastside Union High School District

The Eastside Union High School District in Southern California decided to focus on the classroom and the enhancement of the teacher/student relationship as part of its plan for program improvement. Its technology plan therefore focused on a teacher workstation used as a sort of *interactive chalkboard*. The plan included training in how to use it. Later phases called for (1) connecting the teacher workstation to a variety of technological resources including library resources, classroom management systems, online resources and services, and external research centers; and (2) the development of student workstations in and close to classrooms linked to similar electronic resources.

The school used a number of effective tactics to integrate technology use and subject-matter learning. Teachers applied to receive the teacher stations and were required to attend significant training during the summer in order to receive the stations. The plan allowed departments to choose either *Macintosh* or *PC/Windows* computer systems based on the software they planned to use. Training related technology use to content-area learning. The district hired a full-time technology coordinator and gave him the authority to carry the plan through to implementation. The district now serves as a model for the rest of the country.

I hope reading about these three good scenes has given you hope that your school can use technology well. Now, let me present some information on important factors in getting to those good places:

## Effective Implementation of Technology

Ritchie and Wiburg (1994) researched schools in San Diego County that seemed to be making especially effective use of technology in their instructional programs. The following factors were found to be important:

1. The quality of professional development provided
2. Administrative leadership
3. Pedagogical orientation of the teacher and school
4. Community or outside institutional support

## 1. The Quality of Professional Development Provided

Morgan (1998) surveyed over one hundred schools in Texas and found that the most significant factor in successful integration of technology was the quality of staff development provided. This confirmed what other research studies had suggested about the importance of effective technology-related professional development (Office of Technology Assistance 1995; Fulton 1996; Norton and Gonzales 1997).

Technology staff development efforts have been weak. The Office of Technology Assessment (1995) reported that districts spent less than 15 percent of their technology money on professional development. In some states, such as New Mexico, this is as low as 4 percent (Bingaman 1997). Even when teachers had access to technology, they reported feeling uncomfortable using it, and did not have knowledge of how to use computers in instruction. Many states and districts lack inservice education for both teachers and administrators to integrate technology into their roles. Learning to use new instructional approaches takes time. Showers (1990) suggested that much in-service training is not successful because 1) it is overly focused on the wonders of technology rather than the real educational problems faced by teachers, and 2) little is provided in the training to help teachers transfer learning to the classroom. Joyce and Weil (1995) noted that it takes at least a year or two for teachers to feel comfortable with any new teaching method. While long-term research by the Apple Classroom of Tomorrow team (Dwyer, Ringstaff, and Sandholtz 1990) confirms that integration of technology can have positive and significant effects on the learning environment, it takes several years for teachers to tap the power of these tools. Introducing an innovation is not enough to ensure its implementation.

## 2. Administrative Leadership

As Finkel (1990) noted, research recognizes that the administrator holds the key to the long-range success of any technology plan. What do schools that are successfully integrating technology and teaching have in common? Administrators who were strong users of the technology themselves (Wiburg 1991; Ritchie and Wiburg 1994; Wiburg 1997). In-service education for administrators and support for leadership in technology helps. Bloom (1991) found that administrators who attended an Administrators' Technology Academy sponsored by the San Diego Office in California were significantly more likely to perceive technology as being useful in education and to use it themselves.

## 3. Pedagogical Orientation of the Teacher and School

Everything we do now in education must be considered in view of changing paradigms about what students should know and be able to do, how teachers should teach, and how these new types of learning should be evaluated. The world we must prepare our students to enter is fundamentally different from the one in which we grew up and attended school. Traditional perceptions of what education should look like—lectures to deliver instruction, learning as memorizing, and feeding back facts learned from lectures—do not tap the power of new technologies to support meaningful learning (fig. 13.1).

Just as important as technology professional development and support is the pedagogical orientation of the principal and the school. Schools that have integrated technology with instruction are usually schools in which new instructional strategies and efforts to restructure the curriculum are encouraged. They support innovative teaching as part of the school culture. Honey and Moeller (1990) identified distinctly different pedagogical orientations for those teachers who were high implementers of technology as compared with teachers who were low implementers. High implementers used technology as a tool to stimulate thinking about content in the curriculum. Low implementers tended to fall into one of two groups: those teachers who had had negative experiences with technology and did not feel comfortable using it and those teachers who felt technology exploration would interfere with the lecture and textbook approach they preferred.

**Figure 13.1: Different perceptions of education**

## 4. Community or Outside Institutional Support

There is a final interesting variable that I have found in my experience working with schools. Many of the schools that have been successful in integrating technology have had significant help from an outside group. It might be a business, an institution of higher education, or a service organization. A partnership with a nearby university or college sometimes makes the difference in providing just enough extra help and expertise to make technology integration happen. A New Mexico State University/public school partnership grant in 1995 provided a local school district with a file server, training, and networking help to provide e-mail and Internet connections to the schools. This district is far ahead of neighboring districts in having electronic access in its classrooms (Wiburg, Montoya, and Sandin 1997). Membership in a district, state, or county technology consortium or partnerships with neighborhood community groups such as the Chamber of Commerce, the Boys and Girls Club, or a Senior Citizens center can provide additional support for schools seeking to integrate technology. These types of partnerships are also looked upon favorably by funding institutions and this can result in additional financial and human resources.

# The Steps in Developing
# an Effective Technology Plan

You have read some of my ideas on the factors crucial for making a good vision become a good reality. Now I will share six steps in developing a plan for technology integration. First, I give you an overview of these steps; then I explain each step in more detail.

1.  Creating the future—As you might have guessed by now, I believe the wise use of technology begins with imagining a desirable future and planning how to get there. There are two parts to this first step. You must set up a planning process and structure first, and then work with your planning group to look at what is possible and desirable.
2.  Assessing your school or district—Find out what has been done in the area of technology at your site. Even more important, look at your program improvement goals and find possible technology solutions related to your needs and goals. Below I provide questions to help you complete Step 2.
3.  Establishing strategic goals—In this step you put together the data gathered in step 2 with the vision you developed in step 1 to develop strategic goals that will guide the technology plan.
4.  Building a Technology Integration Plan—Once you have developed strategic goals and gained support for these goals, the next steps are relatively easy. For each of the strategic goals, you specify objectives, activities, staff responsibilities, related hardware/software, costs, student outcomes, and evaluation strategies. Below, I include examples and suggested formats for this.
5.  Making sure the plan is carried out—This is a step that is often missed in technology planning, the process of learning-resource management. You need to develop a structure to ensure that what you planned to happen will happen. At this stage you will need to specify everything, from the design and acquisition of the hardware and the sequences of implementation, to the management of the plan.
6.  Evaluating and adjusting the plan—Did you do what you said you would do? And did it matter? You must develop ways to monitor the impact of your efforts and modify your plan as needed. I suggest ways to do this, both formally and informally.

## Step 1: Creating the Future

The first task for an educator interested in establishing a technology plan is to identify a planning group and give it the time, resources, and authority it needs. This will involve:

- Identification of all people affected by the plan (the stakeholders) and ways for these people to provide input,
- Agreement on the purpose of the plan prior to proceeding,
- A firm commitment to link technology applications to school and program improvement,
- A way to put curriculum and student learning-outcomes first, with technology solutions to follow, and
- An agreed upon timeline for developing and completing the plan with benchmarks along the way. The step-by-step model provided in this chapter can support this process.

Once the planning team is established, the team members need to look at what is possible with technology. While it is common to emphasize computers, do not ignore other technologies. Effective use of video and instructional television, even the use of overhead projectors, can dramatically improve instruction and student learning. Electronic calculators are effective mathematics learning tools. Phones in classrooms serve a variety of instructional purposes and also provide a positive message about teachers as professionals.

Arrange for your planning team to visit a school with a reputation for exciting uses of technology. Or invite speakers to demonstrate the potential of technology for learning, or show some videos on new technology-based learning environments. Vendors can be helpful; for example *Apple, Compaq, IBM, AT&T*, and other companies have excellent videos on how technology can improve learning. No matter what you are told, however, beware: as one administrator put it: *there is no magic bullet.* Too many administrators have trusted vendors to provide a total technology solution only to be disappointed in the results (Wiburg 1996).

## Step 2: Assessing Your School or District

In this step, you work together on two tasks: assessing your school's or district's instructional needs and finding out what has been done with technology so far. Here are some questions to help your planning team think about where they are with technology and where they might like to go:

- What educational problems (gaps between student performance and desired performance) do you see? Which of these gaps do you think technology can help you solve?
- What is your current process for school improvement and how might technology planning fit into this process?
- How are you currently using technology? Are you using it as well as you could be? If not, what is limiting you?
- What concerns do teachers, administrators, and parents have about technology? How are these concerns being addressed?
- How will you ensure buy-in to your technology plan once it is developed?
- What has been your planning process so far? How could it be improved?

One way to assess your school technology needs is to look at weaknesses in the academic areas. In what content areas (reading, writing, mathematics, or science) are students weakest? What process skills (critical thinking, research, or presentation abilities) need to be strengthened? What do you want your students to be able to do that they cannot do now? What do you want your teachers to be able to do? What are other strengths and needs of your school community? What are the community learning needs in the area of technology? Could home-school communication be improved with technology (phones, video, or computers)? *Focus on your educational needs and the right technology solutions will emerge!*

There are a variety of sources to use for your school or district needs-assessment. Different states have different names for the document they use for assessing and guiding their school programs. In California, it is called the *School Report Card*; in Texas, the *Campus Action Plan*; in New Mexico, the *Educational Plan for Student Success*. It is worth the time to re-examine your school plan and align your technology plan with it. You can also use observations, surveys or focused interviews of students, teachers, other staff, and parents. Look at scores (on both criterion- and norm-referenced tests). Use informal teacher tests as part of your needs assessment.

Make a list of your faculty (or in the case of districts, your principals), the kinds of innovations they support, and who would be your obvious change agents in the group. Often innovative teachers without much technology experience can be the best leaders in a technology integration effort. While you want some technology expertise on your team, watch out for techies who want to focus on the tools rather than on how the tools can enhance learning.

Then discuss what in-service education and access to technology will empower these change agents to integrate technology with their teaching. This is my solution to the problem I mentioned above of mis-understanding equity. *Do not try in the beginning to get everyone equal exposure to technology.* Concentrating on your change agents keeps resources from being so diluted that a critical mass of resources is never reached to show what technology can really do. For example, suppose a school bought thirty computers. One way to use them would be to put them in a lab and then let all the students use the lab. This could mean that each student would get twenty minutes of exposure per week to the technology. But in such short periods, neither student nor teacher could do any meaningful work. With such a program, the school can say, "Look we are using computers." But it cannot achieve the greater effect of changing the teaching and learning environment in any substantial way.

Instead of having a lab, suppose you divide the thirty computers into five sets of six each. Then you issue them to five change-agent teachers who would have their students use them in cooperative learning projects, all day, every day. At the end of the year, you could ask those five to share with the rest of the faculty their technology-integrated units and lessons and their evaluations of how things went. Then you could have them help decide how to expand the integration.

## Step 3: Establishing Strategic Goals

In this step you put together the vision you developed in step one with the data gathered in step two to develop strategic goals to guide the technology plan (figure 13.2)

**Figure 13.2: How steps 1, 2, and 3 fit together**

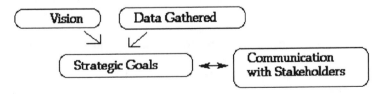

Do not forget that technology planning must be integrated with all other planning or it will be peripheral to the school community and ultimately of little educational value. Strategic planning is a strategy that focuses first on the school's mission and long-term goals prior to developing specific program objectives.

## Example of a Mission Statement and Related Goals

Here is an example of a school district's use of strategic goals as the basis for developing a technology plan. Staff began with this mission statement:

"The Mission of the Educational Technology Plan of the Best School District is to support teachers, students, and administrative and support staff with appropriate technological equipment and solutions for all parts of the educational program."

Once they had established this mission, they developed strategic goals to make their vision a reality:

- To provide all students, teachers, and administrators with the technologies, tools, and skills in using those tools that will enable them to make maximum use of their abilities and the most efficient use of learning and instructional time,
- To provide increased opportunities for critical and creative thinking in all content areas, using the potential of technology to support problem-solving and creative students and teachers. To include in this new curriculum increased access to information and technology applications and—through telecommunications, video, and instructional television—access to knowledge beyond the school,
- To use technology to support expanded and more accurate assessment efforts, with a particular emphasis on assessing student higher-level thinking skills, performance, portfolio development, and other desirable competencies not currently measured on standardized tests,
- To streamline office functions so that meaningful and needed information is readily available for instructional and managerial decision making, and
- To utilize technology so that it strengthens the bridges between home, school, and community through parent classes, desktop publishing services, coordination of school and home use of com-

puters in support of academic programs, and provides opportunities for community input to the school program.

## Student and Staff Outcomes

Some districts subdivide strategic goals into more specific student and staff outcomes. They may also include specific outcomes in terms of improving learning-resource management. Here are some examples of student and teacher outcomes:

- Students will effectively integrate the use of computers and related learning technologies such as CD-ROM'S, Internet resources, instructional television, and video resources in their learning activities.
- Students will use or create technology-based products for researching, presenting, processing, and managing information in all subjects.
- Teachers will use technology to meet the needs of students with different learning preferences and diverse abilities.
- Teachers will use technology to increase communication between the classroom, the school community, and the outside world.

## Step 4: Building a Technology Integration Plan

Once you have developed strategic goals that are supported by stakeholders, the next steps are relatively easy, although they can be tedious. For each of the strategic goals, you specify objectives, activities, staff responsibilities, related hardware/software, student outcomes, and evaluation strategies. You should also estimate costs for each objective. This makes it easier to develop a low-, medium-, or high-cost action plan by adding or subtracting specific objectives. I recommend that the tech-planning committee actually use large butcher paper in the initial stages of Step 4, drawing lines to divide columns and filling in the columns in as each goal is addressed. This takes time, but if you do it well you will have all the information you need to complete your technology plan.

Table 13.1 shows an example of how you can turn a strategic goal into an implementation plan. In this case the strategic goal was to use technology for problem solving within the classroom curriculum. The example shows the use of the World Wide Web and spreadsheet applications to engage students in collaborative problem solving.

**Table 13.1: Sample Partial Action Plan**

Strategic Goal 3: Use Technology for Problem Solving within the Classroom Curriculum

| Objectives | Activities | Timeline | Person Responsible | Hardware/Software | Cost |
|---|---|---|---|---|---|
| 1. Students will be able to use the Web to research answers to problems. | Students will research local problems about the environment. Use teacher pre-selected websites and print resources to solve problem. | Spring 2001 | Team Technology Teacher | 4 Pentium PCs with access to the Internet | [Research and enter current costs of computers and Internet access.] |
| 2. Students will use a spreadsheet to analyze different financial situations. | Students will plan a project to raise funds. They will use a spreadsheet to calculate profits/costs. | Spring 2001 | Team Technology Teacher | Use hardware already obtained. Use Excel in Microsoft Office | [Research and enter current costs of software, e.g., Microsoft Office for Education.] |

# Step 5: Making sure the plan is carried out

Next you need to develop technology and human infrastructures to ensure that what you planned to have happen will happen. It is important to articulate how you will manage the technology resources and enable educators to use them well. In Step 5, you specify all of this.

## *Learning Resource Management*

Many schools do not use their technology resources as well as they could. When you develop a technology plan you must consider how to ensure coordinated and effective use of current and future learning resources. Here are steps to ensure that learning resources management is built into your technology integration plan:

1. *Identify existing resources.* Once you have identified your strategic goals and target population you should identify all existing resources available to implement your plan. An inventory specialist in your district can probably show you a form s/he uses that you can adapt to your purpose.
2. *Consider providing access to resources beyond the school.* Technology opens the school to worldwide sources of information. Connect the classroom and school library to information resources, electronic mail, and news services, as well as to organizations in your community itself. For example, one project linked an elementary school to the local university and the local bank.
3. *Examine current patterns of staff and student uses of resources, and design ways to improve them.* Consider keeping logs of use. Which resources are well used? Which are not? Why? What resources are easy to get to and which are not? Look at the current use patterns for all learning resources from science kits to software.
4. *Examine current curriculum and instruction goals and determine alignment between these goals and current learning resources.* This process can be considered from two directions. There may be many valuable resources that no one has taken the time to align with curriculum goals. Or there may be new curriculum goals that require the acquisition of new kinds of learning resources. Also, consider discarding outdated materials and tools.
5. *Create procedures for aligning and using new resources.* As you consider acquiring new tools, focus on how well they will align

with current and future instructional goals. Describe the strengths and weaknesses of the current resources and develop a plan for strengthening your collection. Specify the procedures you will use for finding and evaluating new learning materials. Decide how you will ensure that selection of new materials is consistent with your school's goals, and how will you ensure increased access to them.

## Planning for Staff Development

Providing high-quality staff development may be the most crucial key to your plan's success. One of the best means of staff development in technology is simply to involve staff in planning for technology use. As teachers clarify their instructional goals, see how new technology materials can be used to meet those goals, and consider how technology might help them evaluate student learning, they grow in understanding. Opportunities to access, preview, and evaluate a variety of software programs will further enhance their learning.

I often suggest to the committee writing the technology plan that they include significant release time for themselves and other staff to develop and implement the plan. One school provided an afternoon a month of release time to the technology planning committee. Each member of this committee learned a piece of exemplary software, developed a sample lesson for using the software, and shared it with the rest of the committee. They called it "each one teach one" and it seemed to work very well.

We know that effective professional development must be sustained, relevant to teachers' needs, and embedded in the workplace, and that it must include adequate time for teacher learning and collaboration (California Dept. of Education 1997; Norton and Gonzales 1997; also see chapter 12 in this book). Provide staff development as close as possible to the school site and as much as possible during teachers' regular workday. Workshops should focus on the same equipment and resources teachers have in their school and classrooms. In addition, give teachers opportunities to design learning environments by integrating technology (Wiggens and McTighe 1998; Norton and Wiburg 1998).

Ensure that all teaching of technology is done in the context of solving real educational problems. For example, many teachers want to develop new methods of assessment. Technology provides a simple way for students to keep electronic portfolios of their writing, and a means for teachers to share student work and progress with parents and

the principals. Teachers can also videotape student learning perform-
ances; have students watch, evaluate, and re-record their presentations;
and send videos home so parents can see what their children are able to
do.

Invest as much as possible in support for teachers. This might
mean hiring a parent or a technology consultant to spend time at the
school working with teachers who are interested in learning how to
integrate technology with the curriculum. Look to local universities,
and ask for student teachers who know how to use technology and who
need experience in classrooms. Even the school's students can be valuable tutors for teachers in the technology area.

Make certain that teachers have adequate and convenient access to
the technology you want them to learn to use. Invest in computers for
teachers. Of course our ultimate goal is that students learn how to use
technology for learning and creating, but that will never happen until
teachers feel comfortable using technology for teaching. All other professionals are given computers, phones, Internet connections, and copy
machines. Until teachers are routinely given the professional tools they
need, technology will not be fully integrated into the classroom.

If your district cannot afford to issue computers to teachers, it
might begin by offering teachers low-cost loans and payroll deductions
for buying personal computers. Or it might offer to provide computers
and other technology tools first to those teachers who are willing to
attend professional development workshops and work to integrate technology in their classrooms.

From my own twenty-five years of experience being a teacher and
working with teachers, I recommend that you do not require everyone
to participate at the beginning. Start with those teachers that really want
to use technology in the classroom and give them the materials and the
support they need. Discuss with the entire staff the necessity of testing
different instructional approaches with technology in order to find out
what works best in this school. Invite teachers to be pioneers and assure
other teachers that it is all right to wait to implement technology fully
in their classrooms. As the non-pioneer teachers begin to see technology being used for learning, they will be more likely to adapt it in their
own way in their own classrooms later. As the innovators begin to
change the learning culture in their classrooms, parents and other
teachers will begin to ask for help in integrating technology in more
classrooms.

## 6. Evaluating and adjusting the plan

You must consider two kinds of evaluation. First you need to develop a way to evaluate your plan itself. Prior to implementation, be sure your plan contains all the elements needed for technology integration. Table 13.2 is an evaluation rubric to help you do this.

Second, you must evaluate the impact of the plan as it is implemented in your district or school. Evaluation components to the technology plan help staff focus on the desired outcomes and determine which aspects of the plan work and which need adjustment. Did you do what you said you would, and did it matter? What effect is technology integration having on student learning? Teaching? Administration? School climate? Parent and community involvement?

Your evaluation design should include both formative and summative components. Formative evaluation occurs during implementation and can be valuable for making adjustments to increase the likelihood of success. They also can sometimes provide the data you need to get continued support from the district and the community.

Summative evaluation occurs at the end of a specified period, usually on a yearly basis, for the purpose of determining programs' successes and failures. At the end of a specified period, a variety of summative data should be collected such as student test scores, surveys from teachers and students, observations, and interviews. The technology committee can then look at the summative data and make decisions about what aspects of the plan should be expanded and/or continued and which aspects are not working and should be changed or eliminated. A technology plan is a living document. A yearly meeting to study the data and modify the plan can be built in from the beginning.
You need to decide the following: What kinds of data do you want to collect and for what purpose? Who will collect and compile the data? What data are you collecting already that might be valuable in terms of evaluating technology integration in your school? What additional instruments or strategies will you use? What will be your timeline for gathering data?

Go back to the implementation/action plan that you completed in Step 4. For each objective, you should specify a student or teacher outcome and a means for evaluating whether the objective was met. These

**Table 13.2: Evaluation Form for your Technology Plan**

Rubric: Partially meets criteria = 1; Meets criteria = 2; Exceeds criteria = 3.

____1. The Context for the Plan. Is there information about the context for the plan, the demographics and structure of the district, school or organization? Does the reader get a quick, clear picture of the organization and its purpose?

____2. Vision of Technology Integration. Is there a clear vision of how technology can be used to meet the needs of the district, school, classroom, or organization? Is the vision for using technology clearly tied to the instructional goals of the organization?

____3. Writing Quality. Is the overall writing clear and concise, easy to read and comprehend?

____4. Needs Assessment. Has the writer completed a situational analysis (needs and strengths assessment)? Is the reader aware of the strengths and weaknesses in the organization as they relate to technology use in the proposed plan?

____5. Problem/Needs/ Goals/Objectives. Are the goals clear? Are objectives or outcomes related to the goals? Do the suggested activities clearly support the proposed outcomes?

____6. Integration with Other Programs. Does the document describe how the technology plan interacts with other efforts for program and organizational improvement?

____7. Evaluation. Is there an evaluation plan aligned with the goals, objectives and activities included in the plan?

____8. Implementation. Are implementation strategies clearly defined? Does the reader know who will do what, when, to whom, and with what resources? Is there a time line that seems reasonable and do-able?

____9. Research-based. Does the plan reflect what we know about the effective uses of technology for teaching, learning, and productivity?

____10. Continuous Improvement. Does the plan include a means for the continues re-evaluation of the plan and supervision of the implementation process?

outcome measures will be the basis of your evaluation plan. Be sure to include ways to assess not only student growth, but also teacher change, changes in classroom and/or school climate, effectiveness of the professional development provided, and effectiveness of the learning resources management. Use your imagination as you develop evaluation strategies. The data you collect can range from the formal to the very informal. Unobtrusive measures such as an increase in daily attendance or the amount of time students spend free reading often tell you as much about a classroom innovation as direct measures of student performance. Research suggests that effective integration of technology can influence positive changes in teacher pedagogy (Becker and Ravitz 1999). Such changes might include increased levels of participation in learning activities by more students. One principal I know often walked through the school and recorded (on a spreadsheet) amount of teacher-talk versus amount of student-talk. She noted who was asking questions in each classroom and also noticed the gender and ethnicity of the students actively participating. Another suggestion is simply to ask the students what they are doing or how they like using computers or other technology. Teachers might also be willing to keep notes on what has worked for them and what has not. Their notes can provide rich information about how technology integration might be influencing their teaching practice. Here are a few additional friendly suggestions I have compiled from my work in helping administrators and teachers integrate technology:

- Keep notes of all technology planning meetings and interviews? Assign a team member to serve as the historian.
- Keep an activity log once the technology is in place. Use a spreadsheet to collect and display the data. Make attractive charts to help everyone see the strengths and weaknesses of the plan.
- Keep samples of work produced using the new technologies.
- Involve teachers in collaborative action research (Sagor 1992). Teachers may be able to come up with the best questions and strategies for evaluating the impact of technology. A local university might be able to provide an instructor and university credits for the teachers' work as collaborative researchers.
- Plan to use technology to support new forms of assessment such as electronic portfolios or videos of student performance.
- Decide which measures of student achievement that you are already collecting are relevant to the plan outcomes, and use these. Do the same with data collected on school and program quality.

- Finally, evaluate frequently and informally. You can learn a lot by asking a few simple questions at the end of a meeting or staff development session, e.g., Did we accomplish what we set out to do? What was still undecided? What do we feel best about? What could we do better next time? In addition you might want to do some focus-group interviews with students. They are likely to give you important insights into how the technology integration plan is working.

Evaluation has been a consideration throughout the technology planning process described in this chapter. Because so much of the curriculum is controlled by the evaluations one uses, it is important to take one last look to make sure that the outcomes you want for your students, teachers, and community are well aligned to the assessments you plan to use.

We are now at the end of this chapter on technology planning. I hope the information is helpful to your situation. If you want to learn more about this topic, visit the websites listed in table 13.3. Remember that the best thing about technology is not the technology itself but the way its effective use can improve the learning and teaching environment.

**Table 13.3: Sources to Consult for Technology Planning**

| Source | Address | Comment |
|--------|---------|---------|
| Kansas Technology Guide | http://pt3.nmsu.edu/ TheSteps/TechGuide/ techguide.html | |
| National Center for Technology Planning | http://www.nctp.com/ | A complete resource for technology planning compiled at Mississippi State |
| Tech Plans | http://www2.msstate.e du/~lsa1/sip/ | A collection of award winning technology plans |
| The Milken Foundation Exchange | http://www.mff.org/ edtech/ | Resources and research on technology use in schools |
| Technet | http://www.technet.nm .org/ | A resource for technology acquisition |
| North Central Regional Educational Laboratory | http://www.ncrel.org/ta ndl/contents.htm | Resources on technology planning from one of our national labs |
| International Society for Technology in Education | http://www.iste.org/ | ISTE offers multiple resources for technology planning |
| Planning for technology | http://www.nes.org | A guidebook for teachers, technology leaders, and school administrators |
| The United States Department of Education | http://www.ed.gov/ Technology | |

# References

Becker, H. J. and J. Ravitz. 1999. The Influence of Computer and Internet Use on Teachers' Pedagogical Practices and Perceptions. *Journal of Research on Computing in Education*, 31(4), 356-384.

Bingaman, J. 1997. Office of U.S. Sentator J. Bingaman. *Bingaman Launches Effort to Improve Technology Training for Teachers: New Measure Would Equip New Mexico Teachers to Teach Students Critical Computer Skills.* Press Release, 5 June 1997. Washington, D.C.

Bloom, H. 1992. The Effect of Participation in the Administrators' Technology Academy on Participants' Perceptions of the Usefulness of Technology in Education. Ph.D. diss., United States International University.

California Department of Education. 1997. *The Elements of High Quality Professional Development*, Second printing. Sacramento, Calif.: California Dept. of Education.

Dede, C. 1998. Technology and learning. In *Annual Yearbook of the Association for Supervision and Curriculum Development.* Alexandria, Va: Association for Supervision and Curriculum Development.

Dwyer, D. C., Ringstaff, C., and J. H. Sandholtz. 1990. Teacher Beliefs and Practices: Patterns of Change. Cupertino, Calif.: Apple Classroom of Tomorrow, Apple Computer, Inc.

Finkel, L. 1990. Moving Your District Toward Technology. *The School Administrator Special Issue: Computer Technology Report*, 35-38.

Fulton, K. 1996. Moving from Boxes and Wires to 21st Century Teaching. *T.H.E Journal*, 24(4), 76-82.

Honey, M., and B. Moeller. 1990. Teachers' Beliefs and Technology Integration: Different Values, Different Understandings. (Report No. ERIC #ED 326 203). New York: Center for Children and Technology in New York City.

Joyce, B. 1996. *Models of teaching*. 5th. ed. Needham Heights, Mass. : Allyn and Bacon.

Knapp, A., and A. Glenn. 1996. *Restructuring Schools with Technology*. Boston, Mass.: Allyn Bacon.

Morgan, M. 1998. Factors Related to Technology Integration in Schools. Ph.D. diss., New Mexico State University.

Norton, P., and C. Gonzales 1997. Regional Educational Technology Assistance (RETA) Initiative: A Model for Statewide Professional Development. Santa Fe: New Mexico State Department of Education.

Norton, P., and K. Wiburg. 1998. *Teaching with Technology*. Ft. Worth, Tex.: Harcourt Brace.

Office of Technology Assessment. 1995. Ed. Fulton, K., *Teachers and Technology: Making the Connection*. Publication No. OTA-EHR-616. Washington D.C: U.S. Government Printing Office.

Ritchie, D., and K. Wiburg. 1994. Educational Variables Influencing Technology Integration. *The Journal of Technology and Teacher Education*. Association for the Advancement of Computers in Education (AACE), 2(2).

Sagor, Richard. 1992. *How to Conduct Collaborative Action Research*, Alexandria, Va.: Association for Supervision and Curriculum Development.

Showers, B. 1990. Aiming for Superior Classroom Instruction for All Children: A comprehensive staff development model. *Remedial and Special Education*, 11 (3), 35-38.

Tapscott, Don. 1998. *Growing Up Digital: The Rise of the Net Generation*. New York: McGraw-Hill.

Tucker, M. 1992. The Genie in the Bottle. *Electronic Learning*, 12 (3), 50. U.S. Congress, Office of Technology Assessment.

Wiburg, K. 1997. Dance of Change: Integrating Technology in Class-rooms. In *Using Technology in the Classroom*, eds. D. L. Johnson, C. D. Maddux, and L. Liu, 171-184. New York: Haworth Press.

Wiburg, K. 1996. Integrated Learning Systems: What Does the Re-search Say? *Computers in Education*. 7th Edition, ed. J. Hirschbuhl. Guilford, Conn.: Duskin Publishing.

Wiburg, K. 1991. Three Schools in Which Teachers Have Successfully Integrated Technology and Teaching. *Technology and Teacher Education Annual*. 1991. Proceedings Publication for the Annual Technology and Teacher Education Conference, 238-243. Char-lottesville, Va.: Association for the Advancement of Computing in Education.

Wiburg, K., N. Montoya, and J. Sandin. 1999. Nuestra Tierra: Univer-sity/Public School Technology Integration Project. *Journal of Edu-cational Computing Research*, 21(2), 183-219.

Wiggens, G., and J. McTighe. 1998. *Understanding by Design*. Alex-andria, Va.: Association for Supervision and Curriculum Devel-opment.

# About the Contributors

**Bruce D. Baker** is assistant professor of Teaching and Leadership at the University of Kansas. He specializes in the areas of school finance policy and the economics of education. His recent work involves the application of dynamic systems modeling for understanding the implications and behavior of state school finance policies

**Carmen L. Gonzales** is a faculty member of the Department of Curriculum and Instruction in the Learning Technologies Program at New Mexico State University. She is currently the Project Director for a multimillion dollar Technology Innovation Challenge Grant from the U.S. Department of Education, a statewide professional development project called Regional Educational Technology Assistance (RETA).

**Gary Ivory** is associate professor of Educational Management and Development at New Mexico State University. Prior to that he was coordinator of research, testing, and evaluation in the Ysleta Independent School District in El Paso. He has taught grades five through eight and at the community college level.

**Steve Leask** is a doctoral student in Educational Management and Development and a scholarly technology specialist, both at New Mexico State University.

**Mario Martinez** is assistant professor of Educational Management and Development at New Mexico State University. He has published in the areas of planning and performance measurement and higher education finance and policy. He is a member of a national advisory panel for the National Center for Public Policy and Higher Education's national higher education report card project.

**Anne C. Moore** most recently served as branch librarian at the Alamogordo campus of New Mexico State University and as the electronic resources librarian at the Zuhl Library of New Mexico State University, Las Cruces. She is currently completing her dissertation on information literacy, in the department of Educational Management and Development at New Mexico State.

**Tom Ryan** has taught for fourteen years and has been an administrator since 1994. He was a high school principal for three years and is currently Executive Director of Learning Technologies for Albuquerque Public Schools. He has provided staff development on technology to administrators throughout New Mexico and is also co-chair of the New Mexico Council on Technology in Education.

**Irma H. Trujillo** is an administrator in the Ysleta Independent School District in El Paso, Texas. She has experience at a variety of administrative levels, including elementary principal, director of bilingual education, and interim superintendent. She has consulted extensively in the area of dual language instruction and the academic achievement of second-language learners.

**Tom Watts** has worked as a technical writer, analyst and information technology director for a school district and for a county government and in the private sector.

**Karin M. Wiburg** is associate professor and coordinates the graduate specialization in learning technologies at New Mexico State. She is principal investigator of "Preparing Tomorrow's Teacher's Today," a U.S. Department of Education initiative to prepare teachers to use technology to improve teaching and learning.

## DATE DUE

| | | |
|---|---|---|
| | | |
| | | |
| | | |
| | | |
| | | |
| | | |
| | | |
| | | |
| | | |
| | | |
| | | |
| | | |
| | | |
| | | |

GAYLORD     #3522PI     Printed in USA